THE STAG OF LOVE

The Chase in Medieval Literature

THE STAG OF LOVE

The Chase in Medieval Literature

Marcelle Thiébaux

Cornell University Press

ITHACA AND LONDON

Cornell University Press gratefully acknowledges
a grant from the Andrew J. Mellon Foundation
that aided in bringing this book to publication.

First published 1974 by Cornell University Press.
Published in the United Kingdom by Cornell University Press Ltd.,
2-4 Brook Street, London W1Y 1AA.

International Standard Book Number 0-8014-0792-3
Library of Congress Catalog Card Number 73-14396

Composition by St. Catherine Press, Ltd.

Printed in the United States of America

Anthony and Giles

Contents

Illustrations

Preface

From the late thirteenth century an anonymous poem has survived whose closing line identifies it as *Li dis dou cerf amoreus* —"the rime of the stag of love." A description of the stag chase in little more than three hundred lines, the poem makes it clear that the hunt is allegorical, that pursuing the quarry is like pursuing a woman "who is the stag of love." This plainly stated parallel, contained in a little work that I believe is the earliest strictly allegorical treatment of the love chase, is the source of the title of my book. It was the late Robert Bossuat who kindly indicated to me the manuscripts in which *Li dis dou cerf amoreus* was included; in 1962, I published the text of the poem in *Studies in Philology*. The poem provided the germ of my investigation of the chase in medieval literature, for it was likely that such a well-worked-out allegory, each of whose stages afforded the author an opportunity to connect the procedures of the stag chase with the procedures of conventionalized love, would not have sprung up in isolation. My search revealed the existence of a number of little-known allegories, as well as other literary genres in which the conventions of divine or earthly love were expressed metaphorically in terms of the hunt. Moreover, the metaphorical hunt was not limited to the expression of love but was adaptable to a variety of experiences. To work both backward and forward from "the stag of love" was to discover that the theme of the hunt was so widespread in medieval literature alone that a complete catalogue would have been impracticable here. I have not attempted to compile a history of the hunt in medieval literature or to trace its many likely sources. Instead, I deal selectively with representative and significant authors whose works, in several periods and languages, manifest the play of individual talent in controlling and enlarging the possibilities of the received subject matter of the hunt. I have concentrated upon the imagery of the stag chase, although wherever it is useful I refer also to the hunt at large.

It should be kept in mind that whatever we know of hunting in the Middle Ages must be reconstructed from literary sources, chiefly from cynegetic handbooks. These handbooks on hunting tended to be "literary," either in the sense that they were rhetorically embellished or that they were marked by a degree of fictitious idealization. From such semi-fictional sources and from the frankly symbolic iconography of the stag in literature and art, we may in large part understand what the medieval imaginative writer had to draw upon and work with when he chose the hunt as his metaphor.

In medieval literature, metaphors of the chase were most often, but not exclusively, applied to love. Three important works, a life of St. Eustace, the *Nibelungenlied*, and *Sir Gawain and the Green Knight*, exemplify other types of pursuit: the sacred chase motivated by a deity; the mortal chase, moving toward the death of the human hunter or human quarry; and the instructive chase or pursuit of wisdom. Each of these metaphorical types could and did merge with the love chase.

The hunt of love had been developed earlier by Greek and Latin authors. Through the works of Ovid in particular, who gathered and transformed many of the conventions, and through other channels of transmission, such as the cynegetic handbooks of antiquity, the love chase was made readily available to the Middle Ages. The work of three medieval authors of unusual merit—Chrétien, Chaucer, and Gottfried—enhanced the complexity of the love chase through a fusion with one or other of the types of pursuit named above, the sacred, the mortal, and the instructive.

The last part of my study is reserved for the work of those

largely forgotten poets who chose the mode of allegory—a body of literature that is little known today but that kept alive an extensive system of hunting images and their amatory equivalents. *Li dis dou cerf amoreus* belongs here with the *Jagd* of Hadamar von Laber, a monumental, difficult, and in many ways fascinating conjunction of the systems of Minne and the ritualized hunt. Hadamar's own ingenious treatment of the subject in the fourteenth century may be regarded as a medieval farewell to the love chase. Nothing after him quite matches his extravagances, and his German followers were left to compose slim imitations of the master.

English translations of quotations in foreign languages have been provided here wherever possible. The location of the original texts is given in the notes.

I would like to thank Peter and Ursula Dronke of Cambridge University for their generous reading of the manuscript and for their valuable advice. I also express my thanks to Seton Hall University for enabling me, through a faculty research grant, to have a term free of teaching in the spring of 1969 at a critical period in my research and writing. I owe considerable debts to the libraries in which I worked: the Bibliothèque Nationale and the Bibliothèque de l'Arsenal in Paris, the New York Public Library, the Pierpont Morgan Library, and the libraries of Columbia and St. John's universities.

MARCELLE THIÉBAUX

New York City

THE STAG OF LOVE

The Chase in Medieval Literature

I

Literature and the Hunt

The hunt was a literary motif especially favored among writers in the Middle Ages. European literature between the eighth and the fifteenth centuries is full of casual allusions to hunts: Heroes hunt on the way to getting somewhere, they hunt as a means of showing their rank and prowess, of seeking out their enemies in disguise, or of agreeably passing the time. A random episode easily culminates in a human encounter. A knight, hawk on fist, approaches Robin's Marion to inquire whether there are any "birds" in her vicinity, but it quickly becomes plain that the knight's preferred game would be played with Marion. A hunting expedition will launch a hero in the direction of important deeds, military triumphs, the founding of cities and cloisters. It may guide him, as it did Guy of Hampton, to his death. Allusions to a hunt can occur briefly in a long poem by way of analogy to the principal heroic action.

In *Beowulf*, for example, the pursuit that is to carry the warriors to the gloomy and incandescent mere of Grendel and his mother inspires King Hrothgar to speak of the waters with foreboding:

> Ðēah þe hǣð-stapa hundum geswenced,
> heorot hornum trum holt-wudu sēce,
> feorran geflȳmed, āēr hē feorh seleð,
> aldor on ōfre, āēr hē in wille,
> hafelan [hȳdan]. Nis þaet hēoru stōw.[1]

[1] C. L. Wrenn (ed.), *Beowulf, With the Finnesburg Fragment*, 2nd ed. rev. and enl. (London, 1958), lines 1368–1372.

Though the heath-stalker, the strong-horned stag,
may seek the forest when harried by hounds, having
been pursued from afar, he will sooner yield his life
and breath upon the bank than [shelter] his head
in [the water]; this is no holy place!

This water, the pursuit that *now* engages the Danes, *this* quarry, implies the speaker, do not belong to an ordinary chase. Whereas the harried stag would habitually plunge into a stream to shake off its pursuers, no stag would plunge here even to avoid its death. But given the fiendish natures of Grendel and his mother, they dive readily into the terrible mere, and given the extraordinary character of Beowulf, he will not abandon the game at the brink but will swim down in pursuit. On their way the warriors scrutinize the track or footprint of Grendel's mother, and trace her visible spoor over the ground and the murky moor. She who carried off her prey, Aeschere, becomes the hunted hunter. In the latter part of the poem, tenuously echoing the mythic pursuit of these earlier adventures, a bloodied track reappears; it is now that of the retreating Swedes Beowulf follows.

Sometimes a hunt in its entirety will form the prelude to a hero's crucial experience. The quarry has been slain or has eluded its pursuers, the crisis of the hunt subsides, the hunter's mood of exhaustion deepens into vision and prophecy. Charlemagne, in the ninth-century poem, "Karolus Magnus et Leo Papa," sleeps after an exhilarating chase during which he has slain a host of boars. His dream of the meeting with Pope Leo at Paderborn looks significantly to the future, to Charles' victory over the Saxons. Paris in the *Roman de Troie* of Benoît de Sainte-Maure sleeps after a hunt during which he has caught nothing, then awakens to issue his momentous judgment in favor of one of the three goddesses who stand before him. Malory's Arthur spurs his horse so severely in pursuit of a great hart that the horse dies under him. While the king waits for another mount he sits down beside a fountain and sinks into thought. His strange vision of the "beeste" whose noise was "lyke unto the questyng of thirty coupyl hounds" precedes the king's slumber and marks the beginning of the linked events leading to the Grail quest. In such instances as these the period of hunters' repose is fuller of significant event than the chase that wearies. The hero's exertion in the hunt, to which he has been drawn by the quarry, induces a state of dreaming receptivity. He beholds a vision that shapes his life.

My purpose here will be to analyze the special literary uses of the hunt, notably the stag chase, which was considered in the Middle Ages to be the "noblest" sport. Indeed, the stag, together with the "noble" boar, is the quarry most often hunted in medieval epics and romances.[2] In the works to be discussed here, the chase has been integrated within the fabric of narrative so as to convey the quality of the hero's consuming experience. These are works of the literary imagination in which the chase constitutes an adventure of magnitude or intensity. The hero's participation in the chase may elicit a sense of his identity; it may define and alter his life. Whether he sees the quarry slain or becomes himself a victim of the enterprise, it is the chase that confers meaning upon his actions.

There is, to be sure, a good deal of medieval literature in which hunting is merely conventional, where its office in initiating adventures, for instance, seems to be understood without there being any apparent demand felt for its development or its expressed relationship to the rest of the narrative. Mysterious animals conduct heroes upon strange paths to exotic adventures, and then disappear—either to heighten the mystification or because the author has not thought of making further use of them. Pursuits abound. So do dart, net, dog, and quarry metaphors. In this study I treat those authors who have most fully exploited the traditional material; in their works, the symbolic chase corresponds to one or more types of event, namely, the sacred, the mortal, the instructive, and—central to my purpose here—the amatory.

[2] Marcelle Thiébaux, "The Mouth of the Boar as a Symbol in Medieval Literature," *Romance Philology* 22 (1968), traces the literary boar hunt and its meanings in detail.

Before we can judge the aptness or even the meaning of the symbolic hunting activities to be encountered in medieval literature, we must know something of the kinds of material that a poet might have referred to for the substance of his metaphors. Did every poet who wrote about hunting engage in the sport himself? Many medieval poets sound very knowing indeed about it. Yet a writer without much firsthand knowledge can always take refuge in his old books or in new ones. Some elaborate literary hunts appear to rely upon received conventions harking back to Greek and Latin authors, while others reflect a knowledge of contemporary practices. There are poets who write as if they were aware of the codifications of the hunting of their day, whether from reading or from experience. It would be difficult to recreate with any certainty a poet's own immediate acquaintance with the hunt; we can, however, examine sources of information available to him, and furthermore, analyze the possible uses of the hunt as a literary structure.

We have these three things to consider, therefore, if we are to understand the poetic transformations of the hunt: the practice of hunting as a craft; the iconographic figure of the coursing stag; and the situation of the hunt taken as a promising narrative vehicle. The first two of these subjects constitute quite separate funds of material—the one procedural, the second "mystical." Both could in the medieval period be drawn upon and converted into poetic currencies. What hunting was all about, its rules and methods can now be reconstructed from various literary sources, and especially from the way they are represented in formal handbooks of instruction. These handbooks were prevalent in the thirteenth and fourteenth centuries; most of them are in French. It will be seen that many authors were in fact attracted to the rhetoric of the hunt and to closely observed procedures, which they imaginatively borrowed with varying skill and enthusiasm. There are also the iconographic images of the stag, shifting in meaning, that arise chiefly from writing of exegetical and spiritual purpose—from allegory, from scriptural glosses, and bestiaries. An author might incorporate within the context of a realistic chase scene a visual iconographic image of the stag, or evoke such an image through his characterization; the effect will be to increase or alter the apparent meaning. Both these classes of literature, the first instructive in the practical sense, the other morally instructive, do not altogether exclude each other, for the same clichés about the stag will often appear in both, say, a manual of the chase and a psalm gloss. And finally, we may consider the narrative shape of the hunt and the sense of plot it will bestow upon any fictional situation in which it is used. Having once grasped the hunt as a procedure consisting of separate stages, we may perceive its overall schematic design, its characteristic forward movement driving toward a climactic contest. It is in these respects that the realistic hunt merges with and fleshes out the familiar narrative framework of the Journey. Desire impells the hunter on his Journey toward the hunted quarry; the force that strikes the hunted quarry to flee is necessity. On the hunter's side, therefore, the plot may move from desire to consummation; on the victim's, from necessity to death or reprieve.

Hunting Practice and Ceremony

It is well acknowledged that men in the Middle Ages were passionately fond of the hunt. The Anglo-Saxon and Norman kings of England restricted vast forest areas for their diversion. William the Conqueror lovingly protected the stag, writes a wry chronicler, "as if he were its father." There were the noble hunters who had legitimate rights, who could afford stables and kennels to indulge their love of the sport as a form of recreation and military exercise. Since such rights were acquired by inheritance or appointment, by purchase, or as the right of warren, by royal licence to kill "vermin"—fox, pheasant, hare, and the like—authorized hunters covered a range of men from barons and honored clerics to tenants and freemen. There were the huntsmen who furnished the king's table in return for clothing, food, a horse, some gold. And the excitement of organized hunts would have been shared by other servants of great households as well, for the aid of numerous officials was required in a hunting party to locate quarry, manage hounds, spread nets, halloo and cry, and do menial chores when the quarry was slain.

Besides the rich and the warranted, men of fewer means and no apparent rights presumed to hunt and to leave records of their pleasures, if, that is, the poaching of household officers and other anonymous sportsmen upon "woody Grounds and fruitful Pastures, privileged for wild Beasts and Fowls of the Forest Chase, and Warren"[3] may be called hunting. The literate game-thief and dreamer of the *Parlement of the Thre Ages* strolls through the evening mists of May, along banks of primrose, periwinkle, wild thyme and daisies; somewhat later he cannily drops the feet of a slain deer into a hole covered over with fern, moss and broom to mislead the game-keeper, having poached his quarry with a bow and a solitary dog. It is possible that the medieval man, whatever his class, found opportunities to hunt whether legally or illegally. He hunted for food, diversion and release; he believed in the sport as a means of maintaining his skill in the play of weaponry; he followed the hunt in the service of his masters. As a cleric he cherished the belling of hounds and hunters' cries as music lovelier than that sung in the King's Chapel. As a poor man he trapped the verminous badger, not that the badger had ever annoyed him, but its hide provided him with the most durable footgear. Outside the law he shot deer "as men that been hungry and mowe [may] no mete finde / and been harde bestad [besieged] under woode-linde [lindenwood]."[4]

There is no lack of medieval evidence of the hunt's widespread practice. Forest assizes and laws, grants of individual privileges, proceedings against poachers, who might be blinded, gelded, fined or arrested, offer factual documentation. Architectural

[3] John Manwood, *Treatise of the Forest Laws*, 5th ed. (London, 1741), pp. 143 ff., "What a Forest Is."

[4] "The Tale of Gamelin," in W. H. French and C. B. Hale (eds.), *Middle English Metrical Romances* (New York, 1930), lines 675–676.

ornamentation, illuminations, manuals of the hunt, and a very considerable body of imaginative literature, reveal the favor the subject found with artists and craftsmen, court writers, and poets. By drawing upon documentary and literary sources modern scholars have made the technical aspects of hunting practice and terminology accessible to readers today. Hermann Werth in the last century, and recently Kurt Lindner, have classified the medieval handbooks;[5] Lindner, moreover, has contributed his monumental *Geschichte des deutschen Weidwerks*.[6] Chief among the Scandinavian scholars who have given us authoritative modern editions of a large number of the hunting books is Gunnar Tilander, editor of the series *Cynegetica*; his etymological "essais" and "mélanges" of the same series deal discursively with the language of the hunt.[7] For the German, David Dalby has provided his invaluable *Lexicon*.[8]

To be sure, the perusal of special dictionaries and modern annotated editions of medieval handbooks will give us an impression of a pastime that was highly stylized and ritualized. The formality of hunting must, of course, have varied a good deal with the epoch and region, the rank, resources, tastes, and degree of urgency of any one hunter. Of Charlemagne in the

---

[5] Hermann Werth, *Altfranzösische Jagdlehrbücher nebst Handschriften-bibliographie der abendländischen Jagdlitteratur* (Halle, 1889); Kurt Lindner, "Über die europaïsche Jagdliteratur des 12-15. Jhs.," *Zeitschrift für Jagdwissenschaft* 1 (1955): 84 f.

[6] Volume 2 of this work is *Die Jagd im frühen Mittelalter* (Berlin, 1937–40).

[7] These are: "Essais d'étymologie cynégétique," *Cynegetica* 1 (Lund, 1953); "Nouveaux Essais d'étymologie cynégétique," *Cynegetica* 4 (Lund, 1957); "Mélanges d'étymologie cynégétique," *Cynegetica* 5 (Lund, 1958); and "Nouveaux mélanges d'étymologie cynégétique," *Cynegetica* 8 (Lund, 1961).

[8] *Lexicon of the Medieval German Hunt: A Lexicon of MHG Terms (1050-1500) Associated with the Chase, Hunting with Bows, Falconry, Trapping, and Fowling* (Berlin, 1965). Dalby often gives perceptive literary judgments within his definitions, to which I am indebted. Apart from Dalby, who in his preface expresses the need for further scholarship on the subject, little else has been written on the imaginative uses of the medieval hunt.

The care of the hounds in the kennels. Miniature in Gaston Phébus, *Livre de chasse, ca.* 1400, ms. 616, folio 52 v°. Bibliothèque Nationale, Département des Manuscrits.

mood of a moralizing practical joker, his biographer relates an exemplary tale. Coming from church one morning, the emperor, with exhortations against idleness, proposed an impromptu hunt to his court and his guests. This company of visiting Venetian ambassadors, opulently got up in ermine, pheasant and peacock feathers, and silks, yellow and purple, was forced to comply. "We can all set out in the clothes which we are wearing at this

Training and caring for the hounds. Miniature in Gaston Phébus, *Livre de chasse*, *ca.* 1440, ms. 619, folio 42 r°. Bibliothèque Nationale, Département des Manuscrits.

moment," declared Charles. He had on his cheap and sturdy sheepskin, but he dragged his bedizened guests with ill-concealed malice and joy (so that he might lecture them later upon their vanity) through mud and thickets. "As they rushed through the woodland gullies they were lacerated by the branches of trees and thorns and briars, they were drenched with rain and they were befouled with the blood of wild beasts and with the stench of the skins."[9] Obviously the business of the hunt as Charles knew it could be organized at a moment's notice, without undue ceremony, and preferably in homely gear.

[9] From Notker's Life of Charlemagne, in Einhard and Notker the Stammerer, *Two Lives of Charlemagne*, trans. Lewis Thorpe (Baltimore, 1969), pp. 165–166.

Handbooks of the sport, however, which begin to appear well after Charles's day, make an effort to claim an elaborate decorum of attitudes, procedures, language, and vesture—green for summer, gray for winter according to one authority. What the handbooks reflect is a set of ideal notions based upon the customs of the greatest households; it would be difficult to believe that even those hunts that were contemporary with the handbooks were conducted according to the letter of all such prescriptions. Of those manuals dealing with the stag directly or indirectly, the earliest are the least pretentious. These date from the middle of the thirteenth century (although older versions may have existed, such as a source for Gottfried von Strassburg's French hunting terms). The pertinent thirteenth-century manuals are Guicennas' *De Arte Bersandi*,[10] Daniel Deloc of Cremona's *Moamin et Ghatrif*,[11] done at Frederick II's Sicilian court, and *La chace du cerf*.[12] The Anglo-Norman *Le Art de Vénerie* of Guillaume Twiti, who was a huntsman at the court of Edward II of England, is dated before 1325, although its language reflects an older usage. Twiti's book provided the basis for an English treatise in dialogue form called *The Craft of Venery*,[13] and is also the main source of Dame Juliana Berners' hunting book printed at St. Albans in 1486.[14] The purpose of these books appears to be purely instructive. They describe types of equipment, set down correct terms and procedures for judging, pursuing, capturing, and breaking different types of quarry, give the various seasons, and advise in the care and cure of hounds and falcons.

---

[10] Ed. Gunnar Tilander, *Cynegetica* 3 (Uppsala, 1956).

[11] Ed. Håkan Tjerneld, *Studia Romanica Holmiensia* 1 (Stockholm, 1945). *Moamin* and *Ghatrif*, respectively Arabic and Persian treatises to begin with, were translated from their Latin versions into Franco-Italian by Daniel for Frederick's son. Versions of both also exist in Old Italian, and of *Moamin* in Old Spanish.

[12] Ed. and tr. into modern French by Tilander, *Cynegetica* 7 (Stockholm, 1960).

[13] Both ed. by Tilander, *Cynegetica* 2 (Uppsala, 1956).

[14] Ed. Tilander, *Cynegetica* 11 (Karlshamn, 1964).

Later fourteenth-century handbooks convey an expanded sense of the hunt's ceremony, composed as they were by more sophisticated writers—most of them noblemen. These books, moreover, are increasingly literary, filled with rhetorical descriptions, moral apologies, exempla, Christian and naturalistic allegories, and the praises of actual and legendary hunters. Principal among the handbooks of this period are the influential *Livres du roy Modus et de la royne Ratio* (ca. 1354–1376) by Henri de Ferrières.[15] The *Livre de chasse* portion of *Modus et Ratio* incorporates allegories of the stag and boar, a debate between hunters and falconers, and memoirs of great hunts. There is Gace de la Buigne, chaplain to three kings, who wrote his long poem *Le roman des deduis* (1359–1377)[16] for the education of one of the sons of King Philip the Bold, Duke of Burgundy. The work includes a range of diverse materials; for example, a contest between Virtues and Vices as well as a debate between *Amour d'oiseaux* and *Amour de chiens*, a falconer and a huntsman. Hardouin de Fontaines-Guérin, a nobleman of Anjou who finished his *Trésor de Vénerie* while imprisoned in Provence in 1394, gives a variety of fanfares, and writes of Placidas, Godfrey of Bouillon, Alexander, Perceval, Charlemagne, and of Julius Caesar's stag.[17] Gaston (called "Phébus" on account of his brilliant hair), Count of Foix, whose person and court Froissart celebrated after he had enjoyed the count's hospitality, writes that he undertook the composition of his *Livre de chasse* on the first of May, 1387.[18] Gaston closely follows parts of *Les livres du roy Modus*, and occasionally Gace's *Roman*. It was this

[15] *Les livres du roy Modus et de la royne Ratio* consist of Vol. 1: *Livre de chasse*, and Vol. 2: *Songe de pestilence*, ed. Tilander (Paris, 1932). The *Livre de chasse* is preserved in 33 mss. Carl Nordenfalk has handsomely reproduced the book's miniatures in *Le livre des deduis du roi Modus et de la reine Ratio* (Stockholm, 1955).

[16] Ed. Åke Blomqvist, *Studia Romanica Holmiensia* 3 (Karlshamn, 1951). Twenty mss. are preserved.

[17] Ed. Henri-Victor Michelant (Metz, 1856).

[18] Ed. Tilander, *Cynegetica* 18 (Karlshamn, 1971). Tilander's edition reproduces the 87 miniatures of ms. 616 of the Bibliothèque Nationale in Paris.

important treatise of Gaston's that was largely translated into English as *The Master of Game* (with some borrowings from Twiti as well)[19] by Edward of Norwich, Second Duke of York (ca. 1406–1413); it also forms the basis for many of the chapters of Jacques du Fouilloux' *La Vénerie* (1561).[20] Finally, an elegant and personal work may be mentioned, the late fifteenth century stanzaic *Chasse*[21] of Jacques de Brézé, Grand Sénéschal of Normandy. A member of one of France's wealthiest families, Jacques hunted with Anne of France, the daughter of Louis XI, and his poem gives an account of the expedition.

The type of chase in which the stag was pursued and captured *à force*, or as Chaucer has it, "with strengthe," by hunters coursing with horses and hounds (as distinguished from stalking with bows, or driving the quarry into a net) is represented in medieval manuals in the following way:

Hunters were early risers; they necessarily avoided the sin of sloth. They might in fact go out the evening before the day of the chase to find and move (the terms *quêter*, *détourner*, *lancer*, and *esmouvoir* appear variously to refer to this initial stage) warrantable deer. The size of the party could be any number from one man upwards, but each one quested independently. The man had to be sharply observant, keeping his eyes fixedly on the ground along the animal's track (*erre*); he looked for its footprints or "slots" (*piés*) and its excrement or "fewmets" (*fumées*). He had to scrutinize the surrounding trees as well for those places where the bark was scraped (*freür*) and the branches bent or broken (*portées*) in the animal's passing. He might find its grazing places (*viander*). The signs he sought would reveal the quarry's size, age, and value. With him, tugging at the leash (*liem* < Lat. *ligamen*) was his scenting hound, the "limer." A sensitive, excitable hound when the scent was fresh, the limer had to be well trained to silent questing. Along the way the

[19] Ed. William A. and Florence Baillie-Groham (London, 1904).

[20] Ed. from the *editio princeps* of 1561 by Tilander, *Cynegetica* 16 (Karlshamn, 1967).

[21] Ed. Tilander, *Cynegetica* 6 (Lund, 1959).

Departure for a royal hunt: the court of Philippe le Bon of France. Fifteenth-century painting in the Musée de Versailles. Photographie Giraudon.

The start of the hunt. The Hunt of the Unicorn. Late fifteenth-century French or Flemish tapestry from the Chateau of Verteuil. The Metropolitan Museum of Art, The Cloisters Collection, Gift of John D. Rockefeller, Jr., 1937.

huntsmen would place branches (*brisiés*) in certain positions; these marks would not only serve him in locating the path upon the company's return, but would establish his priority over other hunters by showing that a defined area (*enceinte*) had already been reconnoitered.

The gathering: hunters feast in the woods while the report is presented on the game to be pursued. Miniature in Gaston Phébus, *Livre de chasse, ca.* 1440, ms. 619, folio 56 r°. Bibliothèque Nationale, Département des Manuscrits.

Having quested, the huntsmen would join the gathering (*assemblée*) of the entire company at a designated place in the forest where the lord of the chase would be waiting to hear the formal reports (*rapports*) of his officials. The men would carry back samples of fewmets in their blouses or hunting horns to present for the lord's inspection. The lord would also look over the hounds of the pack and the horses that were led forth for the purpose. The gathering was a time of banqueting and fellowship. While manuals of the older form do not even mention the gathering, later books emphasize its festal quality and turn the landscape of the occasion into a *locus amoenus* with birdsong, rejoicing Nature, sun's rays, a fresh stream of running water to cool the wines, an agreeable spacing of the trees, and a leafy oak under which the king might sit.

In preparation for the chase itself, the dog varlets set up their "tristes" or relay stations (*relais*), usually choosing older, steadier hounds to be posted as replacements along the way the company expected to ride. Those of the pack (*chiens de meute* < *esmouvoir*) were the young, swift hounds. One source counts a pack of "twelve hounds at least"; another gives "twenty to forty." The varlets' relation to the hounds, cultivated during their feeding and training period, became all-important for the success of the hunt. It was essential to fondle and encourage, to call each by its own name and by endearments: *douce, douce amy, beau frere, petits mignons, mon amy, mon vieux, compains, mon valet, sire,* and *vieux docteur.* One would, as with an intimate, *tutoyer* his hounds. On the other hand, terms of extreme reproach were *vilain* or *mâtin*—"cur."

The party departed to the sound of the horn. Cries of *harro* and *holloa* (from *harer,* to incite the hound towards its prey) would drive the pack on to the pursuit (*mener, pourmener*). The stag could be expected to engage in its habitual slyness (*malice*) of rusing, or doubling: while still far ahead of its pursuers it would turn to retrace its steps *toward* the pack, thus strengthening the scent, then take a wide leap off to the right or the left and flee in this new direction. The hounds would reach the scent with growing excitement, but at the point where this gave out they were brought up short—confused and agitated. The hunters would then lead the dogs back around in widening circles from the spot, urging them with repeated cries of *"Arrière!"* until the scent was recovered. Since a stag might ruse in this way more than once, the hunters did well to remark the first time whether it had chosen to escape to the right or the left, for it would take the same direction again.

An object in the chase was to force the stag out of its haunts, familiar thickets where it could easily hide and evade its pursuers. Once driven out of the forest, it would characteristically

ale et ce donna grant auiserat
de roy retraire. En prens garde
enchacant aquelle main le cerf
que tu chaceras se destourneza
en fuyant ou derir ou a sene
stre car il est de certain que en
faisant ses vuses il se destoine
voulentiers a vne main z ceste
ou il se destourne mam rent
tout le iour comunement.
¶ Ces deux choses que ie tay
dites donnent grant auisent
en chacant cest de faire les
baisees pendans et a mon
auisement aquelle main ils
se destournent. Car ses tes
chiens chacent le contre ongle

cest a dux se reuers par ou ils
seront alez tu le sauas par les
baisees pendans et sidoiement
auisement de retraire ses chies
pour desfaire la vuse. Puis
nous dirons coment sen doit
relaissier vn cerf ce que len
chace ¶ Quant len enuoye
ses chiens au relies sen y doit
enuoiez tel qui ait congnoi
sance du cry des sauges chiens
et la cause si est que si loyent
venir aucune partie des chies
chacant combien que tous
ceulx que len auoit laisse
couue my feussent mie z qt
my eust traue de chiens et q

The pursuit of the stag: hunters riding to the hounds. Miniature in
Le Livre du roy Modus, fifteenth century, ms. M 820, folio 12 r°.
Courtesy Pierpont Morgan Library.

doit mettre son arc sur son de soy et sa main de quoy il tient la corde de son arc si la doit tenir devant son visage en tenant la corde. Et doit avoir les esguilles ferrees contre son fust. Et se la beste vient tost sac get il doit tout en paur ses bras eslongnier et doit commencier attirer son arc doulcement et silz soit tout tire avant que la beste soit endroit lui. Et doit estre son arc si aisie et si douly quil se puisse tenir tout entesie longuement et congnoistre la beste tant quelle soit venue pour oultre lui en asseant sa main et en tenant son corpe tousiours le plus droit et seure contre son fust quil pourra. Et doit tirer la corde de son arc droit a son oreille destre et doit tirer sa sayette iusques au fer et doit

ainsi vous pou te tenir son entoise et essaier si main et laissier aler. Et se la beste vient a top bien tost et elle soit une pou loinge de toy tu dois tirer une pou au devant aussi comme droit aux espaules, mais puis que une beste vient pres tu doit asseoir ta main en milieu corps au devers des espaules. Certe diray ces causes pour quoy tu dois laissier passer la beste qui te vient a fuse avant que tu tirupes et quant elle vient tost et de loing pour oste tu dois tirer au devant. Et tu dois savoir que se la beste qui vient a fuse est en droit toy et tu tires ce si mal fait et contre l'art de l'archerie pour .iij. causes. La premiere est une se tu fiers la beste de travers elle ne mourra. Mais si tost comme

change its course altogether and take to open country, fallow land, and dusty roads. It might in its desperate flight (*menée*) manage to leave its pursuers well behind, a possibility that was termed the "forloyne" (*forloyng*). Hard-pressed and fatigued, the stag would emit a stronger scent because of the sweat it shed, together with blood and froth from its mouth. At these signs, the hounds' eagerness intensified. The excessively harried stag was said to be *malmené*—a word used just as commonly elsewhere in the figurative sense, of heroes, martyrs, and lovers driven to extremes of suffering or to death. The stag in these straits would frequently descend to the water (*battre l'eau*), find a stream in which to cool itself and, it was said, attempt to cover its scent. This plunge, called "soiling," might be signaled according to French handbooks by joyous cries of *"cerf à l'eau"* and *"l'yeaue! fuyt l'yeaue,"* for it indicated that the stag was indeed ready to be taken. A struggle might even occur in the water, with the hounds crowding upon the stag, who in turn tried to push them under the current. The stag might reach the farther bank, or could simply return to the bank from which it had plunged and continue to flee.

When the animal was quite literally at the end of its forces (*sur ses fins*) it would wheel about to face the encircling, frantically baying hounds. Even this need not be the finish of the hunt, for the stag sometimes succeeded in breaking through the circle, wounding hounds and escaping once again. At the final bay, there was yet a danger of the stag's antlers dealing deathly wounds both to hounds and men. It was left to a huntsman to move skillfully behind the stag as it remained imprisoned within the circle of hounds, and to cut the hough-sinew in the hind leg to disable it. Then to end the agony of the animal, the huntsman killed it (*servir le cerf*) by piercing it between the horns and the neck, cutting through the spinal cord to the marrow. He might, alternatively, plunge a sword through to the heart from behind the shoulder. It was less common to slay the stag with bow and arrow in this type of hunt. Immediately the hounds were permitted an adequate opportunity to leap upon (*fouler*) the carcass

The pursuit: nearing the capture. Miniature in Gaston Phébus, *Livre de chasse, ca.* 1400, ms. 616, folio 77 r°. Bibliothèque Nationale, Département des Manuscrits.

to bite the flesh and suck the blood, while the hunters continued to utter cries of the chase, both caressing and urging them.

Breaking (*défaire*) the stag consisted first of placing it on its back with the antlers fixed in the earth on either side of the carcass. The right foot was severed and presented (*lever les droits*) to the king or highest ranking person, perhaps to a lady to be complimented by the "honors of the foot." Now the cods were cut away, and the carcass was flayed (*écorcher le cerf*). The hide was to be left under the carcass, propped up at the corners by sticks to keep the blood from flowing off. The belly was slit open from jowls to pizzle and the entrails taken out. Certain choice morsels of these organs belonged by right to chief personages on the field; they might be consumed at once or arranged on a forked branch (*fourchie*) for presentation. Finally the haunches and the head were removed. Portions of the carcass were reserved for purposes that vary widely from one authority

du cuir tout entour le au bien
pres. Et ne couppe une les
oreilles lesse les en sa teste et
couppe le cuir par derriere les
oreilles en alant en traucrs
en aussant grans bauffres
du cuir pendus. Ainsi souuns
se cerf escorchier si comme on
se doit faire ou mestier de la
nene. Cy deuise coment
et par quelle maniere len
deffait le cerf Et paysant
manicre.

Aprentis
demande coment len
deffait le cerf. prudus respot.
Quant tu deffais le cerf
oste premierement la langue
toute entiere et boute ton

touuel par mi le gosier qui tient
a la langue et fay vne fente
boute ou foursbie de quoy nous
tauons parle icy deuät. puis
oste les antours qui en auant
appellent les neus du cerf. les
antours sont une huille chair
qui est ou coste du col et tont
auir espaules. En cela atu
ners cesse chau somgnant de
lespaule et fay vny peuis en
preste assouter ten doy si la su
lieue de ton doy et couppe au
long du col cesse chau euiron
plain pie de long et fay vng
partuis et met au foursbie
et aussi fens tu de lautre
part. puis pren le pie deuät
deffue du cerf et enaisse tout a

trauers du coste du cerf au
long de lespaule par deucrs
se coste et oste lespaule et
ainsi ostenis tu lespaule de
lautre part. Puis oste la
surgorge cest vne chair qui e

de puis le bout de la hampe
par dessus sa gorge. Enaise
dont par le bout de la hampe
tout atrauers se col iusques
au saerel et garde que tu ne
le couppes. Et couppe cesse

to another: the heart to the lepers; the cartilage of the heart to a pregnant woman or to a lord and a child; the left shoulder to the forester; the liver to his boy; the suet and urine saved for their medicinal value; the head to the master huntsman, or the lord of the household, or even the limer; the pelvic bone—"the corbeles fee"—to the ravens. Throughout the breaking of the stag, the hunters were exhorted to drink wine in plenty—and only wine—and to leave none of it!

The hounds' reward was to be prepared with turned-back sleeves, but without gloves. Their tidbits might be the heart, liver and kidneys according to one source, the lungs, well-cleaned paunch, windpipe, and blood-soaked bread according to another. These were arranged upon the hide, the hounds summoned to the "quarry" but held on leashes and disciplined with sticks to prevent their approaching too impulsively or competing with one another. An important stage for its training value, the quarry was accompanied by continuing fanfares and hunting cries. At the last the remainder of the carcass was trussed and

The quarry: the hounds are given their portions while a hunter sounds the horn. Woodcut in *Les Livres du roy Modus*, Chambéry, 1486, folio b 7 r⁰. Courtesy Pierpont Morgan Library.

Hunters prepare the stag's carcass before their return. The Hunt of the Unicorn: Return from the Hunt. Early sixteenth-century Franco-Flemish tapestry. The Metropolitan Museum of Art, Bequest of Helen Hay Whitney, 1945.

carried to the lord's gate where the company "blew the Prise"—
that is, sounded the fanfare of the capture.

Here in brief were the techniques and the language of the
stag chase as it can be reconstructed from a conflation of medieval
hunting books. While the preceding account is mainly factual,

Two hunters return with the stag's carcass slung over their horse.
Miniature in Marco Polo, *Livre des Merveilles*, fourteenth century, ms.
2810, folio 62 vº. Bibliothèque Nationale, Département des Manuscrits.

medieval handbooks do reflect an acquaintance with certain
iconographic representations and allegorical descriptions of the
stag (and other animals) as they occur in the arts and in literary
materials. To the sources available we may turn for examples
of these iconographic images.

The Iconography of the Stag

The stag could be visually represented in striking, identifiable
attitudes, whether these representations were plastic or verbal.
Five principal iconographical types of the stag can be discerned;
the meanings attached to each type could vary, and in some
instances more than one type became conjoined. The five are:

the thirsting stag, the serpent-slaying stag, the nobly antlered stag, the harried stag, and the transpierced stag.

The original text for the thirsting stag is Psalm 41: 1. "As the hart panteth after the water brooks, so panteth my soul after thee, O God" (*Quemadmodum desiderat cervus ad fontes aquarum, ita desiderat anima mea ad te, Deus*). A simple commentary on this verse is that of Rabanus Maurus, who glosses the stag as the soul of the faithful that eagerly desires great spiritual good. In a lyric by Hildegard of Bingen that praises St. Maximinus, the poet dwells in a verse upon the life-giving waters. She compares the saint to the hart longing for the fountain, the water of His love that issues from Christ himself: "He, the swift hart ran up to the fountain of purest water bubbling from the mightiest stone whose moisture made the sweet perfumes flow."[22]

The legend of the serpent-slaying stag, received from natural historians such as Pliny, Aelian, Oppian, and Lucretius, is repeated by Isidore of Seville in his *Etymologies:* The stag is able to rejuvenate its strength when infirm. It devours a certain venomous serpent which it draws out of the clefts in the rocks by the breath of its nostrils, and so is restored by finding a medicinal value in the poison. Both the thirsting stag and the serpent-slaying stag become fused in Peter Lombard's summarizing gloss of Psalm 41:1. The stag is the catechumen who, having swallowed the poisons of earthly vice (that is, the serpent), thirsts for the waters of the baptismal font. The poison is thus quenched and the catechumen rejoices like the newly youthful stag, for he has become a new man. In a similar manner, the stag of the psalm verse joins with the serpent-killing stag in the *Bestiaire de Gervaise*. Here it is the penitent man who, determined to destroy his snakish sin and thirsting for his soul's renewal, allegorizes the stag. A variation occurs in the *Bestiaire Divin* of Guillaume le Clerc. In this case, however, the meaning alters: the stag is Christ harrowing hell and overcoming the

[22] On the thirsting stag: Rabanus Maurus, *PL* 112. 893a; Hildegard of Bingen, cited in Peter Dronke, *The Medieval Lyric* (London, 1968), p. 76.

serpent, Satan. The stag is said to spew water into the serpent's
hole, so forcing him out to destroy him. Therefore, "in Him
there wells up the clear fountain that is full of wisdom." The
Master of Game cautiously cites the legend of the stag's re-
juvenation through the snake, and its longevity, to introduce a
passage on the medicinal virtues of the various parts of its body:

> An hert lyuoþ lengest of eny beest for he may wel lyve an c. yere,
> and þe eldere he is, þe fairere he is of body and of heed and more
> lecherous, but he is not so swift ne so liȝt ne so myghty. And ȝit
> mony men seyn but I make non affirmacioun vpon þat whan he is
> ryht olde he hetyth a serpent wiþ his foote til she be wrothe, and
> þan he oteth hure and þan gooþ drynk, and þan he rennethe hidere
> and þidere to þe watir, and venyin be medled togydere and makeþ
> hym cast al his euel humours þat he had in his body and makeþ
> his flesshe come al newe.

Sir Thomas Malory evokes the stag's capacity to renew its life,
comparing it to the immortal life of Christ, but does not, however, allude to the serpent:

> And well ought oure Lorde be signifyed to an harte. For the
> harte, whan he ys olde, he waxith yonge agayne in his whyght
> skynne. Ryght so commyth agayne oure Lorde frome deth to
> lyff, for He lost erthely fleysshe, that was the dedly fleyssh whych
> He had takyn in the wombe of the Blyssed Virgyne Mary. And
> for that cause appered oure Lorde as a whyghte harte withoute
> spot.[23]

An allegorical chapter (which also notes briefly the stag's
renewal of its youth) of *Les livres du roy Modus* gives considerable

[23] On the serpent-slaying stag: Isidore of Seville, *Etymologiarum sive
Originum Libri* 20, ed. W. M. Lindsay, 2 vols. (Oxford, 1911), 12.1.
18–19; Peter Lombard, *PL* 191. 415a–416a-c; *Bestiaire de Gervaise*, ed.
Paul Meyer, *Romania* 1 (1872): 420; *Le Bestiaire: Das Tierbuch des
normannischen Dichters Guillaume le Clerc*, ed. Robert Reinsch (Leipzig,
1892; rpt. Wiesbaden, 1967), lines 2761–2762; *The Master of Game*,
p. 20; *The Works of Sir Thomas Malory*, ed. Eugène Vinaver (New York,
1954), p. 718. A useful summary of the patristic background of Christ
the stag is given in Carl Pschmadt, *Die Sage von der verfolgte Hindin*
(Greifswald, 1911), pp. 35–37.

attention to the type I have distinguished as the nobly antlered stag. Queen Ratio provides the apprentice with the desired "moralités et figures" of the stag. In all cases she makes its antlers analogous to some human power or virtue that glorifies God or that God has bestowed. First, just as Our Lord has given the stag the ten branches of its antlers to defend itself against its three enemies, men, hounds and wolves, so has Christ given men the ten commandments of the law by which he may defend himself against the flesh, the devil and the world. Secondly, we are reminded how God showed himself crucified to St. Eustace (see below, p. 60) by allowing his image to be mirrored forth among these commandments, that is, amidst a stag's antlers. The antlers may be figuratively explained as the ten fingers of the priests as they elevate bread and wine before the people, substances converted through God's "great nobility" into the body and blood of Christ. Thirdly, through the same nobility, good men, both cleric and lay, obey and keep in their own heads the ten commandments to be beheld in the antlers of the stag's head. Finally, the fallow deer and the roe deer bear horns that represent crowns; so these beasts can be compared to emperors and kings and to all those of noble rank who sustain the faith. While oriental analogues have been proposed for the mystically horned stag, whose radiant antlers form a crown or a nimbus, Queen Ratio's allegories are, so far as I know, individual.[24]

A fourth iconographic type, the harried stag, may be observed in examples reflecting both a classical and a Christian tradition, each with differing meanings. The simile of the chase that turns up in the *Song of Roland* belongs to the epic genre. While treacherous Ganelon pretends that Roland would blow his horn mightily for a hare only, Roland's quarry is in fact the Saracens who flee from him like the stag from the hounds. The lintel at Angoulême repeats the iconographic stag chase in which

---

[24] On the nobly antlered stag: *Les livres du roy Modus*, 1, chap. 74; Pschmadt, *Die sage von der verfolgte Hindin*; Hippolyte Delehaye, *Mélanges d'Hagiographie Grecque et Latine* (Brussels, 1966), p. 235.

Christians and pagans figure. These must be regarded as
Virgilian imitations, for in the *Aeneid* it is a doomed and in-
effectual Turnus who as the stag (*cervus*) is to be done to death
by that worthy hunting dog (*canis venator*), Aeneas. This is the
sort of simile found so frequently in Homer, for instance,
Achilles' swooping upon Hector like a falcon after a dove. The
doomed stags of the *Aeneid* and the *Song of Roland* are the
enemy, and the fiercely harrying hounds their righteous pursuers.

No less doomed is the harried stag of the Christian tradition;
its significance, however, is for everyman; its pursuers, fleshly
ills, devils, vices, and Death. Hunts had been depicted on funerary monuments and sarcophagi during Roman times. The
pursued animal, like the psychopomp Hermes, conducted the
hunter-soul over the threshold of mortality. Christian craftsmen
copied this motif in their funerary art, probably, as Cumont has
suggested, without recognizing the animal psychopomp as the
emissary of a pagan divinity such as Dionysus-Zagreus. But in
the medieval form of this type of hunt, it is the stag who is the
driven soul. Explicit examples are to be seen in tapestries and
miniatures of the sixteenth century. Each of the five panels of
one tapestry, for example, portrays a stage of the stag's pursuit
through life by various dogs and hunters. *Nature* first leads
forth the limer *Jeunesse*, while hounds representing pride, doubt,
care, sorrow, age and other such forces are driven by hunters
among whom are *Ignorance, Vanité, Vieillesse, Maladie. La Mort*
deals the last blow.

The allegory of man's life as that of a driven animal may be
found earlier in literary texts as well. 'A iesu hwuder schal ich
fleon hwon þe deouel hunteð efter me bute to þine rode?' [Ah,
Jesu, which way shall I flee when the devil hunts me but to
your cross?] ends the *Orison to our Lord*. The sinner's agitated
flight from vice is expressed various ways in Chaucer's lyric,
"An ABC," a translation from De Guilleville. In one stanza the
sinner acknowledges that he is a beast—later "prey"—that flees
from the world's enemy and beseeches the Virgin's aid:

Al have I ben a beste in wil and deede,
Yit, ladi, thou me clothe with thi grace.
Thin enemy and myn—ladi, tak heede!—
Unto my deth in poynt is me to chace!

Chaucer's Parson corroborates the devil's manner of hunting his "praye," man:

The feend seith, "I wole chace and pursue the man by wikked suggestioun, and I wole hente [seize] hym by moevynge or styringe of synne."

That the "stirring of sin" could be a beguiling means of harrying man is made clear in the English *Gesta Romanorum*'s legend of Constance. Referring to the notion that the hunted deer was apt to be entranced by the sweet belling of the hounds and would stop to listen, the allegorical passage describes the hind's heeding, to its sorrow, the seductive baying of the dogs, "evil thoughts":

And an hynde ariseth vp, scil. dilectacion of synne, and all þe wittys rennyth after, Thorow werkyng of synfull werkys; and houndys, scil. shrewde thowtys, euermor berkith, and entisith so, þat a man, scil. þe flesh, and þe soule stondith and abidith stille.[25]

The last iconographic image to be exemplified here is the transpierced stag—and hind. When Hugo of St. Victor allegorized the hind as the pure soul of mankind smitten by illicit

---

[25] On the harried stag: *La Chanson de Roland*, ed. T. A. Jenkins (Boston, 1924; rpt. 1965), lines 1874–75; *Aeneid* 12. 750–751; Rita Lejeune and Jacques Stiennon, *La légende de Roland dans l'art du Moyen âge* (Brussels, 1966), p. 38; Franz Cumont, *Recherches sur le symbolisme funéraire des Romains* (Paris, 1942), pp. 455, 438 ff.; Emil Picot, "Le cerf allégorique dans les tapisseries et les miniatures," *Bulletin de la société française de reproductions de manuscrits à peintures*, 3ᵉ année (Paris, 1913), pp. 57–67, with 11 plates; *Old English Homilies and Homiletic Treatises of the Twelfth and Thirteenth Centuries*, ed. Richard Morris, *EETS* (London, 1868), 34: 203; "An ABC"; "The Parson's Tale" in *The Complete Works of Geoffrey Chaucer*, ed. F. N. Robinson (London, 1957), pp. 525, 238; *The Early English Versions of The Gesta Romanorum*, ed. Sidney J. H. Herrtage, *EETS ES* (London, 1879), 33: 320.

longings, his inspiration may have been Virgil. A fuller consideration of Eros the hunter, and Virgil's Dido as a wounded hind, properly belongs in the next chapter on the Love Chase. But it is to the point to be reminded of them here: Hugo writes: "Cerva est casta et munda anima. Sagittae sunt desideria mala. Venatores sunt daemones. . . ." Day by day our souls are chased by diabolical hunters who seek to ensnare us with our own nets of the five senses or shoot us from afar with their deadly arrows of evil desires.

However, the arrows of desire need not be evil always, even in a Christian context. Much earlier, in his gloss upon the Canticles, Origen had called God the archer that strikes man with his chosen arrow (*sagitta electa*), opening within his soul the burning wound of love. Origen does not explain what sort of animal man is. Perhaps he is simply man. Origen's passage on the stag remains distinct from the wound of love, for there he reiterates the legend of the serpent-killing stag, suggesting thereby that the *caprea*, the roe of the Canticles, may be understood as the Savior. But if we think of the wound of love as a blessed, as well as a cruel stroke, our understanding of the later, medieval figure of Christ as the transpierced stag becomes enhanced. If man is the wounded beast of the devil's chase, and yet may be the recipient of the dart of divine love, then Christ shares man's part. For, made flesh, he became the transpierced victim of men's cruel pursuit, at the same time that he bore the wound for love of mankind. A brief image in a thirteenth-century lyric remembers, in the midst of the Virgin's tears, that Christ was made quarry:

> He was to-drawe,
> so dur islawe
> in chace.[26]

---

[26] On the transpierced stag: *PL* 177. 575a; Origen, *Homélies sur le Cantique des Cantiques*, ed. and tr. Dom O. Rousseau (Paris, 1953), pp. 95, 98–99; "A springtide song of redemption," *English Lyrics of the XIIIth Century*, ed. Carleton Brown (Oxford, 1932), p. 110.

The Hunt as a Literary Structure

Medieval writers found ways of using the icon of the stag in its diversity of appearances, as they found that the stages and indeed the whole procedure of the stag chase lent themselves to fictional ends. The action of a hunt could be seen to follow a pattern that made it conformable to patterns of literary action. Even in its simplest form the hunt meant movement toward conflict. The sense of a heroic contest between hunter and quarry emerges from a number of medieval authors. St. Augustine used the word *venator* to mean "gladiator," a fighter of wild beasts. Aelfric's *Colloquy* depicts the huntsman's craft as one demanding courageous confrontation: "How did you dare to kill the bear?" asks the Master. "I stood opposing him and slew him with a sudden blow." To the Master's admiring, "You were so brave!" comes the understated reply, "A huntsman shouldn't be fearful." Both ancient and medieval writers understand the fusion of the hunt's disciplined violence with the heroic exploit in accounts of the toils of Hercules, the slayer of beasts who over and over captures his quarry. Forced to expiate his wrongs by pursuing and controlling fantastic and noxious beasts, manifestations of destructive nature, he is the very type of the ascendant hunter. In one of the many medieval translations of Boethius's *Consolation of Philosophy*, Chaucer enumerates his triumphs: "He dawntide [daunted] the proude Centauris, and he byrafte the despoilynge fro the cruel lyoun; . . . he smote the brides . . . he drowh [drew] Cerberus (*the hound of helle*), by his treble cheyne . . . and he, Hercules, slowh [slew] Idra the serpent and brende the venym. . . ." (Book 4, poem 7). The exemplum concludes with an exhortation to courage: "Goth now thanne, ye stronge men, ther as the heye wey of the greet ensaumple ledith yow."

If such authors made a connection between the actual hunting and slaying of animals and heroic or manly action, the authors of hunting manuals made similar correspondences. We have remarked that it was not unusual for these books of instruction to incorporate the conventions of poetry. It would be difficult to say who was imitating whom, for the reciprocal exchange of influence between poets and the authors of manuals of the chase was one of long standing. Certainly a literary treatment of the business of hunting was not a medieval innovation. Among the Greek and Latin authors of hunting books, there is an attitude of rivalling the poets. One of the most interesting from this point of view is the third century writer Oppian who dedicated his Greek treatise, *Cynegetica*, which is really a "little epic," to the Roman Emperor Caracallus. It is a charged and buoyant celebration of the pleasures of hunting. Oppian has the poets in mind from the beginning. Calliope and Artemis call on him, and he opens with a dialogue between the author and Artemis. In it the goddess urges him to leave the usual subjects of heroes, Argonauts, Dionysus, and Aphrodite, and to "Sing the battles of the wild beasts and hunting men; sing of the breeds of hounds and the varied tribes of horses; the quick-witted counsels; the deeds of skilful tracking." His hunted animals acquired the status of characters with their "bridal chambers," "tearless love," their births in need of "no midwifery," their friendships and their feuds. However, when he writes about the intense longing of the hound, stirred by the scent of its prey, Oppian temporarily forsakes the epic mode and indulges in an extravagant simile of yearning reminiscent of romances:

> Even as when a girl in the tenth lunar month, smitten by the birth-pangs of her first child, undoes her hair and undoes the drapery of her breasts and, poor girl, without tunic and without snood, roams everywhere about the house, and in her anguish now goes to the hall and anon rushes to her bed, and sometimes throws herself in the dust and mars her rosy cheeks; so the dog, distressed by devouring grief, rushes this way and that and searches every stone in turn and every knoll and every path and trees and garden vines and dykes and threshing floors. And when at last he hits the airy trail, he gives tongue and whines for joy; even as the little calves leap about the uddered cows, so the dog rejoices exceedingly.[27]

[27] *Oppian, Colluthus, Tryphiodorus*, Oppian's *Cynegetica*, ed. and tr. A. W. Mair (Cambridge, 1928; rpt. 1958), pp. 5 ff., 51–53.

If the actual hunt could be accorded literary treatment in this fashion, the converse was also true, in ancient as in medieval times: the hunt might become a metaphorical, symbolic, or structural element in literature. We may go back to Xenophon (430–354 B.C.), himself one of the earliest authors of a treatise on hunting, the *Cynegeticus*, in which he lists Homeric heroes— Nestor, Odysseus, Peleus, Achilles—as worthy hunters. His *Cyropaedia*, the education of Cyrus the Elder who established the Persian Empire, was a form combining history, biography, the theory of rule, and romance. While Xenophon in fact believed in the hunt as an important military exercise, he also turns it into a narrative element in the life of his boy hero. Cyrus's first hunt leads to a military triumph. Battle takes place between the youth and the enemy Assyrians who have dared to take game in Median territory. The hunters are in turn hunted by Cyrus and he slaughters them. By its placement in the narrative the hunting expedition serves as a crucial coming-of-age feat that marks the blooding of the young ruler. Generalizing on the virtue of the hunt for Persian youth, Xenophon writes what is to become a medieval commonplace, repeated also eventually by Machiavelli and Cervantes:

> The training it gives seems to be the best preparation for war itself. For it accustoms them to rise early in the morning and to endure both heat and cold, and it gives them practice in taking long tramps and runs, and they have to shoot or spear a wild beast whenever it comes their way. And they must often whet their courage when one of the fierce beasts shows fight. . . . In a word, it is not easy to find any quality required in war that is not required also in the chase.[28]

In an elaborated form, the hunt offers a narrative pattern of quest and conflict, with a dénouement. Both in actuality and in fiction, the dénouement of a hunt could vary. A hunter might "win" the contest, that is by defeating and possessing his quarry. "Losing" could mean that the animal has eluded him, or it

[28] Ed. and tr. Walter Miller, 2 vols. (Cambridge, Mass., 1914), 1:19.

could mean that the hunter dies in the pursuit. In hunts in which the hunter himself is slain, it could be said that he has in effect, although unwittingly, become the victim of his chase. This situation formed a paradox dear to many medieval writers. There is a third possible outcome, a fictional one to be sure, suggested by the actuality of long and frustrating hunts: that the obsessed hunter, unable to give up, becomes forever chained to his pursuit. Instead of the hoped-for conflict with the quarry, there is the anguish of an eternal quest. Examples are to be found among the earliest writers of all three types of dénouement —the hunter successful, the hunter turned victim and the hunter doomed to an endless chase.

Consider Plato's metaphors of the hunts of war and learning. Words constructed upon θηρ-, a wild creature or beast of prey, contain the idea of urgent pursuit, whatever the object. Generalship is an art of hunting men ((Θηρευτική τις ἥδε γέ ἐστι τέχνη ἀνθρώπων) in the shape of cities and armies. Xenophon dispraised such hunters of men, and closed his *Cynegeticus* declaring that true hunters toil in the service of their fellow citizens, unlike the politicians who selfishly plunder other men. As for geometers, astronomers, and calculators, Plato called these "hunters in their way" into the nature of being. For the general, the geometer, the astronomer, and the calculator—as for the actual hunter—the most important part of their sport is "the chase and the capture" ((θηρεῦσαι καὶ χειρώσασθαι), as distinct from the knowing use of their booty afterwards. Thereupon, like huntsmen and fishermen, all will turn over the spoil of their respective hunting to those who will know what use to make of them, the winnings of the investigators, for example, being made over to those versed in dialectic. The philosophical hunter becomes a butt of satire in Aristophanes' *Clouds:* thus, Strepsiades is mocked with "We greet you, old man, hunter of the Muses' lore!" But the philosopher's chase is soon to be a cliché, a flattened image, and the notion of hunting simply becomes buried in the language of scientific or philosophical research. Cicero's aside, defining the physical philosopher as a hunter, can be no more: "Should not therefore the physicist, that is, the searcher and hunter of nature (*speculator venatorque naturae*), feel ashamed to seek out evidence of the truth from minds steeped in habit?" The nouns *venator* and *vestigium* (a footprint), and verbs signifying stages of the hunt: *venor*, *indago* (track down), *vestigo* (follow a footprint, from which "investigate") will recur commonly in the language of inquiry—as for example in Thomas Aquinas' *venatur secundum particulam definitionis.*[29]

The paradox of the hunter who becomes his own victim is handled with elaborate emphasis in the work of two dramatists —Sophocles and Euripides—who may be cited here. In Sophocles' *Oedipus Tyrannos* the search for information leads not to the nature of external reality, as with the philosophers' quest, but to self-discovery. The booty of the chase proves larger than the pursuer had expected. Both the hunter and victim of his irascible chase, Oedipus unwittingly tracks himself down to exposure and defeat. When he inveighs against Creon, Oedipus accuses him of hunting for power ($\tau\nu\rho\alpha\nu\nu\iota\delta\alpha$ / $\theta\eta\rho\hat{\alpha}\nu$, 541–2). Bernard Knox writes: "He sees Creon as the foolish hunter who is not equipped for the chase, a contrast to himself who has long ago captured the prey."[30] Ironically, Oedipus echoes the theme of his own chase for Laius's murderer, which has long ago been sounded in the play. It was, in fact, Oedipus who initiated the metaphor upon hearing the word of the oracle that Creon brought: "Where shall it be found, this track ($\ddot{\iota}\chi\nu\sigma$) of an ancient guilt, difficult to trace?" (109), Creon replies: "If

[29] The metaphor of the philosopher's hunt is to be seen in Plato, *Euthydemus* 290b, c, and d, ed. and tr. W. R. M. Lamb (Cambridge, Mass., 1924, rpt. 1962); Aristophanes, *Nubes*, ed. K. J. Dover (Oxford, 1968), line 358; Cicero's *De Natura Deorum*, ed. Arthur Stanley Pease, 2 vols. (Cambridge, 1955), 1:83; Aquinas' *Commentaria in 3 libros Aristotelis de Anima* 2. 1. 3.

[30] *Oedipus at Thebes* (Yale University Press: New Haven, 1957), p. 112. See also p. 111 and notes, pp. 234–235. Words for tracking and starting game are abundant in *Oedipus*, as Bernard Knox has shown, although the chase forms just one of the metaphorical schemes within the play. The translations used here are Knox's.

you search for it you can catch it (τὸ δεξητούμενον / ἁλωτόν) but if you neglect it, it escapes" (110–111). When Tiresias is driven to pronounce the dire word "polluter" of Oedipus, the king upbraids him for his shamelessness: "You flush from cover (ἐξεκίνησας, i. e. start game) such a word!" (354–55). The chorus enlarges upon the theme of the hunted beast, singing of the fugitive, and touches ironically upon the maimed foot of the one who flees:

> It is time for him to move in flight a foot swifter than wind-swift mares . . . . The divine command has flashed from Parnassus to track down (ἰχνεύειν) by all means in our power the man who has left no trace (τὸν ἄδηλον, a vanished spoor). For he ranges under the shade of the wild forest, among caves and rocks, like the bull, solitary in misery, with miserable foot. [464 ff.]

At the last, caught by his own pursuing, Oedipus pleads to be permitted to return to the mountains.

The tragic hero becomes incorporated here in the act of the chase. The frontier passed by Oedipus is a psychic one: the truths he pursues and captures are those in his doomed nature. Like many hunts in literature that impel the protagonist to contest and destruction, it is one that proves irresistible. A divinity controls the hunt and its outcome at the same time that Oedipus brings about his own catastrophe. Even while fleeing from himself, his character drives him running to meet his destiny.

The hunting that pervades the *Bacchae* of Euripides is more specifically rooted in the role of the god Dionysus whose power the play celebrates. The Greek Dionysus was both a hunter and sacred victim whose functions and epithets had syncretized with those of the Cretan divinity Zagreus—"lord of the wild animals," "great hunter," a god of death and the underworld who hunted his victims. In the *Bacchae* different characters are victims at different times, and finally the mortal hunter-king Pentheus is sacrificed so that the god may be glorified and live. Throughout, the Maenads' ritual tearing of their victim (probably a re-enactment of the tearing of Dionysus by the Titans) is expressed as the climax of a hunt. The women are "fleet hounds," for instance (977). Upon their return from dismembering their victim, Agave exults: "Happy was the hunting!" (1171, 1183). But the "quarry" is precisely that king, Pentheus, who had persecuted the god and his cult, ordering that *they* be hunted down as beasts (226–27). His attendant refers to them as "quarry" and "prey" (435–36). So Pentheus as would-be hunter is to become the hunter entrapped (1019), his fate a repetition of Actaeon's (1293), most renowned among the hunter-victims. The Bacchae as hounds of the god return from the mountains with their "quarry of the chase" (1204), praising Bacchus "the hunter" who "lashed the Maenads against his prey" (1191–92). More terribly ironic is a further exchange of the roles of hunter and victim, however, for the Maenad Agave as one of the god's "hounds" discovers too late that in their frenzy she and the other women have dismembered her son, who was Pentheus. Thus, even while revering and serving the god as one of his hunters, she must fall victim to his inexorable power, her child's own slayer.[31]

What of a pursuit that never ends? So long as the chase continues unresolved, hunter and hunted remain locked in their antithetical relationship of flight and pursuit. The myth of the hound that never fails to seize its prey and the prey that is destined never to be captured is preserved by Apollodorus in his *Library* and by Ovid in the *Metamorphoses*: Minos gave Procris, his mistress, such a hunting hound whose name was Laelaps. The hound went in pursuit of an uncapturable vixen that had been ravaging the country. But given the properties of the pursuer and the quarry, no consummation of this chase would ever be possible. Through the intervention of Zeus, both hound and quarry became transfixed into stone, resulting in the paradox of a moving yet arrested pursuit, incompleted except as the artist has captured it.

[31] References to the *Bacchae* are from David Grene and Richmond Lattimore (eds.), *The Complete Greek Tragedies* (University of Chicago Press: Chicago, 1958), Vol. 4, Euripides, tr. William Arrowsmith.

Later versions of the unresolved hunt occur as legends of the wild chase. Where the climactic joining of the two, hunter and victim in a contest, fails to take place, where the hunter rides endlessly and the perpetually elusive quarry dooms him to this course, the hunter can be regarded as a victim. Imprisoned in a repetitious, futile, and seemingly unchanging act, the obsessed pursuer takes part in a train of the hunting dead or damned. Medieval accounts survive of processions of souls or demonically possessed beings driven and led by powers like Herodias, Hellekin, and Diana. Can such reports as these of routs of women, "witches" riding on animals, sweeping up infants to devour them, have stemmed from relics or memories of Bacchic sects? Known in the early Roman centuries, such minorities were publicly threatening and very hard to eradicate. Heightened stories of bands of frantic religious devotees bent upon their grisly prey may well have nourished those Christian legends of the hunting and hunted damned.[32]

Eventually, medieval eyewitnesses were not wanting for lurid reports of these processions. Ordericus Vitalis in the *Historia Ecclesiastica* tells of a wretched string of souls, goaded by the giant Herlechinus, that a priest of Bonneval, near Chartres, caught sight of in January 1091. A rout of recognizable clerics, monks, judges, and bishops, as well as certain women, were glimpsed riding through the forest. Among the torments they endured was that of a burning nail affixed to the saddle, wounding the nates of the howling rider. The terrified curate recalled "harlequin," and murmured to himself, "Haec sine dubio familia Herlechini est. . . ." The *Peterborough Chronicle* for 1127 describes a mob of twenty or thirty hunters seen riding to the

---

[32] On the wild chase, see Burchard, Bishop of Worms, "Decretorum libri XX," bk. xix, called "the Corrector," *PL* 140. 963d; Cumont, "Les mystères de Bacchus à Rome," in *Les religions orientales dans le paganisme romain* (Paris, 1929), pp. 195–204; Tenney Frank, "The Bacchanalian Cult of 186 B.C.," *Classical Quarterly* 21 (1927): 128–132; Richard Bernheimer, *Wildmen in the Middle Ages: A Study in Art, Sentiment, and Demonology* (Cambridge, Mass. 1952); Hanns Bächtold-Stäubli, "Wilde Jagd," *Handwörterbuch des deutschen Aberglaubens*.

hounds on rams and horses, blowing their horns continually by
night between Stanford and Peterborough during Lent. Hunters,
hounds, rams and horses, were black and loathly. In another
instance a woman was seen running from a wild company from
whose ranks were heard "þe voys of feendys, lyche þe voys of
hunters and of here houndys wyth orrible hornys and cryes."
And along with these testified accounts, there arises the transformed poetic version of that fairy company of the dead that
Sir Orfeo beheld, engaged in a ghostly chase during which they
took no beast:

> He miȝt se him bisides
> Oft in hot undertides
> þe king o fairy wiþ his rout
> Com to hunt him al about,
> Wiþ dim cri and bloweing;
> And houndes also wiþ him berking;
> Ac no best þai no nome,
> No never he nist whider þai bicome.[33]

Thus, the design to which any hunt, however complex, might

[33] The medieval accounts are in Ordericus Vitalis, ed. Augustus le
Prévost (Paris, 1845; rpt. New York and London, 1965) 3:367 ff.; *Jacob's
Well*, ed. Arthur Brandeis, *EETS* (London, 1900), 115: Pt. 1, pp. 166–67;
The Peterborough Chronicle, 1070–1154, ed. Cecily Clark (London, 1958),
p. 50; *Sir Orfeo*, ed. A. J. Bliss (Oxford, 1954), lines 281–288.
At length, the legend of the preternatural wild hunter who did mortals
mischief became relegated to the realm of young wives' tales, like the
one recounted by Mistress Page to Mistress Ford:

> "There is an old tale goes that Herne the hunter,
> Sometime a keeper here in Windsor forest,
> Doth all the winter-time, at still midnight,
> Walk round about an oak, with great ragg'd-horns;
> And there he blasts the tree, and takes the cattle,
> And makes milch-kine yield blood, and shakes a chain
> In a most hideous and dreadful manner.
> You have heard of such a spirit, and well you know
> The superstitious idle-headed eld
> Receiv'd and did deliver to our age
> This tale of Herne the hunter for a truth."
> [*Merry Wives of Windsor*, IV.iv. 28–38]

be resolved—the romantic quest, the epic contest, and the various dénouements—was capable of being exploited with individual results by early writers. In its developed literary form the hunt became a Journey upon which the protagonist was swept more or less irresistibly, impelled as he was by his desire for the quarry. Along the path of his Journey, the hunter would observe rules corresponding to the rules of the chase, perform necessary rituals, overcome obstacles in the landscape. All that he did marked stages in the hunt's progress and in his own. He might meet guides and rivals who would assist in determining the outcome of the hunt. Throughout this foreward movement of the Journey, a sense of conflict was strenuously maintained in the perpetual dialectic of flight and pursuit,[34] a dialectic broken at the last in the climactic encounter between the hunter and the animal. The pursued game acted as a lure, a guide, or psychopomp to draw the hunter ineluctably on his course from known surroundings into an unfamiliar, unsuspected, or forbidden territory where a crucial contest would take place, one that would change his life. This pursued animal often had uncanny qualities—whiteness for instance characterizes one type of quarry from the white hart and boar of Graelent and Partonopeus to the Whale that doomed Ahab to his infernal chase, or more whimsically, Alice's white Rabbit. Such quarry would entice the intent pursuer into an alien setting, an actual or psychic wilderness where he must wrestle with the beast. A function of the quarry therefore was to achieve the separation of the protagonist from his familiar notions of reality and order and procure for him his isolation.

The hunter would at length confront his prey, or he would engage in some adventure to which the hunted game had led him. For the animal itself might turn out to be of secondary importance: the original contest between man and quarry that belongs to an actual hunt might become transferred to some other power or adversary. The protagonist might even engage in

[34] The observation is in Jacques Aymard, *Les Chasses Romaines* (Paris, 1951), p. 142n.

his contest in the course of another person's hunting, thus assuming the quarry's or the hunter's role.

A turning point in the contest propelled the adventure to one of its possible conclusions. The hero triumphs; he captures, perhaps slays the animal, and is permitted to return with his spoils, perhaps to be established or re-confirmed within an order of his society. By his own act he has achieved a moral or practical victory and this completed his passage to a new condition. The quarry may here function as an extension of the hero's own nature, a restless, uncontrolled, or older aspect of himself. Details of the quarry's dismemberment may correspond to the hero's conquest of this former self, which he is now enabled to cast from him. On the other hand, the prize of the contest may not be the animal he originally set out to capture, but some other acquisition or burden of wisdom with which he must learn to endure.

An alternate conclusion is one of the two we have already observed. The encounter with the quarry or the struggle to which the quarry has conducted the hero may result in the dissolution of his former or human identity, perhaps the loss of his life. The hunter himself becomes the hunt's object; he, not the quarry, is sacrificed. Failing to survive the crisis to which the hunt has brought him, he is annihilated in the act. Or failing altogether to meet his quarry, the hunter becomes forever absorbed, like those engaged in the eternal chase, in the world of the hunt.

Metaphorically and symbolically, therefore, the chase becomes an imperative Journey by which a mortal is transported to a condition charged with experience: a preternatural region where he may be tested or placed under an enchantment; a transcendent universe; or the menacing reaches of the self. The act of the chase may reflect not only the compulsion arising from within his own nature to undergo change, but also an external force that imposes this necessity on him: that is, the god. For we are frequently aware of some power outside the hunter himself, with which his own will is made to coincide, both of

these driving, luring, compelling him. The hunts in which
Oedipus, Pentheus, and Actaeon engage are divinely controlled.
The god may be the beast that baits the man, or it may be the
god that makes of the man his victim, either as possessed hunter
or as captured object. When the mortal advances in to the next
world, he will sustain the shock, or he will fail; either his
humanity is enabled to take on something of the power of the
god, or willessly, he falls into the god's dominion.

There are four principal types of experience traditionally expressed in the form of a hunt in literature: The sacred chase,
the mortal chase, the instructive chase, and the amatory chase.
These four types are not mutually exclusive and will often occur
in combination. In the sacred chase, the quarry draws the hunting
protagonist to an encounter with a divinity where his conversion
is effected. The sacred chase may also encompass the hero's
death, however, in which case it will converge with the mortal
chase. The mortal chase in a nonreligious context uses the hunt
as a conductor from life to death. The instructive chase initiates
the hero: Hunting guides him from a condition of ignorance to
one of knowledge or self-knowledge. The amatory chase, which
will be the main burden of this book's investigation, drives the
hero—as hunter or victim or both—to the experience of passionate love.

II

The Chase in
Medieval Narrative

The Sacred Chase: Aelfric's Passion of St. Eustace

Among Greek and Latin pre-Christian authors, the hunts
that are devised by gods usually spell destruction for the mortal
who is lured to become involved in them. The hunt's purposes
are retributive and punitive. Sent by an angry deity whose altars
have been neglected, the quarry can cause havoc. Before or
after the general destruction, however, there may be a moment
of recognition, an acknowledgment of the wrong done, or a
stunning confrontation with the godhead. One example of such
a chase is that described in a legend that Pausanias recorded in
his *Description of Greece*. Moved to vengeance by the omission
of her rites at Stymphalos, Artemis sent a stag to entice a certain
hunter. The animal attracted the man to the abandoned and now
flooded Stymphalian plain. Having followed his quarry to the
flood that verged on an abyss there, the hunter was so inflamed
by the pursuit as to be incapable of withdrawing at the brink.
He plunged into the water after the stag and all three—man,
quarry, and lake, were washed down into the chasm, sacrifices
to the goddess's displeasure. The malice of the goddess of the
chase was familiar enough in the Middle Ages. A similar
reference to her and her emissary, the ravaging Calydonian boar,
is recorded in the *Roman de Thèbes*, where she takes retribution
against the father of Oeneus for his failure to fulfill her rites.
Chaucer gives the tale in his *Troilus*, and he also depicts the fate

of Actaeon, widely repeated among medieval authors, in his
Temple of Diana of the Knight's Tale:

> Ther saugh I Attheon an hert ymaked,
> For vengeaunce that he saugh Diane al naked;
> I saugh how that his houndes have hym caught
> And freeten [devoured] hym . . .[1]

The meeting with the god in Christian hunts might be just
as stunning as Actaeon's witnessing of Diana in the bath, but in
Christendom the figure of the divinely sent emissary of the stag
is benevolent in its purpose. Aelfric's Passion of St. Eustace
points up the Anglo-Saxon author's identification of Christ with

St. Eustace and the cruciferous stag. Woodcut in *Les Livres du roy
Modus*, Chambéry, 1486, folio f 5 v°. Courtesy Pierpont Morgan Library.

[1] The references to the vengeful Artemis are in Pausanias, *Description
of Greece*, ed. and tr. W. H. S. Jones (Cambridge, Mass., 1954), bk. 8,
chap. 22, "Arcadia"; *Roman de Thèbes*, ed. Léopold Constans (Paris,
1890), 1, lines 761–764; Chaucer, *Troilus*, 5.1464 ff.; "The Knight's
Tale," *Works*, p. 37, lines 2065–2068.

the stag, and he achieves something more. By his choice of punning language during the scene of Placidas's conversion (before he takes the baptismal name of Eustace), Aelfric infuses the familiar paradox of pursuer's and victim's exchanging roles with the Christian concept of the victim victorious. While the narrative episodes of the legend, as Aelfric received it, already carry out this theme of the hunter's assumption of the victim's role as the man grows more like the god, it is Aelfric who stresses this through his use of language. The legend is as follows:[2]

Placidas, so called from birth, was a military tribune living in the days of the emperor Trajan's reign. Pagan though he was, Placidas and his wife lived virtuously, generously aiding those who were persecuted, needy, or otherwise unfortunate. Placidas loved to hunt with his soldiers, and one day as they followed a herd of stags Placidas remarked an animal greater and more beautiful than the rest. Pursuing this creature who separated itself from the herd, Placidas became separated from his companions. Alone and over difficult ground Placidas hastened after his quarry, until all at once the stag leaped up on a rocky ledge. The chase suspended, Placidas stopping long to admire the greatness of the stag, the quarry began to speak: (in accents reminiscent of those heard by Paul on the road to Damascus) "Placidas why do you pursue me? I am Jesus Christ whom you worship unknowingly." Placidas fell to the earth; restored to his senses at length he was told to be baptised together with his wife and sons, and to return to the place. These things he did, and, as Eustachius, he returned to the mountain to hear that he would undergo trials with his family. Choosing to suffer these

---

[2] The legend appears in *PG* 105. 375 ff., accompanied by a Latin text. The most faithful Latin version of the Greek original (which itself is at least as old as A.D. 726), is that, according to Holger Petersen, in Bonino Mombrizio (ed.), *Sanctuarium seu Vitae Sanctorum* (Paris, 1510; rpt. Paris, 1910). See Petersen, *La Vie de St. Eustache* (Paris, 1958), and Angelo Monteverdi, "I testi della leggenda di S. Eustachio," *Studi Medievali* 3 (1910): 392–498. Aelfric's version has been edited by W. W. Skeat, *EETS* (London, 1900) 94: 190–219.

at once, Eustachius saw within days a plague destroy his servants and animals. Thieves took his goods and clothing. He decided to leave his country, and embarked with his family for Egypt. But as he had no money to pay for the passage, Eustachius saw his wife taken from him by the ship's captain, who had fallen in love with her. Eustachius had no choice but to disembark with his children. At a point in his journey, finding himself prevented from proceeding by a river, he crossed over with one child on his back, and left him on the farther bank while returning for the second. With a child left on each bank, Eustachius endured the anguish of seeing a lion on the one shore take one son, and a wolf on the other carry off the second. Resisting the temptation to throw himself in the river, he trusted in God and made his way to a village where he labored for many years to earn his living. After various adventures Eustachius and his family became miraculously restored to one another. The children had actually been rescued from their wild predators by kindly farmers and shepherds, unknown to Eustachius, while his wife had been released from her captor by his death. But this worldly happiness was not to endure. In the course of time Trajan was succeeded by Hadrian, who became the instrument of Eustachius's final suffering and joyful death. Hadrian on the occasion of a victory urged his subjects to worship in Apollo's temple, which of course Eustachius and his family refused to do. When throwing the victims to the lions proved to be in-effectual since the lion would not attack them, the emperor had them enclosed to die in a fire-heated bronze bull. There, their deaths were painless, their bodies left miraculously intact.

The scene of Placidas's conversion is worth observing, as Aelfric tells it:

> Truly, between the stag's horns shone the likeness of Christ's holy cross, brighter than the radiance of the sun, and the image of our Lord, Christ the Savior. And He sent the speech of men into the stag and called to Placidas, saying, "Ah, Placidas, why do you persecute me? Indeed, for your sake I have come now, so that through this animal I might reveal myself to you. I am the Christ

that you unknowingly worship. The alms you give to the poor are
before me. And I came so that I might reveal myself through
this stag, and in his place, hunt and capture you instead, with
the nets of my mercy."

Witodlice betwux þaes heortes hornum glitenode gelicnys þaere
halgan cristes rode breohtre þonne sunnan leoma. and seo an-
licnysse ures drihtnes haelendes cristes. and he mennisce spraece
asende on þone heort. and clypode to placidam þus cwaeþende .
"Eala placida . hwi ehtest þu min . efne for þinum intingum ic com
nu . þaet ic þurh þis *nyten* þe mé aetywde . Ic eom se crist þe þu
nytende wurðast . þa aelmyssan þe þu þearfum dest . beforan me
syndon . and ic com þaet ic me þe aetywde þurh þysne *heort* . and
for hine þe ge-huntian . and gefón . mid þam nettum minre
mildheortnysse." [41-50]

Two sets of homonymic word-pairs, which I have italicized
and which are the feature exclusively of Aelfric's Old English,
draw attention echoically to the subtle exchange of roles between mortal hunter and divine victim. The primary pair is
heort, stag, and *mild-heort*, mild; the secondary pair is *nyten*,
animal, and *nytende*, ignorant. "The merciful and benign God"
(*se mild-heorta and se welwillenda god*, 17) who wishes to reward
Placidas for his good deeds is mentioned just before the hunt is
introduced with its *micelne floc heorta* (26), thus establishing a
link between God's mercy and the stag as the divine victim that
seems to offer itself. The passage quoted above ends with Christ's
revelation of Himself "through this stag" (*þurh þysne heort*, 49),
yet He makes it immediately clear that the hart has been a
decoy, a means of ensnaring Placidas as much as are the nets of
His mercy (*mid þam nettum minre mildheortnysse*). The stag that
began as prey is identified, like the mercy of God, as a pursuer.
Placidas, the apparent hunter, is to be the victim of this chase
in his eventual martyr's role. While the principal pair of hom-
onyms reveals the quarry to be the hunter, the secondary pair,
near-homonyms, links the ignorantly (*nytende*, 47) Christian
Placidas to the animal (*nyten*, 46) of this chase whom he, in
his sufferings, will have to replace. Christ has shown Himself

through this beast (*nyten*); Placidas who unknowingly (*nytende*) reveres Christ will imitate the passion of the divine victim who, in turn, has ensnared his soul.[3]

Placidas falls to earth twice during this meeting, and when he revives, Christ speaks further; the stag is no more mentioned here. When Placidas returns home, he and his wife and two young sons receive baptism. The next day Eustachius, as he is now called, goes out to the same place, sends away him companions as if for the purpose of hunting, and beholds the same vision (*þa ylcan gesihðe*, 102–3). Again he converses with Christ directly, as lord (*drihten*) and savior (*haelend*). But the image of the powerful, gentle quarry that had originally led him to Christ, face to face, anticipates the form of subsequent trials of Eustachius. Wild beasts, now predatory and menacing, will present themselves in their hunters' aspects to try the saint, but will in fact leave him unscathed. Eustachius must watch helplessly when the lion and wolf drag off his young sons; since he does not learn of their rescues until many years later, his anguish for his children is protracted. When at last he and his reunited family are condemned to die, the emperor Adrian has them thrown to a strong lioness. Instead of devouring them, however, the beast bows and falls at the feet of Eustachius. These three encounters with wild beasts form a pattern, both reversing and paralleling the narrative's original hunt scene, in which the human hunter stood before the divine quarry. It is now the beasts who threaten the man, and yet, as in that earlier scene, there is no combat. The expected climactic onset of the hunt does not occur at that first meeting, and continues to be postponed until the moment of Eustachius' death. At the last, a beast does devour Eustachius—but it is a beast of bronze. The flesh and blood lioness failing, the emperor has the device of

[3] Frances R. Lipp, "Aelfric's Old English Prose Style," *Studies in Philology* 66 (1969): 689–718, discusses this very feature of Aelfric's style, and gives examples, different from those in my analysis, of "the use of rhyme and of other similarities in sounds and, incidentally, of word play and repetition as well," drawing attention to balanced, parallel or antithetical words and phrases (692–694, 700).

the bronze bull (*aenne aerenne oxan*, 421) heated in the fire. It is as if the saint's initial bond with the divine quarry has become diffused and repeated throughout the story in the form of his other meetings with animals: no natural beast can touch him, only an "unnatural" one, forged by a pagan artificer. The legend's conclusion, moreover, distorts the conventional laudatory image of Hadrian as a hunter of imperial grandeur.[4] Here he is rather paltry. Managing badly with the lioness, he sets the bronze bull at his Christian quarry and succeeds in bringing about the consummation of a loftier chase than any of his own.

In Aelfric's hagiographic narrative, the mutually dependent and interchangeable polarities of hunter and hunted that were familiar in the sacral hunts of antiquity (notably the Dionysian) become converted to a paradox meaningful in terms of the Christian sacrifice. The Christian martyr both pursues and emulates the divine victim, who in turn permits Himself to be harried to the death in order to allure and captivate mankind. The revelation of the cruciferous stag provides a vision of Christ both divine and mortal. When eventually St. Hubert (b. 655) replaced Eustace in popularity, the miraculous elements in the older saint's life became attached to a substantial core of facts that made up the biography of St. Hubert. That the latter's fame spread wide is indicated by the many medieval orders of the Knights of St. Hubert, together with the founding of St. Hubert's Abbey where hunting dogs were raised. In the eleventh century St. Hubert's *vita* absorbed the motif of the cruciferous stag, probably as a result of his other associations with hunting. It is a suaver, more worldly account of the quarry's effect: revealing its gleaming cross, the stag instructs the hunting saint to go into the service of the current bishop whom he would eventually succeed.

From the thirteenth century, vernacular lives of St. Eustace proliferate; in French there are fourteen versions, eleven of them in verse. It is the legend of Eustace's cruciferous stag that

---

[4] The importance of Hadrian's hunts receives attention in Aymard, *Les Chasses Romaines*, pp. 173–184; 523–535.

provides the hunting book of *Modus et Ratio* with its point of departure for the allegory of the stag.

The Mortal Chase: Siegfried's Death in the *Nibelungenlied*

There are no supernatural elements evident in the *Nibelungen-lied*[5] to vindicate the harshness of fate or console men for their anguish. The procedure by which Siegfried exchanges his role of hunter for that of a victim is not redeemed by any other-wordly glory or even any wisdom in this world. This exchange of roles demonstrates how Siegfried is forced to bend to the single universally recognized and inexorable force in that dark epic-romance, the power of death. In terms of narrative structure the chase in the sixteenth âventiure works to conduct the hero from the world of the poem, an event that is necessary in motivating the subsequent behavior of his wife and bringing about the climax of the *Nibelungenlied*. The poet exploits hunting in its various details for the sake of irony, foreshadowing what is to come, and reflecting earlier occurrences. Siegfried hunts in such a way as to manifest his whole character and to recall for us his earlier achievements; at the same time his actions gradually anticipate the manner in which he will become the quarry of Hagen and Gunther, the two "boars" of Kriemhild's prophetic dream: she has seen them giving chase to Siegfried over the heath, reddening its blossoms. Siegfried's victim nature, increasingly emergent in the sixteenth âventiure, may also receive some strength from hints of his stag aspect, recalled during his death scene from earlier versions of his legend. For example, Sigurth in the *Thidreks Saga* was nourished in infancy by a hind; in the *Volsunga Saga* Brynhild explained Gudrun's dream of a great hart with golden hair as the coming of Siegfried.[6]

---

[5] References are to Karl Bartsch (ed.), *Das Nibelungenlied*, 18th ed. rev. (Wiesbaden, 1965).

[6] This characteristic of Siegfried is discussed in Otto Höfler, *Siegfried, Arminius und die Symbolik* (Heidelberg, 1961), pp. 48 ff.

The hunting adventure consists of three stages: the first shows Siegfried's brilliant and fantastic venatic performance; the second his comic-heroic grappling with the bear; and the third his curiously passive death. The three parts present contrasting spectacles, mounting in intensity, and revealing Siegfried's subtle passage from human to animal condition, from life to death.

Siegfried hunts competitively, with that insensitive superiority to the others which Hagen, finally exulting when Siegfried is slain, had found so invidious. The narrative draws attention repeatedly to his excellence, and these praises begin to ring hollowly against the insistent allusions to his fate as the hunt's prime victim:

> Den lop er vor in allen an dem jegde gewan. [934,4]
>
> Er was in allen dingen biderbe genuoc.   [935,1]

> He above all others won praise in the chase.
>
> He was most accomplished in every respect.

But his death is forecast with certainty. The first game slain that day is Siegfried's; the last will be Siegfried himself. This first quarry of his is according to one reading a young boar (*halpful*); the boar is the device of Hagen, Siegfried's murderer. Then in rapid succession he brings down a remarkable number and variety of game: a lion, a bison, an elk, four aurochs, a grim (possibly, a supernatural) stag, and finally another huge boar which he slays face to face with his sword in the best style. He will not be able to do this with the last boar, Hagen. The diversity and strength of these beasts recall the astonishing variety of Siegfried's former triumphs: his combat against the dragon; his winning of the gold; Brunhild's rescue; his daunting of Brunhild both on the field and in the bedchamber; his noble marriage; his victory against the Burgundians' foes. All these deeds, while they work against him to arouse envy, will also accrue to the profit of the Burgundians. In the same way, it is the Burgundians who order the spoils of his hunting to be

heaped onto wagons and carried to Worms, once the race for
his death has begun. Moreover, Siegfried's hunting looks forward to the poem's final carnage when, to avenge him, so many
men must die at Etzel's court. The declaration that "many
beasts there had to lose their lives" (*dô muosen vil der tiere
verliesen dâ daz leben*, 942,1), when the hunters vie with the
matchless Siegfried, is an echo of a prophetic line at the opening
of the *Nibelungenlied*, refer to that ultimate slaughter: "for this
(referring to Kriemhild) many heroes had to lose their lives"
(*dar umbe muosen degene vil verliesen den lîp*, 2, 4). Such numbers
of animals does Siegfried quell that the others express anxiety
lest nothing be left in the wood for them to kill—nothing, that
is, except Siegfried himself. At length the hunt is over, yet it is
not altogether finished (*daz jagt was ergangen und doch niht gar*,
943, 1) for he is still alive.

The intermediate episode, between Siegfried hunter and
Siegfried victim, is that in which the party rouses a great bear
with the noise of horns, actually intended to recall the party
to camp for their repast. Siegfried decides to provide amusement
for his companions. He chases the bear on foot, grapples with it
and binds it to his saddle. Through his hand-to-hand confrontation Siegfried begins to enter into his animal aspect, for he
takes on the bear as an equal without the benefit of any weapons.
It is not so much a hunt as a wrestling match between two
powerful opponents. A description of Siegfried interrupts this
scene: for the first and only time he is fully pictured for us in
his splendor: his horn, spear and sword, bow, quiver, and
arrows; his gold, his silks and the variety of animal furs he
wears—sable, panther, otter, and a patchwork of the pelts of
various animals. The interruption falls in a crucial place: it is a
formal presentation of the magnificent animal to be slain. Codifications of hunting practice would eventually recommend that
a stag selected by hunters should be described in all its aspects:
color, slope of the belly, the height of its buttocks, the thickness
of neck and shoulder, and an account of tail and antlers. Of
Siegfried we are told:

And in what magnificent style Siegfried rode! He bore a great spear, stout of shaft and broad of head; his handsome sword reached down to his spurs; and the fine horn which this lord carried was one of the reddest gold. Nor have I ever heard tell of a better hunting outfit: he wore a surcoat of costly black silk and a splendid hat of sable, and you should have seen the gorgeous silken tassels on his quiver, which was covered in panther-skin for the sake of its fragrant odour! He also bore a bow so strong that apart from Siegfried any who wished to span it would have had to use a rack. His hunting suit was all of otter-skin, varied throughout its length with furs of other kinds from whose shining hair clasps of gold gleamed out on either side of this daring lord of the hunt. The handsome sword that he wore was Balmung, a weapon so keen and with such excellent edges that it never failed to bite when swung against a helmet. No wonder this splendid hunter was proud and gay.[7]

The bear incident is resumed. Back at the camp, Siegfried frees the bear, the hounds attack and panic breaks out. As the frantic bear attempts flight to the wood, he dashes among the cooks, scattering the fires, the pots, the food, the men. Hounds and hunters give him chase, but it is Siegfried who, one last time, prevails, slaying the beast with his sword (as he will shortly be slain with Hagen's spear) and arousing general comment upon his strength:

Dô sprâchen die daz sâhen, er waere ein kreftec man. [963,1]

Those who saw this said he was a powerful man.

The pattern of the bear's behavior foreshadows the action of Siegfried during his death-throes, which are imminent. Like the maddened bear, Siegfried will run at Hagen, thrashing at him with his shield, from whose shattering pieces the gems will fly in all directions, creating a chaos like that of the fragments of the disintegrating kitchen scene, comical now, horrible later when Siegfried's death fulfills its meaning.

[7] Tr. A. T. Hatto, *The Nibelungenlied* (Harmondsworth, 1965), pp. 127–128.

The final stage of the chase, in which Siegfried is the quarry, follows immediately upon the bear's death. Siegfried burns with thirst since Hagen has hidden the wine. It is now that Siegfried's animal attributes begin to emerge more pronouncedly. Like the hunted stag that will take to water at the point of death, Siegfried races with Hagen to the spring. Hagen, who lags behind, begins to look more like a pursuer than a rival in a game. As for Siegfried, he will three times lie down passively at the foot of his king. He offers at the outset to prostrate himself as a generous handicap; the second time he lies down to drink and is there pierced to the heart. The last time death fells him and he reddens the flowers beneath him with his blood. This uncharacteristic humility of Siegfried's immediately signals his role as victim, reinforced by those residual qualities that Siegfried inherits from earlier legends, namely, aspects of his stag nature. The opening of the 17th âventiure then sums up the theme of the chase and the quarry:

> Von helden kunde nimmer wirs gejaget sîn.
> Ein tier daz si sluogen, daz weinten edliu kint. [1002, 2-3]

> There was no hunting done by warriors which was worse than this; one of the animals they slew was mourned by noble maidens.

The poet has admirably integrated the chase into the fabric of his narrative, for he has made it relevant not only to the hero's own experience, his past, his future, his very nature, but also to the poem's other events. The hunt carries the hero from life to death, and conducts him, too, from the world of the poem, so that Kriemhild's revenge may develop and be permitted to control the subsequent action. When at the last Siegfried's slayers fight against their attackers in the 32nd and 33rd âventiuren, their men are compared in their ferocity to boars. Dancwart fights *als ein eberswîn / ze walde tuot vor hunden*, Volkêr, *als ein eber wilde*. They, as if noble quarry in their turn, must succumb to the death that closes the poem.

The Instructive Chase:
Sir Gawain and the Green Knight

The hunting accounts that occupy so conspicuous a place in the Christmas festivities of Sir Bertilak's court, and provide so telling a background for the probing of Sir Gawain, were composed, it will be remembered, during the period that saw the expansive development of books about hunting. The details of the poem's three hunts themselves, as well as the circumstances leading to and from these hunts, reflect a corpus of developed learning and information concerning not only how men engaged in the sport but what was believed of the hunt's virtuous and moral effects upon its practitioners. By the late fourteenth century, practices and attitudes were well enough known by certain writers to occur in other literature than that technically devoted to sport. Praises of the chase were usual even in earlier handbooks. The thirteenth century treatise, *La chace du cerf*, the first to appear in a vernacular, tends to be largely informative; yet it also states that "the sport is so noble, that there is neither king nor count, nor even Gawain himself, who, if he were alive and loved it well, would not be the more honored for it."

> Li deduiz est si souverains
> Qu'i n'est rois ne cuens, ne Gauvains,
> S'il estoit vis et bien l'amoit,
> Qui plus honorez n'en ceroit
> De touz ciaus qui s'i entendoient.[8]

Whether or not the author of *Sir Gawain and the Green Knight*[9] had encountered such a suggestion as this to inspire him in the composition of a romance in which his hero very certainly would have been removed from harm's way had he been an enthusiastic hunter, cannot, unfortunately, be determined here, if it is to be determined at all. Yet the Gawain poet was indeed aware of the various traditions associated with the

---

[8] Ed. and tr. Tilander, *Cynegetica* 7 (Stockholm, 1960), lines 24–27.

[9] The edition referred to is J. R. R. Tolkien and E. V. Gordon, 2nd ed. rev. by Norman Davis (Oxford, 1968).

chase, written or oral, as well as of its practice. It is to such
reserves of authority as are contained in the hunting manuals
and other informed accounts and figurative uses of the chase
that we may turn to clarify the relation of Bertilak's hunting to
Gawain's experiences in the romance. One of the principal
effects to proceed from the instructive hunting of the host is
the young hero's enlarged self-awareness.

Before Gawain's arrival at Sir Bertilak's castle the poet has
been restrained in what he suggests of the hero's inner nature.
In the initial full portrait we have of him being armed in splendor,
what we know of him chiefly is what emerges symbolically from
his investiture. There is as as yet little of the humorously (though
sympathetically) discomfited, inwardly tergiversating captive
that he is to become. The Pentangle and all his accoutrements
obscure that secret man from our full view. Externally beheld
he seems a model of military and religious perfection, Mary's
knight. As for his early thoughts and speeches, they gently
reveal him a conventional if appealing hero. When he requests
permission to take the challenge from Arthur, he displays a
courteously humble manner:

> I am þe wakkest, I wot, and of wyt feblest,
> And lest lur of my lyf, quo laytes þe soþe—
> Bot for as much as ʒe ar myn em I am only to prayse:
> No bounté bot your blod I in my bodé knowe. [354-357]

> I am the weakest, I know, and least in understanding and smallest
> would be my life's loss, if anyone should seek the truth—I am
> only praiseworthy in so far as you are my uncle: I know no virtue
> in my body but your kinship's blood.

We have a glimpse of the inward man when the poet admonishes
Sir Gawain to "þenk wel" (487 f.) that he not shrink (*wonde*)
from peril, and as if in delayed response the knight "mad ay
god chere and sayde 'Quat schuld I wonde?' " (563). We may
infer his growing anxiety as the seasons pass: we hear that he
bids the court "goud day / He wende for euermore" (668-669).
In the wintry forest on the verge of despair he prays for a lodging

place where he may hear mass, and matins on the next day. Yet
his speech in the wilderness, his steadfast praying for guidance
as he "cryed for his misdede" (760) really confirm and extend
the impression afforded us during his arming and his earlier
utterances—that of a correct, brave, devout and honorable
young knight. Dinner at the table and the flattery lavished upon
the guest at Bertilak's castle do not as yet elicit a glimmering of
the private, susceptible man ironically conceived by the poet.

It is at the beginning of the third fitt[10] that our knowledge of
Gawain suddenly widens and deepens, as does the self-consciousness he reveals. Here is the point at which the young man
vnlouked his yʒe-lyddeʒ (1201), affording us a view within, while
Bertilak's chase drives and urges in the background. From the
moment his hostess Lady Bertilak steps into Gawain's bedchamber we are permitted the happily imperfect view of him,
his embarrassments, pretences, hesitations, doubts, and eventually his "wallande joy," in short, his entire quandary as a man
in an awkward moral and social situation, needing to make a
decorous choice and ingeniously temporizing. With the un-
locking of his eyelids, we gain the equivocal inner perspective
which will continue on to the scene at the Green Chapel where
the hero looks down at the drops of his own blood in the snow.
Self-consciousness and the interior vision begun in the bedchamber culminate, with the confrontation with his host at the
Green Chapel, in the hero's discovery and acknowledgment of
human failings. After having endured two arrested blows and
a genuine, though slight, third, he finds himself by his own
admission a dupable man—like Adam and Samson, by a woman
—a man "fawty and falce" capable of "cowarddyse and couetyse," "trecherye and vntrawþe" and all because of his "surfet,"
"þe faut and þe fayntyse of þe flesche," and "pryde." His precise

[10] Or, to accept the manuscript evidence of the poem's divisions as
discerned by L. L. Hill, the third section consists of parts 5, 6, and 7 of
the poem's 9 parts. ("Madden's Divisions of *Sir Gawain* and the 'Large
Initial Capitals' of *Cotton Nero A X*," *Speculum* 21 [1946]: 67–71.) The
871 lines of these three parts, the three days' hunting, in fact take up a
little over a third of the entire romance.

acknowledgment of wrong actions now improves upon his original politely conventional confession of unworthiness in that scene where he took the challenge from Arthur. What is now especially of interest is not the particular faults that are "confessed," (he may be mistaken about them anyhow, as Larry D. Benson suggests), but the fact that the Knight of the Pentangle is filled with a sense of being somehow flawed. An upshot of the poem is, that "he has learned something about knighthood and himself. The 'fol chevalier' has become wiser through an initiation into a broader life than knighthood comprehends."[11] What has Sir Bertilak's ferocious hunting to do with this initiation?

In contrast to Gawain, who progresses from near-opacity to a winningly awkward transparency, from innocence to awareness, Sir Bertilak emerges as the poem's most complex personage on all counts, as well as being the least comprehensible to us. He is energetic, capable, versatile, the richest in experience— witness his ability to appear at will as different beings at different times. He is, above all, formidably knowing as a hunter who always gets his prey. We are not allowed to forget how he and Lady Bertilak drive their captive guest. His "enmy kene," the lady urged, "rehayted" (1744) him with her rich words, to a love that would undo him just as the huntsman "rehayted" (1422) the dogs on the field, and as on that first night at dinner Sir Bertilak "rehayted" his guest to take "penance" (895), facetiously referring to the feast he was offering, though his urging Gawain to a literal penance would indeed be fulfilled by the poem's climax when the younger man confesses, repents, and is forgiven. Both "hunters"[12] goad him to the discoveries

---

[11] *Art and Tradition in Sir Gawain and the Green Knight* (New Brunswick, 1965), p. 239.

[12] The seminal and still valuable essay on the importance of hunting in the poem is that of H. L. Savage, "Symbolism and Allegory in *Sir Gawain and the Green Knight*," in *The Gawain-Poet* (Chapel Hill, 1956): "She [Lady Bertilak] finds herself, like her husband, pursuing noble game," and, "like her husband in the forest, she has again roused noble game" (p. 36). A. K. Hieatt, "Sir Gawain: Pentangle, Luf-lace, Numerical Structure," in *Silent Poetry: Essays in Numerological Analysis*, ed.

that reach their height at the Green Chapel. It is a hunt of knowledge in which the victim becomes the pupil, like that more terrible one of Oedipus in which the victim gained—as a result of his unwitting self-harrying—dire wisdom.

Expert in the chase, Sir Bertilak also manifests an accurate acquaintance with the vices and virtues connected with hunting, according to what was known and believed in the fourteenth century. It is he who has with sly intent immobilized the young man where he may be tenderly assaulted by Lady Bertilak. How often Bertilak cajoles the knight to lie at his ease and how often we are reminded of this dangerous relaxation (in contrast to the violently energetic business of the hunters) with the use of "linger," "lie" and "ease"—*lenge, ly(ʒ)e, ese!* How insistent is Bertilak in urging idleness upon the guest! He coaxes him to put off his departure for the Green Chapel appointment: "now leng þe byhoues" (1068). Gawain again asks permission to go, but the host prevents him from leaving after the boar chase. He persuades him, "to lenge hym resteyed" (1672): and so "Gawayn is lenged" (1683). Even more pertinent are the host's exhortations to rest while he himself rides to the hounds. He presses him to lie in bed, although hunting would have been, in the light of contemporary handbooks, the universally recognized preparation for combat.

Before the first day's hunting, Gawain was urged to keep his bed: "Bot ʒe schal be in yowre bed, burne, at þyn ese" (1071), and "ʒe schal lenge in your lofte, and lyʒe in your ese" (1096). Similarly, before the fox chase: "Forþy þow lye in þy loft and lach þyn ese / And I schal hunt in þis holt" (1676–77). Not only does the host insist upon this fatal ease but the poet reminds us of Gawain's lying, lurking and lingering, wryly savoring his hero's vulnerability. On the first day while Bertilak unharbors

---

Alastair Fowler (London, 1970), has significantly pointed out that the love-lace of the lady is a noose (one of the meanings of *laas*) with which she snares Gawain (pp. 118–119). The *laas* is an attribute both of Venus and Satan in medieval literature. On the further use of binding, snaring, and leashing in the love chase, see below, pp. 90, 178, 205.

a deer, "Gawayn þe god mon in gay bed lygez, / Lurkkez quyl
þe dayly3t lemed on þe wowes" (1179–80). And when the lady
enters, "þe lede lay lurked a ful longe quyle" (1195). Sir Bertilak
dangerously pursues the enraged boar "whyle oure luflych lede
lys in his bedde" (1469). Before the fox hunt, the lord tends to
his affairs while "Sir Gawayn lis and slepes" (1686); during
that same hunt the poet exclaims with irony, "Now hym lenge
in þat lee [that sheltered place!] þer luf hym bityde!" (1893).
Once Gawain has accepted the fox's pelt, imagining he has
deceived his host, the poet writes, "Let hym ly3e þere stille"
(1994). Gawain's easeful lying, his abstinence from energetic
activity, may evoke a recollection of his harsher rest when, a
knight in the wilderness, near slain with sleet, he "sleped in his
yrnes," his freezing armor (729).

Gawain's lounging and lurking, in contrast to the hunters'
early rising prepare him for downfall. Not only does he lie in his
lofte waiting to be scented out like quarry (while being exposed
by the poet), but he is doing precisely the thing that will make
him susceptible. Lying in bed, especially in the morning, instead of rising to work, pray or hunt, for instance, invites temptation. "Ese, etynge, and drynkinge" are the conditions in which
Lechery thrives; "Slepynge longe in greet quiete is eek a greet
norice to Leccherie" says Chaucer's Parson in his Tale. To
Melibee, Dame Prudence cites Cato against idleness: "Enclyneth
nat yow over-muchel for to slepe for over-muchel reste norisseth
and causeth manye vices." Idleness, "the ministre and the norice
unto vices," "roten slogardye" indeed make one prey to the
devil's hunt:

> For he that with his thousand cordes slye
> Continuelly us waiteth to biclappe,
> Whan he may man in ydelnesse espye,
> He kan so lightly cache hym in his trappe,
> Til that a man be hent right by the lappe,
> He nys nat war the feend hath hym in honde.[13]

[13] See, in Chaucer's *Works:* The Parson's Tale, p. 260, lines 951–952;
The Tale of Melibee, p. 182, line 1593; The Second Nun's Tale, p. 207,

Observe the dangerous sloth of those who linger excessively in their bed-chambers: Troilus, Chretien's Erec, and Arthur at the beginning of *Yvain*.

The notion that hunting and idleness are at odds is a commonplace of the hunting manuals.[14] Guicennas' *De Arte Bersandi* begins by saying that whoever would be perfect in this craft must apply heart and will to it, and must be eager, not sluggish: "Qui vult scire et esse perfectus in arte ista, primo debet apponere cor et etiam voluntatem et debet esse levis et non piger" (p. 18). The prologue of the *Livres du roy Modus* informs us that Modus despises idleness and that he has organized the diversions of the hunt to enable us to escape this vice:

Il ordena tous les deduis,
Affin que ne fussons oysis,
De cerfs, de sengliers et de dains. [109-11]

He devised all the sports—
so that we wouldn't be idle—
concerning stags, boar, and roebuck.

Et que nous ne fussons oysis,
Nous fist un livre de deduis. [127-129]

And so that we wouldn't be idle,
he composed for us a book of sport.

---

lines 17, 7-13. By the fifteenth century, the ill effect of late rising has become the subject of a reformist tirade by the tutor Ponocrates in Rabelais' *Gargantua*. Deploring his pupil's pernicious, "medieval" habit of lying in bed until eight or nine o'clock in the morning (on the strength of the Psalmist's saw: *Vanum est vobis ante lucem surgere, Ps.* 126:2), Ponocrates has him up at four. (*Gargantua*, ed. Pierre Grimal [Paris, 1939], chap. 21.)

[14] Various classical antecedents of this commonplace are gathered in Aymard, *Chasses Romaines*, p. 493 and nn. A list of patristic references to idleness is given in D. W. Robertson, Jr., *Preface to Chaucer* (Princeton, 1963), p. 92n. Cf. Tilander's note, Jacques du Fouilloux, *La Vénerie et l'Adolescence*, p. 168n.

And finally:

> Il faut proceder sur le livre
> Que Modus avoit ordené
> Contre l'estat d'uisivité. [150-152]

> We must go on to the book
> that Modus devised
> against the condition of idleness.

Hardouin de Fontaines-Guérin states near the conclusion of his treatise that nobles when not engaged in war should first hear mass, then go to the hunt. In this way they will pursue no vicious activity, but by using their time for sport and delight keep out of the way of sin:

> Eulz doivent au commencement
> Oyr messe primièrement,
> Et après aler à la chasse.
> Ainsi à nul mal ne pourchasse
> Cilz qui ensy son temps emploie,
> Pour vices prent déduit et joie:
> Car, comme j'ay dit, bien sachies,
> Hors de mettent de mains pechiés
> Ceulz qui la chasse oient souvent. [1841-1849]

Especially of interest is the variation on this commonplace that pits hunting against perilous bed-lounging. It makes the chase the preserver of virtue inasmuch as it prevents a man from harboring lascivious thoughts in his bed, either forcing him to rise early or fatiguing him by the day's end. Gaston Phébus in his *Livre de chasse* reiterates this praise of the hunter who, having ridden all day to the hounds, can lie down contentedly in his bed at night and enjoy a sound, virtuous sleep. Moreover, Gaston claims that the hunter is more certain than are other men to gain some region of Paradise, whether he reaches its lower courts or its suburbs, simply because he has eschewed that root of all the vices, idleness: "pour oster cause d'ocieuseté qui est fondement de tous maulx." *The Master of Game*, largely

a translation of Gaston, dwells lengthily upon the theme of
"idelnesse," arguing that "the game causeth often man to eschew
þe vij deedly synnes. . . ." Then follows the bedchamber topos:

> Now shal I preue þe how an huntere ne may by no reson falle
> yn any of the seuene dedly synnes. ffor whanne a man is ydel &
> reccheles wiþ oute trauayle and men ben not occupyed to be
> doyng some þinges & abideþ oþer yn þeire bed oþer in chambres,
> hit is a þing þe which draweþ men to ymagynacioun of fleshly
> lust & plaisere.[15]

Developing his theme, the author then offers an extensive
account of all that a hunter must do, going in quest of his
quarry, coming to the gathering of hunters, ordering and un-
coupling his hounds, giving chase, undoing the quarry. In each
of these stages, "is he lasse ydel . . . for he hath ynowe to do to
ymagine, and to þenk on his office."

A noteworthy treatment of this theme appears in the penitential *Livre des Seyntz Medicines* of Henry of Lancaster (whose
allegorical fox hunt will be discussed below). There we find a
passage on the sin of "peresce" (Sloth or Idleness) that bears a
close relation to the idleness topos of the hunting books. It
proposes the virtuous businesses of the chase and of morning
worship as alternatives to lying in bed and engaging in amorous
thoughts:

> Car au matyn, quant jeo deusse lever pur vous, Sire, servir et
> ascune bien faire, en l'eure saut par la bouche: "Il est uncore
> matyn, il fait male temps, nous ne poons aler au boys ne en
> ryvers" ou "il est jour de feste, qe ferroi jeo quant jeo serray
> levee, forsqe d'estre plus a male aese qe jeo ore ne su ?"

> And in the morning, when I ought to arise for you, Lord, to
> serve or do some other good, immediately the words leap to my
> lips— "it is still early, the weather is bad, we cannot go to the

---

[15] *The Master of Game*, Prologue, p. 5. The edition, however, is faulty
in the printing of this passage. I am extremely grateful to Douglas Gray,
who very kindly transcribed for me the version given here from ms.
Bodley 546, fol. 7 v⁰.

woods or to the river [hunting or hawking]"—or—"it is a holiday, what will I do when I get up except to be less well at ease than I now am ?"

Or, instead of rising for morning services, the indolent man will murmur: "Lessez moi dormir ou penser en mes amors." At nightfall, too, he will think again of his ease:

Alons cocher et gardetz qe le lit soit bien fait a aise, si qe je puisse veoir comme longement jeo puisse dormir.

Let us go to sleep and make certain that the bed is well made for ease, so that I can see how long I can sleep.

Dame Peresce is the evil enchantress that is responsible, and she causes the loss of many a good thing.[16]

It is Lady Bertilak who plays a part like that of Dame Peresce, tucking the covers tightly around, and refusing to allow her disconcerted guest to rise out of his bed. There he must remain, ignorant prey to the temptations his host and hostess have devised, but moving slowly, as he reveals himself, in the direction of enlightenment. Meanwhile Bertilak hunts in fact the quarry of woods and fields, but his long-range object is Gawain. As the green challenger and consenting partner to his wife's insincerely amorous invitations, and as the wielder of the Danish axe, and the "spetos sparþe," Bertilak has a fiendish aspect. He seems to be pursuing Gawain as the devil pursues men to ensnare them. But ultimately, putting aside his malicious aspect, Bertilak reveals a sympathetically didactic quality during the meeting at the Green Chapel. As the Green Knight there, he becomes peculiarly paternal, even genially respectful. Now his previous harrying of Gawain, which has brought his pupil-victim to a juncture where he may be enlightened, chastised, confessed, and absolved, appears after all to have its salubrious and instructive side. We may begin to discern the link between his venatorial aspect, unfailing slayer of beasts, and his function

[16] *Livre des Seyntz Medicines*, ed. E. J. Arnould (Oxford, 1940), pp. 22–23.

in eliciting a penitent self-awareness from Gawain, who like the game animals must bend his neck to the poem's hunter. The Green Knight will, in his punishing role, draw drops of his victim's blood, as if to mortify the fault that lurks within, just as he has routed out and slain animals in the field. Then, amicably, the Green Knight gathers the young man to him and grants forgiveness.

Hunters of men who teach and correct wrongdoers may be a figure deriving from Scripture, namely Jeremiah 16:16, a passage which, according to D. W. Robertson, Jr., prefigures for the medieval reader the work of "true Christian prelates":[17]

> Behold I will send for many fishers, saith the Lord, and they shall fish them; and after will I send for many hunters, and they shall hunt them from every mountein, and from every hill, and out of the holes of rocks.

But medieval literature also offers at least two instances of an explicitly metaphorical hunt for men's souls: the earlier is in the *Ormulum*[18] on the apostolic chase—"to huntenn affterr sawless" and "to slaetenn [track] affterr sawless." Perhaps through a fusion of the "fishers of men" texts of the New Testament (Matthew 4:19 and Mark 1:17) with the passage from Jeremiah, the *Ormulum* directs the apostles Philip, Andrew, and Simon:

> To spellenn alle lede,
> & hunntenn affterr sawless swa
> Wiþþ haliȝ lare & bisne,
> To turrnenn hemm till Crisstenndom
> All fra þe defless walde;

[17] D. W. Robertson, Jr., *A Preface to Chaucer*, p. 225.
[18] Robert Holt (ed.), *Ormulum*, 2 vols. (Oxford, 1878), 2:113–114, lines 13459–75. A diabolical inversion of the didactic hunt for souls is demonstrated by Chaucer's Friar's Tale. "Teche me . . ." says the summonour to the demon in hunter's guise, "how that I may moost wynne." As they go about for prey, the pupil then offers to instruct the instructor, and is rewarded for his pains with a promise of learning secrets in hell, "Moore than a maister of dyvynytee."

All þiss wass þurrh Beþþsayda
Full opennliȝ bitacnedd,
Forr itt bitacneþþ hunntess hus,
Forr þatt teȝȝ sholldenn hunntenn,
Acc nohht wiþþ hundess affterr der,
Acc affterr menn wiþþ spelless,
& Forrþi þatt Sannt Anndrew wass
Rihht god & haȝherr hunnte,
Ne dwalde he nohht, son summ he fand
Hiss broþerr Sannte Peterr,
To lacchenn himm wiþþ spelless nett
To brinngenn himm to Criste.

To preach to all men and hunt for souls, thus with holy learning and by example to turn them to Christianity and away from the Devil's power. This was because of what Bethsaida [their city] plainly signified, for it means "hunter's house." Therefore they were to hunt—But not with hounds after beasts, but after men with gospel. And since St. Andrew was a very good and skilled hunter he did not delay, but soon found a certain man, his brother St. Peter, to entrap with the net of gospel and bring him to Christ.

Even more pertinent is the developed allegory of hunting the fox in Henry's *Livre des Seyntz Medicines*.[19] Reintroducing the theme of *Peresce* with its fostering of sin, Henry begins with the figure of the fox's lair. *Peresce* is now the female fox, mother of the vices; Henry reminds the reader of the stench of the fox,

---

[19] A detailed comparison between the meanings of the fox chase in *Sir Gawain* and in Henry's *Livre des Seyntz Medicines* (pp. 105–107) appears in Marcelle Thiébaux, "*Sir Gawain*, The Fox Hunt and Henry of Lancaster," *Neuphilologische Mitteilungen* 71 (1970): 469–479. On the nature of the fox, Kenneth Varty, *Reynard the Fox: A Study of the Fox in Medieval English Art* (Leicester University Press, 1967), is of literary interest. The whelps of the fox are mentioned in the *Ancrene Wisse, Edited from Ms. Corpus Christi College Cambridge 402* by J. R. R. Tolkien, *EETS* (New York, 1962), 249:105. There "þe Vox of ȝisceunge [covetousness]" has its offspring such as "triccherie" and "gile." In Chaucer's *Boece*, Book 4, prose 3, men are compared to various beasts: "If he be a pryve awaytour yhid, and rejoiseth hym to ravyssche be wiles, thou schalt seyn hym lik to the fox whelpes."

Foxes and foxholes in a hunting manual. Foxhunting frequently served an allegorical purpose among imaginative authors. Miniature in *Le Livre du roy Modus*, fifteenth century, ms. M 820, folio 28 r°. Courtesy Pierpont Morgan Library.

comparing the fox's den, with its entrances, to the body and its orifices. Within is a corner, a man's heart, where the vixen cohabits with the male, *Orgoil*, to bring forth their whelps, the five other mortal sins. Foxes hide in their dens during the day but range abroad by night, seeking their prey. Henry gives the meaning: the evil of the human heart is generally kept concealed from the world's recognition, but at night the vices issue forth privily to do harm. Hunting the foxes and routing them out of their hole by various methods constitutes the work, allegorically, of the father confessor. He is both hunter in this sense and game warden, for he protects other game, the virtues, from the ravaging foxes:

> La veneour ou le forester, c'est mon confessour qi chacee si com veneour lez pecchés hors de moi, et sicom forester ou parker garde sa baille out tout son poair et destruit tout vermyne, ensi fait le prodhomme qi mette tout sa peyne a moi garder en bons vertues et en chacer toutez males vices. [111, 19-24]

Once he has drawn forth a confession of the sins, that is, forced out, captured, and slain the foxes, the hunter-confessor has their pelts stripped off to be brought back to the lord's hall. There the pelts will be displayed upon the wall so that the lord and all other men may behold them. The retention of the foxes' skins may be allegorized, continues Henry, as the perpetual memory, however painful and shaming, of the sins that are to be kept always before the eyes of the heart.

> La peel de renard fait homme pendre en la sale, si qe le seignur et touz autres la poent veoir; et plus voluntiers de vynt qe d'un tout soul. . . . Ensi doit homme faire de pecchés: retenir la peel, c'est la remenbrance avoir toutdys com pendu en la sael devant les oeux, c'est a dire overtement devant les oeux de coer, si qe il puisse avoir joie com il appartient—c'est fyn dolour et honte; et doit voloir qe les vicez soient veues et conues de touz com le peel de renard. [115, 10-21]

Is it possible that Henry of Lancaster's allegory of the fox-chase was known to the author of *Sir Gawain?* The third day's hunt is the crucial one in the poem. The fox's dodges immediately anticipate Gawain's efforts to elude both his promise to Bertilak and the beheading axe of his green challenger by withholding the lady's green girdle. As the fox fails in his ruses, so does Gawain fail to conceal his actions from his host. Moreover, the public display at Camelot of the green lace (counterpart to the "foule fox felle," and "token of vntrawþe") closely resembles the penitential exhibiting, in Henry's allegory, of the fox's pelts as reminders of sin.

Bertilak plays a baffling series of parts: as the baroquely magnificent Green Knight he roughly challenges, and eventually he tests, punishes, and shrives his guest. But, aside from the entertainment he affords us, the unpredictable host justifies his behavior ultimately in what he teaches the young man. A sly teacher, he has induced his pupil to err so that he may catch him and make him cognizant of his human weakness. He hunts, he teaches, he hears the pupil's confession. The ambiguity of Bertilak's role corresponds to the ambiguity of the symbolic business of the hunter, for if Gawain had failed to maintain his *trawþe*, Bertilak would presumably have killed him. Thus the poet, by evoking the idleness-venery topos and an association of hunting with teaching and the correction of sin, negotiates a connection between the very literate hunting knowledge of his day and the demands of his romance.

While Gawain appears to be pursuing adventure, he is nonetheless made victim and novice in the hunt of knowledge. Through the uses of the verbs *cache*, *fonge*, and *take*, Gawain's fluctuations between capturing and being captured form a muted current in the poem. The verb "catch," from *chasser*, is the most evident. Gawain *cachez* the Green Knight's weapon from Arthur, thus assuming responsibility for the challenge (368). On the night of his arrival at Bertilak's castle, Gawain and the younger lady *caȝten* comfort from their mutual company (1011); but she refers to him on her first visit to his bedroom as "my knyȝt þat I kaȝt haue" (1225), and on retiring from him "*cachez* hym in armez" (1305). Bertilak comments, ironically, to his guest on how much good fortune "ȝe *cach*" (1938). But at the turning point of his luck, Gawain "*kaȝt* to þe knot"—the betraying lace—to tear it loose, and acknowledges finally that it is "couardise and couetyse þat I haf *caȝt* there" (2376, 2508).

When he is *fonged* at the castle, he is received and welcomed; but *fonge* may also mean "capture" as in *Pearl*, 439, "Fele here porchaseȝ & fongeȝ pray [Many here pursue and seize prey]." Delightedly the court of Bertilak exclaim, "We haf *fonged* þat fyne fader of nurture" (919), and the poet adds "Watz neuer freke fayrer *fonge*" (1315). As Gawain moves forward to receive the boar's carcass, he greets Bertilak and goes "his feez þer for to *fonge*" (1622). The verb *take* is more frequent, more general in meaning, but it too serves to indicate the hero's ambiguous relationship to his adventure. For instance, in the first fitt, he thinks it unseemly for Arthur to *take* the challenge (350); he agrees to *take* the buffet in a twelvemonth (383); is ordered by the Green Knight to "*ta*" and wield the grim tool (413); and is enjoined by the poet at the fitt's close to reflect well on the adventure "þat þou hatz *tan* on honde" (490). Once at Bertilak's house, however, he begins to be taken—between the old and the young lady, who "*tan* him . . . to chambre . . . to chemné" (977–978). Visiting his room the first morning, Lady Bertilak gleefully announces, "Now you are taken, all at once" ("Now ar ȝe *tan* as-tyt") (1210). At the Green Chapel, Gawain is ordered to take—not a weapon but a blow: "þat tappe *ta* þe" (2357). Ruefully the young man exclaims, once all has been made plain, that it is "vntrawþe þat I am *tan* inne" (2509), echoing perhaps how earlier "þay *tan* Reynarde" (1920) before stripping him of his coat.

Finally there is the varying reiteration of a word that occurs chiefly during Gawain's stay at the castle and his visit to the Green Chapel: this is *pris*, in both its principal sense of the praise, reputation, esteem, or reward (OF *pris* < *pretium*) that the knight hopes to win and maintain for his excellence, value and worth (also *pris* < *pretium*), and its other meaning pertaining to the capture or conquest (OF *prise* < *prehensus* < *prehendere*) of quarry, as well as the fanfare that signalled the animal's death.

The *pris* in the hunting sense—as in *The Craft of Venery*'s "blow the pris"—occurs after the Green Knight's hunts of the first and second days: "Baldely þay blw *prys*, bayed thayr rachchez, / Syþen fonge þay her flesche" (1362–63) when the deer is slain, and upon the death of the boar, "There watz blawyng of *prys* in mony breme horne" (1601). While Gawain philanders tentatively under stress of courtesy, yet keeps his promise to Bertilak, the Death blows warningly (could he but hear it) as if to herald the fate that may be in store for him if he errs badly. We are made mindful of the capture of the quarry and Gawain is being tracked, worried, tested. Meanwhile many flattering words heap upon the guest: one of these refers to his *pris*. The court flocks about him, for they have heard

> þat alle *prys* and prowes and pured þewes
> Apendes to hys persoun, and praysed is euer. [912-913]

> That all worth and prowess and pure conduct belong to his person, and ever is he praised.

Gawain wishes, in the bedroom, that he might by word or action aspire to the sheer pleasure of the lady's praise of him:

> Bi God, I were glad, and yow god þoȝt,
> At saȝe oþer at seruyce þat I sett myȝt
> To þe plesaunce of your *prys*. [1245-47]

She immediately rejoins that she could not underestimate his *prys* (1249). In a moment he responds to her further blandishments by expressing pride in the *prys* she attributes to him (1277).

But the etymological sense of the word emerges when Bertilak, returning with the venison asks, "how payez you þis play? Haf I *prys* wonnen?" Asking for his "pay" connects this utterance to the pattern of commercial figures recurring in the poem, for example, the words in which the Green Knight first menaces Gawain in promising him the same "wages" *he* has been dealt (396). At the Green Chapel the challenger bids him to take his "pay." (2247) Throughout, the Green Knight has "cheaped" and "chaffered" and done "chevisaunce," until we begin to see that the theme of moral worth has its basis in physical payments. Gawain seems to be earning severe wages for his initial courage, his courtesy, his sufferings of dilemma and discomfiture. The theme of price moreover recurs with respect to the green lace that he "buys" so dearly. The lady slyly puts a value upon it: anyone who knew its power would "hit prayse at more *prys*" (1850), she insists, pressing it upon him. Sarcastically the lord assesses the third day's kisses (the valuable lace being withheld) highly against the fox's pelt that is "ful pore for to pay for suche *prys* thinges" (1945). But the Green Knight's last words in the scene of their reconciliation neutralize the sarcasm when he straightforwardly declares:

> As perle bi þe quite pese is of *prys* more,
> So is Gawayn, in god fayth, bi oþer gay knyȝtez. [2364-65]

> As the pearl beside white peas is worth a higher price, So is Gawain, in good faith, beside other brilliant knights.

So Gawain is remunerated; he has earned his gains of self-knowledge and his reassessed worth through humiliation and sorrow. His harsh pay becomes transvalued to the magnanimous conferral of praise; his reward is, at the last, that he is to be prized as a pearl among peas for what he has learned and endured, not to be made the destroyed prize of a shrewd hunter's stalking. The disconcerting Bertilak bestows the praise having implanted the lesson. He has been a very hunting devil for enticing this man to temptation, and then a holy hunter of men to teach and shrive him.

III

The Love Chase

Images of the Love Chase from Antiquity

The hunt of love occurs at least as early as Plato's *Sophist* where the hunt provides an overriding metaphor: human affairs become narrow subdivisions of a great pursuit. All men prey upon one another in diverse ways—through war, tyranny, piracy, oratory, law, and conversation. Love, finally, emerges as one category of the private, persuasive land hunt. "Have you never seen the ways lovers hunt each other?" is the query rhetorically raised.

As a simile or metaphor love's hunting had already been used by Greek playwrights and would continue to reappear in lyric poetry and in prose. Aeschylus writes in *Prometheus Bound* of a consanguine union where young men pursue their cousin brides like falcons after wood-pigeons, "hunting unhuntable marriages." In the opening monologue of Euripides' *Helena*, the heroine speaks of a now deceased suitor whose "son hunts me in marriage" while Achilles in *Iphigeneia in Aulis* boasts of the "thousands of girls hunting my couch." In her lovesick delirium, Phaedra, of the *Hippolytus*, longs to drink from springs and lie beneath poplars in a meadow—the wooded and grassy places where her beloved Hippolytus might be found hunting. Her wish would make her, by implication, his passive quarry. Abruptly her fantasy changes: it is Phaedra who would hunt, and she disguises her desire for Hippolytus in imagining herself actively engaged in the frenetic pursuit of game:

Bring me to the mountains! I *will* go to the mountains. Among the pine trees, where the [hounds tread seeking the wild things' blood, hot on the heels of the dappled deer] God, how I long to set the hounds on, shouting! And poise the Thessalian javelin drawing it back—here where my fair hair hangs above the ear— I would hold in my hand a spear with a steel point.[1]

Xenophon, whose *Cynegeticus* we have remarked upon, gives us in his *Memorabilia of Socrates* an arch exchange between the gadfly of Athens and the wealthy courtesan Theodota on the "art of catching friends," an art likened in detail to the efforts of hunters to entangle hares in their nets. "By what art of this kind, then," said she, "can I catch friends?" "If," said he, "instead of a dog, you get somebody to track and discover the wealthy and the lovers of beauty, and who, when he has found them, will contrive to drive them into your nets." "And what nets have I?" said she. "You have one at least," he replied, "and one that closely embraces its prey, your person. . . ." "Why do not you, then, Socrates," said she, "become my helper in securing friends?" "I will indeed," said he, "if you can persuade me."[2]

[1] *Hippolytus*, tr. David Grene, *Three Greek Tragedies in Translation* (Chicago [1942]), p. 178; bracketed section tr. from Euripides, *Hippolytos: Ed. with Introduction and Commentary* by W. S. Barrett (Oxford, 1964), p. 202.

[2] Xenophon, *The Anabasis or Expedition of Cyrus, and the Memorabilia of Socrates*, tr. J. S. Watson (London, 1854), p. 459. Analogous images of the net signifying the girl's hold over her lover may be seen in the Arabic verse of Ibn Hazm from the *Ring of the Dove*, tr. Arthur Arberry (London, 1953), p. 244:

> O thou, who makest of thy women's shame
> A net, to snare young roebucks in the same,
> I see thy net is torn to pieces, and
> Thou holdest but dishonour in thy hand.

and in Chaucer's *Troilus* (III. 1732 ff.). No other lady's beauty

> Kan nought the montance of a knotte unbynde,
> Aboute his herte, of al Criseydes net.
> He was so narwe ymasked and yknet,
> That it undon on any manere syde,
> That nyl naught ben, for aught that may bitide.

In the literature of the ancients, as in the Middle Ages, the prey (especially when wounded) of the love chase often signified the partner who was overly compliant, meek, or impassioned, who thus might be an object of pity or scorn. The Alexandrian poet Callimachus writes that the hunter in pursuit of hare and hind will lose interest in the already wounded, the easily available game. The hunter cares more for the chase itself than for the quarry, a sentiment which Plato anticipates with his observations upon the philosopher's hunt. "Thus too my love," concludes the poet; "He hunts only what flees, and ignores that which lies before him."³ Horace later paraphrased Callimachus in his first Satire:

> As the hunter chases the hare in the deep snow, but will not touch it once it is laid before him (he recites and then applies it), so too with my love: it passes over what is in the open and seizes eagerly what flees before.⁴

In a lyric⁵ Horace writes as a lover seeking to quiet the terrors of the girl who mistakenly defines his pursuit as a sport that will destroy her; in reality, pleads the lover, his longing for her is only like one of the many sounds of Spring that harmlessly startle a stag. The simile of the frightened deer breaks at the last, however, on a suddenly literal note, in which the poet disclaims the figures of hunting in order to urge a reciprocal human love—it is she too who must engage in some of the pursuing:

> You flee from me like a young stag, Chloe, searching for its trembling mother over pathless hills, needlessly fearful of breezes and woods.
> For whether Spring's coming should cause the moving leaves to shudder, or green lizards scatter through the brambles, a stag quivers in its heart and its knees.

³ Callimachus *Hymni et Epigrammata* 2.31, ed. Rudolf Pfeiffer (Oxford, 1953), p. 89.
⁴ Q. Horatii Flacci, "Sermonum Liber," 1. 2. 105–108, *Opera*, ed. E. C. Wickham (Oxford, 1959).
⁵ Ibid., "Carminum Liber," 1.23.

Yet I do not pursue you like a savage tiger or an African lion, to crush you to pieces. Follow your mother no longer, for it is time to follow a lover instead.

In expressing a lover's rapacious longing for a coy mistress, the chase may appear an all too obvious image. Its situation contains the antithetical and complementary acts of flight and pursuit; the completed chase includes the hunter's sense of conquest and pleasure when he wounds the body of his quarry, sheds its blood, uses its flesh for food. Whether the metaphorical pursuer is animal or human, the hunt's climax and dénouement may be seen as adaptable by any moderately imaginative poet to an amatory purpose. In such a rudimentary form the chase as a premeditated and violent sexual pursuit will continue to recur, still a workable image for instance in Shakespeare's *Titus Andronicus*, where a huntress is to be made booty of men:

> My lords, a solemn hunting is in hand:
> There will the lovely Roman ladies troop;
> The forest walks are wide and spacious;
> And many unfrequented plots there are,
> Fitted by kind for rape and villainy.
> Single you thither then this dainty doe,
> And strike her home by force, if not by words. [II.i. 118]

And again:

> Chiron, we hunt not, we, with horse nor hound,
> But hope to pluck a dainty doe to ground. [II.ii. 25-26]

But the love chase does not correspond necessarily to brutal action, where a preying lover seeks, "snares," "captures," and "slays" his victim. The Horatian ode raised the possibility of one wild creature's hunger for another only to disclaim its appropriateness to love. And, as in other types of literary hunts, the lover may be a victim himself. Many of the love hunts of antiquity—and later under their influence, of the Middle Ages —show the workings of the divine principle, of Eros. For while the lover may believe he is hunting his beloved independently, he is at the same time the spoil of Eros, "the terrible hunter," who, as Diotima explains to Socrates in the *Symposium*, "is always weaving some strategem." Like other forms of the symbolic hunt, the hunt of love will often, inconspicuously or overtly, reveal the manipulating presence of an external power, a god. A mortal will enter the realm of influence of some divinity whose power to drive him to love is ultimately traceable to Eros, "the oldest, most revered, most powerful of the gods." A chase initiates him to the discovery or rediscovery of desire. Whether he is lured by his actual or supernatural prey, driven like a hound to an irresistible chase, or whether he finds himself the stricken beast, the lover seldom assumes command. Eros or Aphrodite govern him; later it may be Nature, Amours, Lady Venus or Frau Minne that delivers the blow to render him the impassioned quarry or drives him to his inescapable hunting. One aspect of the fierce, divine predator appears in the Greek Anthology: "Surely mad Love [a rabid dog] has fixed his bitter tooth in me and made my soul the prey of his frenzies."[6] It persists in Petrarch's "Ne la stagion ch'il ciel rapido inchina." At nightfall, others find untroubled repose—"But then, Ah! fierce Love, do you drive me all the more to follow the voice, the footprint, and the track of a savage thing that destroys me. And you do not close in upon her who hides and flees,"[7] and in Racine's "C'est Vénus toute entière à sa proie attachée" where Phèdre is the spoil.

It is Virgil's Dido who represents in classical antiquity the developed type of love's hunted victim within a divinely arranged chase, whose whole meaning and purpose she will never know. Cast briefly, metaphorically, as the stricken hind that is soon to die, Dido becomes essential to the experience of Aeneas through her passion and sacrifice.

[6] From the Byzantine poet, Paulus Silentarius (A.D. 560), ed. and tr. J. W. Mackail, *Select Epigrams from the Greek Anthology* (London, 1890), p. 96.

[7] *Le Rime di Francesco Petrarca*, ed. Giosuè Carducci and S. Ferrari (Florence, 1899), Canzone 50, p. 73, lines 39–42.

Unhappy Dido burns and wanders frenzied all through the city, like a hind struck by an arrow. The hind had walked heedlessly through the Cretan grove, and a shepherd, hurling his shaft, struck her from a distance, unaware that he had left his swift iron in her. The hind flies through the Dictaean woods and valleys with the arrow in her side. [4. 68-73]

The sum of Dido's fate is succinctly contained in the single image: the hind that wanders in pain through the wood with the hunter's weapon still in her flank.[8] Past, present, future concentrate here: there is the evidence of a hunt that has already

---

[8] We may compare this with several examples of the woman as a gazelle that are found among Arab poets during the medieval period; for instance from an anthology assembled in thirteenth century Spain, come the following passages:

> Of a lovely maid I tell:
> Sombre eyes of a gazelle,
> Throat of hind, and wine-red lip . . . [from Ibn Khafaja (1058-1138)]

> Treacherous gazelle,
> Mistress of delay
> In your troth, and well
> Tutored to betray . . . [from Al-Mustazhir (d. 1204)]

> Among the shy gazelles
> Ran lovely fawns, whose spells
> Enslaved my mind, whose art
> Bewitching stole my heart. [from Hamda (fl. 12th c.); Arthur Arberry, tr., *Moorish Poetry. A Translation of "The Pennants,"* an Anthology compiled in 1243 by the Andalusian Ibn Sa'id (Cambridge, 1953), pp. 146, 53, 98.]

One refers specifically to the hunt of such a creature:

> O lovely fawn, huntable indeed for those who may enjoy her
> but to me denied—and would to God she were lawful to me—
> I sent my slave-girl to her, telling her, "Off with you now,
> scout out news of her for me, and tell me truly."
> She said, "I saw the enemy were off their guard
> and the fawn was attainable to any good marksman."
> As she turned, her throat was like a young antilope's,
> the throat of a tender gazelle-fawn with spotted upper lip. [Arthur Arberry, tr., *The Seven Odes* (London, 1957), from "The Black Knight", p. 182.]

taken place, the present anguish of the hind, the future certainty of death for Dido, in spirit as in body.

Nearly as brief is Virgil's account of the hunting party that takes place afterward. Already "wounded," Dido organizes a royal chase, but instead of this diversion's proving a *remedium amoris*, as Ovid said it should be, it becomes the occasion for consummating her passion for Aeneas. Dido is now both huntress, and figuratively, smitten prey. The love of Dido and Aeneas, of which she is the victim, serves to effect Aeneas's development from a heedless sensual delectation to his stinging self-examination and a renewed sense of duty. He knows Dido's love for a time, and survives it. The love chase in which these two are temporarily caught up is part of the epic's larger hunt. Aeneas, a hunter of his own destiny, a hunter after Rome and the hunter of Turnus, is himself a man whom Juno and the fates toss and harry (*jactant, impellunt, agunt*).[9] The seemingly accidental quality of Dido's plight that the simile of the stricken hind suggests—the hind had been unwary (*incauta*), the hunter unaware (*nescius*)—falls within the framework of the gods' deliberate plotting at cross-purposes. Venus, appearing to Aeneas in huntress's guise, soon stirs her other son Cupid to make Dido his spoil. Juno sees to it that the hunting party will be the scene of a sylvan marriage. Jove intervenes to separate the lovers, allowing Dido to be sacrificed in order to liberate a stronger, more determined Aeneas.

[9] M. C. J. Putnam, in *The Poetry of the Aeneid: Four Studies in Imaginative Unity and Design* (Cambridge [Mass.], 1965), examines the imagery of the chase and makes several penetrating observations on the role of Aeneas as hunter (pp. 154–55, 157, 187–88). Aeneas is *venator canis* in the *Aeneid* 12.751, while Turnus is *cervum*, 12.750, in the simile beginning on line 748. On the occurrence of *vestigo* in Aeneas' search for Turnus, see Putnam, pp. 171–72, 176.

Fulgentius explains Aeneas' conduct so as to include hunting among his early faults: "The spirit of adolescence, on holiday from paternal control, goes off hunting, is inflamed by passion and, driven on by storm and cloud, that is, by confusion of mind, commits adultery." *Fulgentius the Mythographer*, tr. L. G. Whitbread (Columbus, 1971), p. 127.

Ovid and the Middle Ages

The chase of love controlled from afar by a divinity is perhaps nowhere so pervasive among poets of the ancient world as in Ovid. In the *Metamorphoses* (1. 456 ff.) the tale of Apollo's passion for Daphne, the god pressing on and the beloved enticing, epitomizes the quandary of a lover caught between two forces. Exulting in his conquest of the Python, Phoebus errs when he deprecates Cupid's skill: "What have you, wanton boy, to do with serious weapons? You contentedly do—I don't know what—with *that* [your torch] to ignite lovers' fires—don't lay claim to my honors!" Cupid shoots the careless boaster, retorting to him: "Your dart may strike all, Phoebus, but mine strikes you." He drives Apollo to a new chase, not one of his choosing, and causes him to fly after Daphne as the dog pursues the hare.

Failure to aknowledge Love's power brings about punishment in the *Metamorphoses*. Ovid shows men and women who resist normal sexual love menaced with destruction or with the deprivation of their humanity, that is, with change either into beasts or into other humbler shapes of nature. Often those who strive persistently to ignore their amorous pursuers will devote themselves instead to hunting, that other "chase of Phoebus's sister." Their impassioned quests for wild beasts form the prelude to their becoming victims themselves. Daphne, preferring the delights of the chase to Apollo's importuning, eludes him to become transformed into a laurel tree. Picus denies the passionate Circe and she lures him to pursue a boar; hotly he presses after the quarry until he is metamorphosed into a bird (14. 320 ff.). Adonis, too eager for the boar chase, spurns Venus and dies to change into a flower. Narcissus, exhausted by the chase, seeks the cool water when he evades the amorous Echo. Now, contemplating his image, he discovers a strange new passion, death, and metamorphosis. Too fervid a dedication to the chaste pursuits of Diana, a renunciation of Cupid's hunting, results in the loss of human form.

In his specifically amatory poems, Ovid continually employs images of the chase. Sappho in the *Heroides* (15. 51) laments her loss of Phaon: "New prey (*nova praeda*), the girls of Sicily, now come to you."[10] Phaedra, like Euripides' heroine, feverishly longs to enter Hippolytus's world of the chase—"to drive the deer into the net, and to urge on the fleet hound over the highest ridge, or with arm shot forth to let fly the quivering spear, or to lay my body on the grassy ground" (4. 41–44). Men and women hunt together, as the bereft Oenone reminds Paris: "Who was it pointed out to you the coverts apt for the chase? . . . Often have I gone with you to stretch the hunting net with the wide mesh" (5. 17, 19). Such are the figures diffused as well throughout the *Arts Amatoria*.[11] The hunt for all types of game—hares, birds, boar, fish, deer—pervades the work. The metaphor is established early: "The hunter knows well where to spread his nets for the stag, well knows he in what glen the boar with gnashing teeth abides; familiar are the copses to the fowlers, and he who holds the hook is aware in what waters many fish are swimming" (1. 45 ff.). Women are "spoil" (*praeda*, 1. 126), as in Sappho's letter to Phaon. "Let assurance come to your minds," the author amiably encourages the reader, "that all women can be caught; spread but your nets and you will catch them" (1. 269–270). The hunt forms the basis of an *adynaton:* sooner will nature reverse itself, "the hound of Maenalus flee before the hare than will a woman persuasively wooed resist a lover" (1. 272–73). Methods must vary to suit the type of quarry: "A grown hind will regard the snare from further away" (1. 766). "Some fish are taken with the spear, others with hooks; still others dragged with taut ropes in hollow nets" (1. 763–764). Nor does the poet address only the young man in these terms: in 3. 662 he advises the woman: "Do not let that hare [the woman's lover] be hunted by others."

[10] *Heroides and Amores*, ed. and tr. Grant Showerman (Cambridge, Mass., 1914; rpt. 1963).
[11] *The Art of Love and Other Poems*, ed. and tr. J. H. Mozley (Cambridge, Mass., 1929; rpt. 1962).

As for the *Remedia Amoris*, it prescribes actual hunting as a recourse for those who want to forget about love. As early as the *Cynegeticus*, Xenophon had rhetorically made a similar claim for hunting the hare: "So pleasant is the sight, that to see the hare tracked, found, pursued, and caught, is enough to make a man forget the one he loves.[12] Ovid now counsels the unhappy lover to take up the chase to distract his thoughts. Here the account of various hunts echoes in its details the metaphors of the first books:

> Or cultivate the pleasures of the chase: ofttimes has Venus, vanquished by Phoebus' sister, beaten a base retreat. Now pursue with cunning hound the forward-straining hare, now stretch your nets on leafy ridges; either with varied panic alarm the timid deer, or meet the boar and fell him with your spear-thrust. Tired out, at nightfall sleep, not thoughts of a girl, will await you, and refresh your limbs with healthy repose. It is a milder pleasure (yet a pleasure, it is), to seek a humble prize by snaring birds with net or reed, or to hide in the suspended bait the brazen hook, which the greedy fish may swallow to his hurt with ravening mouth. By these or other pursuits, until you unlearn your love, you must craftily deceive yourself.[13]

The authority of Ovid persists in medieval literature. His observation in the *Remedia Amoris* that hunting fatigues the would-be lover sufficiently to still his night thoughts became a commonplace of manuals of the chase to protest the virtuousness of the sport, although in these it is not attributed to Ovid. Jean Lefevre's rendering, *La Vieille*, of the thirteenth century *Vetula* (a poem based freely on the *Ars Amatoria*), proclaimed Ovid to be a lover and a hunter of beasts.[14] Other imitators of the *Ars Amatoria* incorporated its imagery of the various kinds of hunts, occasionally with touches of individuality. One of the earliest of

[12] Cited and tr. in Bernard Knox, *Oedipus at Thebes*, p. 234, n. 7.
[13] *Remedia Amoris* (tr. Showerman, *op. cit.*), lines 199–212.
[14] *La Vieille ou les derniers Amours d'Ovide*, ed. Hippolyte Cocheris (Paris, 1861) recounts a love affair of the poet's in which he was deceived by a go-between, and describes his pursuit of the stag, boar, fox, and other beasts, as well as his fowling and fishing exploits.

these imitators, the author of the *comoedia*, *Pamphilus*,[15] opens
with a lamenting lover bending to the advice of Venus. She
stresses the *art* by which all desirable things are won, and uses
the Ovidian figure of the hooked fish: *Et piscis liquidis deprenditur
arte sub undis* (85).

The analogy between love and fishing recurs in the most
celebrated of medieval arts of love, that of Andreas Capellanus.
Amor comes from *hamus*, a hook; the etymology is found in
Isidore of Seville.[16] "Just as a skillful fisherman tries to attract
fishes by his bait and to capture them on his crooked hook, so
the man who is a captive of love tries to attract another person
by his allurements."[17] Chaucer would write in the *Troilus* of
Diomede's efforts to win Criseyde: "To fisshen hire, he leyde
out hook and lyne." For the most part Andreas bases his hunting
imagery in *De arte honeste amandi* upon the pursuit of one kind
of creature for another: tercels, hawks and falcons pursue par-
tridges and pheasants or other small birds; a dog pursues a boar.
Yet the work opens with an allusion to the whole matter of love
in terms of a man's hunting, and this human-animal relationship
is never dropped. In the preface, Andreas affirms to his friend
Gualterus that "this kind of hunting" isn't suitable for a prudent
man. In the third dialogue the question arises concerning
"hunters' rights": should the one who has "wounded" a wild
beast have the prior right to it, or can another hunter claim it?
The verdict is that the first hunter, that is, the earlier suitor,
has the higher right. A mark, however, of Andreas's departure
from Ovid is his employment of images of the chase to dramatize
the struggle between men and women of different social rank.
Not concerned with an exploration of sexual love alone, but
with manners, and modes of argument, Andreas uses the chase,
with its reciprocal gestures of flight and pursuit, as an appro-

[15] Gustave Cohen (ed.), *La Comédie Latine en France en XII*ᵉ *Siècle*,
2 vols. (Paris, 1931), 2:194–223.
[16] Ed. W. M. Lindsay, 2 vols. (Oxford, 1911), 2:x, 'de Vocabulis': A.5.
[17] Andreas Capellanus, *Trattato d'Amore* (*Andreae Capellani regii
francorum "de Amore Libri Tres"*), ed. and tr. Salvatore Battaglia (Rome,
1947), p. 12.

priate means of charting the moves of social and intellectual contenders in the field of love. "Are you not hunting game other than you are worthy to take?" asks the woman of the highest nobility of the middle class man in the third dialogue. Two allusions converge here, one to the prohibitions of social rank, one to the limits of judgment. The *vilain* could not hunt "noble quarry" but had the "right of warren," that is, he could hunt for small, noisome game or vermin. Secondly, is there not a reverberation of the *hubris* of Adonis (*Metamorphoses* 10. 705 ff.) when he pursued the boar despite the warnings of Venus? Hunting beasts that are too large and dangerous, if one doesn't know what one is about, can lead to disaster. So too, with Chaucer's Troilus, when after the glorious intimacies of Book III the lovers recede from our view and we glimpse him on the periphery of our vision, hunting at the close of that Book only the most fierce quarry, ignoring the small tame beasts, and moving all unknowing toward his fall.

Among the thirteenth-century adaptations[18] of Ovid's *Ars Amatoria*, briefer, less original borrowings occur of the hunting images. Both Maître Elie of Winchester and the author of *La Clef d'Amors* urge the amorous prowler to learn how to spread his nets. *La Clef d'Amors* counsels caution, "for the bird may recognize the signs of the spread net." Maître Elie also refers to fishing and adds a line reminiscent of Ovid's title and of the *Pamphilus: par art prent li chiens le gorpil* (15). Both *La Clef d'Amors* and *l'Art d'Amors* of Jacques d'Amiens make use of the *adynaton*: sooner would the chase reverse its order, the hounds run from the hares or become friendly with them than will a woman resist ultimate capture. Limited and conventional in their use of Ovid, such writers nonetheless helped to keep current his images of the love chase.

[18] Elie of Winchester: *Maître Elie's Ueberarbeitung der ältesten französischen Übertragung Ars Amatoria*, ed. Heinrich Kühne and Edmund Stengel (Marburg, 1886); *La Clef d'Amors*, ed. Auguste Doutrepont (Halle, 1890); Jakes d'Amiens, *"L'Art d'Amors" und "Li Remedes d'Amors": zwei altfranzösische Lehrgedichte*, ed. Gustav Körting (Leipzig, 1868).

Less obviously dependent upon Ovid, yet sharing something of his subject and tone, is the twelfth-century lyric from Ripoll, *Quomodo primum amavit.*[19] Here Cupid and his mother are shown as hunters who can divert men's wills from the hunts of Diana. The irreconcilability of the two hunts, the literal and the erotic, together with the awesome power of the god, recall the scene of the *Metamorphoses.* But the medieval lyric contains something more. The boy god's insinuating, gently bullying mockery proves sufficient to drive the mortal hunter earthward "as if in terror." The spoil of Amor, this hunter burns as a result of conversation with the god—no arrow, gold or iron, has pierced him, nor has any quarry enticed him: he succumbs to the mere talk of "playing inside Venus's walls." The poet's light malice in treating this relation between the lover and the god, indeed enamorment in general, is not far from the wry and worldly style of the *Ars Amatoria:*

> In April when groves are leafy and the meadow is covered with rose blossoms, tender young men and maids burn with love. They burn with love, the tender young men and maids, when every little bird sings devotedly in harmony, and the blackbird in the wood sweetly chants. Then Amor, with Venus, his mother, makes war, endlessly bending his ivory bow so as to increase her kingdom. At that time I was returning from the chase, and although the sun had gone down, bending toward the pole, I began to search for my strayed whelps. I looked all about, but could not find them anywhere; I grieved at this more than a little, and kept searching for the lost ones.
>
> While I kept searching thus, Venus's son, leaning on his bow in the guise of a god, spoke to me: "Where are you rushing, charming boy? Diana's quivers have once more been broken, and Cupid's bow must now be taken up: Therefore, I advise you, leave your pursuit. Leave your pursuit, I therefore advise you; it isn't appropriate at such a time. We must instead play the game of venery. Do you perhaps not know Cupid's sport? Why surely, it ill becomes a young man like you never to have played inside the

[19] F. J. E. Raby, *Secular Latin Poetry*, 2 vols. (Oxford, 1957), 2:238–39.

wall of Venus' court. If you play only once in that court, you
never will abandon it, no matter how you suffer, but will serve
there always with all your heart."
At his admonition, I trembled all over. I fell to the earth as if in
terror; and suddenly I burned with a new fire.

Daylight, which makes all things seem clear and familiar, has
ended. The hunter had become separated from his hounds.
These whelps anticipate a feature that will recur in various
allegorical hunting poems—the hounds embodying an aspect of
the man himself. Here the lost whelps suggest the narrator's
loss of touch with the known and predictable world, as well as
his imminent loss of freedom. Cupid tells him that he must
change once he has played within the palace of Venus. By the
end of the lyric the narrator sinks to earth and experiences a
"new fire." Despite the repetition of "play" (*ludere*, *ludit*,
luderis), moving from the impersonality of the infinitive to the
pointed intimacy of the second person, the words of Cupid leave
a hint of menace, for the playground enclosure may also be a
place of bondage from which return will be impossible. If the
poem concerns itself with the power of hunting Eros and his
victim's lightning-stroke initiation to a sensual awareness, it
does so, however, with a suave irreverence that tends to be
absent from the vernacular treatments of a similar subject. When
the god of love stalks and shoots the dreamer of the *Roman de la
Rose*, the awful cruelty of his harrying is already a commonplace
among French writers.

Combined Forms of the Love Chase
in Medieval Literature

From the twelfth century the amatory hunt will continue to
recur in vernacular poetry both as an occasional metaphor and
as a controlling or crucial figure in a given work. Love, divine
and human—the latter in its idealized as in its more robust
manifestations—is a major literary theme: it preoccupies lyric
and romance writers, and finds expression in works as erudite

and as diverse in style and matter as St. Bernard's allegorization
of the Canticles, Alan of Lille's *De Planctu Naturae*, the treatise
and dialogues of Andreas Capellanus, and the joined composition of Guillaume de Lorris and Jean de Meun. When
writing about love, authors sought new vocabularies. Gérard
Paré noted Jean's proliferation of scholastic terms in treating of
love: *enseignement, espondre* < *exponere, gloser* < *glossare, question*
< *questio, despute* < *disputatio*, and of course the university
chaiere for which *la Vieille* declares her qualifications.[20] From
the same epoch as the *Roman de la Rose* our earliest medieval
handbooks of the chase survive, giving evidence of an interest
in recording cynegetic practices and correct hunting form. It is
not too surprising, therefore, to find secular amatory poets
diversifying their expression by drawing upon a vocabulary that
their aristocratic auditors would know and enjoy, and developing their hunting figures in great technical detail. After
the later twelfth century, poets choosing the love chase as a
literary device could find material available to them not only
from the Ovidian books and from Christian writings that included commentaries upon Scripture and upon ancient authors,
but also from the growing corpus of learning that dealt with
the praise and practice of the hunt. The stag of love had become
more than the elusive quarry of the chase as in the *Metamorphoses*,
a Galatea desired by a despairing Cyclops—"more fleeting than
the stag driven before the clear-barking hounds." The stag had
been rendered complex by its important appearances in a variety
of contexts; having been charged with meanings often in conflict
with one another, it afforded a figure of remarkable richness to
secular love poets. Its natural properties and habits were the
concern of handbooks of the chase, and these freely incorporated allegorical material as well. This allegorical material
grew out of a Christian and classical tradition, as we have already
observed. Scarcely less complex is the hound of the chase that
desires the stag of love. "Chiens chace par nature," wrote

[20] *Les idées et les lettres au XIIIᵉ siècle: Le Roman de la Rose* (Montreal,
1947), chap. I, "Vocabulaire Scolaire et Scolastique," pp. 15–52, *passim*.

Brunetto Latini;[21] the pursuant hound in the amatory tradition is, with few exceptions, an extension of one of the lovers, a principle of motion that urges change as the stag lures, a volatile connective between innocence and experience, or between a present state of love and an imminent one.

Medieval poets writing narratives of love seemed to be almost effortlessly receptive to any suggestion of a chase, even of the briefest sort, figurative or otherwise, in which to involve their heroes. Hunting lovers and amatory hunters begin to abound in vernacular literature late in the twelfth century and thereafter. As hunting became increasingly a craft whose divisions could be committed to writing and learned, it afforded poets a pattern whose defined stages could be matched to a wooer's pursuit, and whose methods could provide material for rich and structured images. Metaphors of the chase recur pointedly in *Aucassin and Nicolete*, where each of the lovers sees the other as a hunter: "dites li," says Nicolete to the little shepherds, "qu'il a une beste en ceste forest et qu'il le viegne cacier . . . Le beste a tel mecine que Aucassins ert garis de son mehaing." ("Tell him that there is a beast in this forest and that he must come to hunt it. The beast has such healing power that Aucassin will be cured of his wound.") To the grotesque woodsman who has no head for metaphors, Aucassin laments that he has lost and seeks a white greyhound, the most beautiful in the world.[22] So, too, does the hunting work reciprocally in *Partonope of Blois* where Melior lures Partonope to hunt on her preserves, providing him with her own magical limers:

> They where as soffte as eny selke,
> And ther-to whyte as eny mylke.[23]

[21] Brunetto Latini, *Li Livres dou Trésor*, ed. F. J. Carmody (Berkeley, 1948), 1:184, pp. 161–162, "Des chiens."

[22] *Aucassin et Nicolete*, ed. Mario Roques (Paris, 1963), xviii, 17–18, 30–31; xxii, 39–41.

[23] *Partonope du Blois*, ed. A. Trampe Bödtker, *EETS ES* (London, 1912), 109:65–70, lines 2237–38. The hunting episode, including the rewards of love, covers lines 2192–2314.

His pursuit and slaying of a wild boar with the lady's hounds, whose softness and whiteness might be those of her very body, precede their becoming lovers that same night. Frequently the love chase will merge with another type of symbolic hunt; for instance, shades of the mortal chase and of the supernatural chase suffuse in a macabre way the hunt of love in the *Decameron* (the fifth day, the eighth tale). There the spurned lover, Nastagio, has a horrific noon-day vision of a Knight who chases his shrieking lady in the forest, has her torn apart by his hounds and throws her unyielding heart to them. Immediately thereupon, the lady rises up, apparently unscathed, and the whole chase and capture are re-enacted. There are vestiges too of a supernatural chase arranged by a willful Diana in the manner of the lady Niniane's luring her lovers, notably Merlin, across a ford or by a fountain.[24]

It is to such combined forms that I should like first to draw attention, works in which an amatory hunt has joined with and been altered by its conjunction with another figurative type. Without attempting to explore with completeness the whole range of amatory hunts in medieval literature, I propose to select for close analysis those contexts within a small number of poems where the love chase fuses with one of the other three symbolic types of pursuits: the sacred or supernatural chase, the moral chase, and the instructive chase. In each case, love is the principal theme, while the poet, knowing in literary traditions associated with the hunt, employs its images and events to achieve a pattern whose variations will express a changed condition for one or more of the principal characters of his narrative. The pursuit that led to an other-world meeting with a divinity, like the chase of St. Eustace, undergoes a secular transformation where the quarry draws a hero to an other-world mistress: her love and its power acquire a strangeness that is almost preter-

[24] Lucy Allen Paton, "La Damoisele Cacheresse," *Studies in the Fairy Mythology of Arthurian Romance*, pp. 228–47 (2nd ed. rev. and enl. by Roger Sherman Loomis; New York, 1960) suggests Diana as Niniane's original.

natural, seeming to arise from the "otherness" of her origins.
The chase of death in which a hero like Siegfried became the
slain quarry combines with the death of the beloved to inform
the vision of the poet in *The Book of the Duchess*. And the
detailed matter of the hunting books, such as that which affords
an understanding of the nature of Gawain's self-discovery,
functions in a romance that is devoted to the celebration of love.
Gottfried's *Tristan* is possessed of a knowingness in the chase
that guides him inescapably to a new experience, that of Minne:
it is his cynegetic knowledge that becomes the instrument of
his initiation into Minne's hunt.

The Sacred Chase Transformed: Love and the Other World.
"Manerius" and *Erec*.

An anonymous Latin lyric, "Manerius," and Chrétien de
Troyes' romance, *Erec*, embody hunts that lead their heroes to
love in alien countries. The exoticism of the place in which the
hunting hero loses himself, the uncommon or unfamiliar circumstances accompanying his discovery of it, emphasize the shock
of the erotic encounter—the difference in the mind when desire
takes its hold upon the body. *Amor*, as such poems would show,
is always in some sense *"de lonh"*—foreign, dislocating, capable
of carrying one a great distance from comfortable reality; in
short, a force imposing change. The hero separates from the
landscape he is acquainted with, from his companions, all that
he customarily relies upon (cf. the whelps in *Quomodo primum
amavit*), to be existentially alone; and in such a condition he is
prepared to encounter love. Such is the unadorned pattern of
the other-world chase, and "Manerius"[25] exemplifies it in as
pure a version as we may hope to find in medieval literature.
The chase is the whole poem; its climax is the hunter's union
with the king's daughter.

> Rising up in the early dawn, Manerius
> took up his quiver and golden bow;

[25] Raby, *Secular Latin Poetry*, 2:310–312.

coupling his hounds with a double leash,
he went to the forest eager for the chase.
He coursed through the groves and crossed the uplands,
joyously unharbored a stag of sixteen points.
Yet though he pursued it all the day long
he could not overtake the wild creature.
His companions were tired and his hounds worn out,
all scattered; he called them back with shouts,
and taking up his horn, his strength renewed,
sent its notes forth to every grove.
At the sound a high-born maiden
trembled all over, about to enter her father's land.
The young man glimpsed her and hastened towards her.
He saw her and spoke with her, felt his lips kissing hers.
Then he and that king's daughter, deliberating,
traversed the utmost boundary of love.

Perhaps what distinguishes "Manerius" from the vernacular poems it resembles, like *Tyolet* and *Guigemar*, is the hero's decisiveness even though he is lost in the "other country" and meets its "enchantress" face to face. It isn't Manerius who tremblingly falls into the power of the princess of the forest, but she who responds trembling to the sound of his horn. Sounding the horn is his first emphatic act; at the point of exhaustion, he suddenly reveals an access of renewed strength. He behaves resolutely with the king's daughter, traveling with this unknown girl by their mutual agreement to love's farthest "boundary"—a territorial metaphor[26] that culminates the "other-country" aspect of their meeting. That the trembling princess rises suddenly before Manerius as a replacement for the elusive wild hart, and that the sexual union of man and princess supplants the hunter's triumph over his quarry are plain in the poem. But what country is it that she was about to enter, and what is its king? Can Manerius, having so loved, ever return homeward? The poem's silences as to these matters, its initially

[26] Peter Dronke, *Medieval Latin and the Rise of the European Love-Lyric*, 2:488–89, on the *quinque lineae amoris* topos traced from Ovid and Latin grammarians.

strong, then fading references to the chase, yielding to an ever-sharpening focus upon the erotic encounter, all unite to create the poem's important effects—those of the sudden strangeness of enamorment, the great moral distances traversed to that "territory," and the isolation of lovers from the web of familiar relationships and activities.

The variation upon this narrative pattern that occurs in Chrétien's *Erec* is not only more complex but diffuse, and explores more thoroughly the enchantment of sensuality. The chase first assumes a similar structural purpose in separating Erec from the court, but it then contributes to an expression of the lovers' relation to one another. The chase of love to a distant country occupies the whole of the Manerius poem; in *Erec*, the old quaint custom of hunting the white stag for a kiss—"*l'usage Pendragon*" (1767)[27] functions only in the poem's first third. This announced chase brings the hero, though indirectly and even willy-nilly, to an experience of love which will temporarily have the force of a paralyzing enchantment. Chrétien always tends to rationalize the fairy elements in his romances, exploiting them in his own way to demonstrate the problems besetting his heroes and heroines, their methods of resolving them, and their human development. The fatal dominion which Enide exercises for a time over Erec apparently arises from the lovers' newly discovered sensuality. This dominion bears a literary kinship, however, to the great power of Enide's originals, fairies of the type ranging from a Circe to a Morgan, and looking ahead to Spenser's Duessa—sorceresses who deprive their lovers of their masculine will.[28] Erec's too delicious

[27] References are to Mario Roques (ed.), *Erec et Enide, d'après la copie du scribe Guiot*, BN. fr. 794 (Paris, 1953).

[28] Through an exacting comparison of the analogues and the possible sources for motifs in Chrétien's romance, R. S. Loomis showed the fairy origins of Enide, especially her kinship with Morgan La Fée. The sparrow-hawk with which she is associated, as well as the white stag, occur in legends of Celtic provenience as attributes of, guides to, or contests arranged by, fairy mistresses. (*Arthurian Tradition and Chrétien de Troyes* [New York, 1949], pp. 68–70, 99–100, 118–120.)

Rachel Bromwich ("Celtic Dynastic Themes and the Breton Lays,"

marriage is his enchantment, and it makes him lose his inclination for military activity. Enide, Chrétien hastens to say, used no incantations or charms when she laced his armor. But Erec eventually has to free himself from her power: (she feels herself blamed for having ensnared and captured him and caused his loss of worth) by assuming a steeliness of heart that enables him to subject Enide to punishing tests.

While the stag chase that lures a hero to erotic adventure became common in vernacular *lais*,[29] Chrétien contrives a parallel to it—the battle for the sparrowhawk—and permits these two episodes to reflect something of the nature of both Erec and Enide and of the undeveloped love they bear each other during their courtship and the early part of their marriage. The stag chase, and its counterpart the sparrowhawk combat, both very much in the forefront of the romance until the lovers embrace on the night of their wedding, reflect their evolution toward an innocent sensuality before a deeper understanding changes their relationship and prepares them for their life roles as a king and queen. Thereafter, the stag and the hawk cease to be relevant to them. Except for the occasions when Erec and Enide, in the course of their hard wandering, encounter Arthur again engaged in his customary sport in a wood full of quarry (3920 ff.), or when Erec knows that Arthur may be found

---

Études Celtiques 9 [1961]: 442 ff.) has shown the recurrence in Irish mythology of a white stag chase that drew the hero to his sovereignty over a kingdom. Often the motif is conjoined with that of a hag he must lie with (the divinity symbolizing the new land) before she becomes transformed into a young and lovely bride. Inasmuch as Chrétien tells us that he translated the *Commandemenz d'Ovide*, he must have acquainted himself with the images of the amatory hunt stemming from that quarter as well.

[29] In *Guigemar*, ed. Jeanne Lods, *Les Lais de Marie de France* (Paris, 1959), the hero wounds not only himself but a beast, all white, with a stag's antlers on its head (lines 91–92). His wound will be curable by a beloved woman for whom he must search. Graelent (ed. E. M. Grimes, *The Lays of Desiré, Graelent and Melion* [New York, 1928]) follows a white hind—whiter than the snow that lies on the branch (lines 211–212) —to a fatal enchantress.

hunting the stag, animals of the chase are no longer associated with these two.

The romance opens in a spirit of contentiousness. With the announcement of the chase for the *blanc cerf*, in which Arthur's lords must vie with one another to capture the stag, Gawain foresees further wrangling. There will be *"maus . . . molt granz"* (49), *"noise et bataille"* (306) when the winning knight comes to grant his salute to the fairest woman. The usual strife of the chase, that contest between hunter and hunted, is to occur among the hunters as well, and then continue in the court circle among the five hundred damsels of high degree, each of whom has a knight to champion her. The honor of the white stag, then, is to be a contest of ability and beauty for both a man and a woman who can meet its terms; it will eventually prove Enide's surpassing beauty, though as yet no one has heard of her.

From this announced competition, Erec hangs back. He joins Guinevere with his sword, but without hunting arms. Behind the rest of the party he rides with her entourage for no other reason than to keep her company. He has no intention of joining the chase, yet it is the chase that gives him this opportunity to refuse to conform, "conducting" him to his adventure in the *rear* of its train where he and the queen lose their companions. Once out of earshot (*ne pueent oïr rien, | ne cor, | ne chaceor, | ne chien*, 131–132), he finds himself in a provocative situation with the unpredictable dwarf (whose conduct is never explained) that carries him directly to the country of his enchanting mistress. Thus, despite his efforts to have nothing to do with the white stag, Erec will bear his love back to court to receive the honor, *l'enor del blanc cerf* (1744).

Why should not the narrative have allowed Erec himself to pursue and capture the white stag as well as the fairest girl? Why not have the stag lead, as in so many analogous instances, directly to her? But Chrétien manipulates the familiar romance elements in a new way, and achieves several ends. The character of Erec begins to emerge. His deliberately ignoring the old

custom of the stag suggests his diffidence, or lack of interest
for the moment in love; there is apparently no one upon whom
he would bestow the kiss. It shows especially the characteristic
independence with which he will continue to behave: he will
choose a poor girl, bring her back in rags and insist that the
Queen dress her, refuse to play the role of the courtly love
servant, and train Enide, according to his own irascible notions
of justice, to be a devoted wife.[30] Moreover, Chrétien succeeds
in densifying the atmosphere of enchantment: though resolutely
avoiding the white stag contest, with its amorous motive, Erec
becomes fatefully drawn into the midst of it and into a seemingly
ill-omened love.

Finally the exclusion of Erec from the chase of the white stag
places Enide at the contest's center; it enables her to receive
the regal salute as a blessing (as she will later receive the Queen's
robe), and identifies her with the stag in the King's view, which
must be impartial. Gawain had foreseen that every knight must
be prejudiced in favor of his mistress. Only the King rises, by
virtue of his position, above the rivalry; only his choice of the
fairest (with which Guinevere agrees) could be regarded as dis-
interested. While Erec races after the dwarf, thus bypassing the
stag and galloping straight into the unknown, Arthur slays the
stag. Because of the King's immunity from the general squab-
bling that the knights can be counted on to engage in, the royal
kiss can be said plausibly to testify to Enide's singular worth.
She is unique as the stag is unique; together they become the
object of the King's ritual. Arthur's capture of the stag earns
him the enjoyment of hunter's rights, the kiss he takes from
Enide, though the honor is hers. In the *Mabinogion* version of
the romance, *Geraint son of Erbin*, Arthur gives the stag's head
to Enid, "and from that time forth her fame increased thereby."
There the lady wins the honors of the chase directly, whereas
Chrétien divides the ritual, so that the lady receives the honor
and the King the "portion." Hartman von Aue, in his *Erec*,

---

[30] Z. P. Zaddy, "The Structure of Chrétien's *Erec*," *Modern Language
Review* 62 (1967): 613–615, gives an idea of "Erec's imperious nature."

establishes clearly that Arthur takes the kiss as his *rëht*, the word meaning the hunter's right.[31] There is a further detail that subtly connects Enide to the *blanc cerf*. Before Chrétien tells her name for the first time, before Guinevere clothes her, Enide's *senhal* derives from the whiteness of her plain garment: she is *la pucele au chainse blanc* (1071, 1339, 1612). Erec, having shunned the white stag, returns with the girl in white who wins the white stag's honor. This honor can reflect solely upon Enide, as Chrétien tells the tale, since her lover had removed himself from the rules of the contest. Instead Erec reserves his efforts for the hawk competition, which he enters with sudden fixedness of purpose.

Riding into the strange town, Erec remarks at once knights and ladies feeding and tending falcons. He is now in the realm of the sparrowhawk. Once he has beheld Enide, he will pointedly seek the bird out. The stag has "led" him to the unknown; the sparrowhawk involves him in what he thinks is the known—winning Enide—but he cannot yet foresee the hardships she will bring to them both. Once again this contest is meant to try the worth of both the man and his mistress. He must be daring; she must be beautiful and good. In the heat of the fight, he draws strength from her loveliness.

Gradually Chrétien arrives at a symbolic identification of Erec with the hawk as he has identified Enide with the stag. A hawk is customarily a pursuer, while a stag is pursued. Because of Erec's battle prowess, Enide wins the hawk as she has won Erec with her beauty. Just before the contest, Erec brusquely insults his rival's maiden: "Away, young lady, go amuse yourself with some other bird, for you have no right to this one." But Enide gains, through Erec, her right to the bird, and it becomes, together with Erec, her only wealth. The honor, joy, and renown she has achieved that day, her inner happiness,

---

[31] The analogues are in Gwyn and Thomas Jones (trs.), *The Mabinogion* (London, 1957), pp. 241, 246; Hartmann von Aue (ed. Albert Leitzmann [Halle, 1957]), lines 1104–1111; 1753–1760, cited by David Dalby, *A Lexicon of MHG Terms Associated with the Chase*, s.v. *rëht*.

depend upon Erec; yet she focusses her attention both upon her hawk and her lord.[32] Explicitly, then, Chrétien fixes these implied identifications between the lovers and the two animals of the chase. In the climax to the romance's first part, the account of the wedding, he isolates the images of stag and hawk from the two contests that have led to the discovery and winning of the bride. To convey the lovers' new, voluptuous joy, he employs these images in a new way, concentrating upon the animals' hunger and thirst, both in the heat of the chase and in training for it:

Cers chaciez qui de soif alainne
ne desirre tant la fontainne,
n'espreviers ne vient a reclain
si volantiers quant il a fain,
que plus volantiers n'i venissent,
einçois que il s'antre tenissent.
Cele nuit ont tant restoré
de ce qu'il ont tant demoré.
Quant vuidiee lor fu la chanbre,
lor droit randent a chascun manbre.

The hunted stag that pants for thirst does not so desire the fountain, nor does the sparrowhawk respond so willingly to the lure when it is hungry, as did they come willingly together as soon as they might clasp one another. That night they had much consolation for what they had so long awaited. Once the chamber was voided they rendered to each sense its right.[33]

Each the apparent "quarry" in a love contest, the stag and the hawk first served to bring the hero and heroine together, and now have become converted to images expressive of the lovers' individual longings for each other. Their love's consummation incorporates yet another figure of the hunt, the *droit*—the portion due the limer, or leadhound. Yet as the images are

[32] This detail is noted on p. 216 of Roques' edition, from BN ms. f. fr. 1450 (described in Roques' Introduction, pp. xxviii-ix).
[33] Roques (ed.), lines 2027–2036.

conceived in this passage, the stag and hawk do not really "unite" since each thirsts and hungers for a fulfillment that cannot take the other into account. Chrétien's allusions to animals of the hunt here point to an incomplete union, which is what the events of the romance also go on to reveal. Man and wife will not join in perfect unanimity until much later, after their suffering together.

Ironically, too, what the love contests proved turns out to have been the superficial and conventional attributes of the two lovers. They are seen to be perfectly matched, well suited for each other's love, in the generalized language of romances: They were wholly matched and equal, as to courtesy, beauty and graciousness (*molt estoient igal et per | de corteisie et de biauté | et de grant deboneretê*), begins the account (1484 ff.). The contests thus elicit what can readily be observed or is already known— Erec's superior force of arms, Enide's splendid loveliness—and bring these qualities into play as each lover responds to the other. These are the requisites, the conventionally acceptable, even endearing traits that cause them initially to love. Yet in this early stage of love, compared to the stag's thirst and the hawk's hunger, Erec becomes temporarily enlaced in the enchantment of their sensuality. As is usual with Chrétien, the first joy of hero and heroine is insufficient: after a peak of ecstatic happiness Enide and Erec must proceed to test their deeper and enduring love. Perhaps it is significant that Erec and Enide do not participate in any more of Arthur's diversions in the forest. Instead, the narrative reports Arthur's hunting as though at a distance from the lovers, as when Erec rides by chance into the king's outdoor court among his pavilions and cannot be persuaded to stay (3920 ff.), or when, once again (4492), Erec guesses that Arthur may be found hunting the stag within five leagues. For the lovers, mature in their unanimity, the pastimes of Arthur's court now seem remote, belonging with the pleasures of their less happy innocence when they had first received their marriage blessing from Arthur and Guinevere. Once and for all, Chrétien drops the figure.

As distinct from this courtly hunting of Arthur's, the symbolic hunt has a meaning for Chrétien that is related to Ovid's in the *Ars Amatoria*, though Chrétien's emphasis is upon the animals' separate desires rather than upon the bond that locks hunter and prey. In addition, these figures acquire a further depth from their association with fairy legend and myth, which invest hawk and stag with magical energy. The voluptuous joys to which they conduct the hero and heroine have the strength of a dire, otherworldly spell that only their human suffering can break.

The Mortal Chase Transformed: The Poet's Vision of the Death of the Hart. *The Book of the Duchess.*

The chase, fragmented though it is and consigned to less than five percent of the poem,[34] nonetheless works with economy both thematically and structurally in Chaucer's *Book of the Duchess*. The twin themes of this elegiac poem are love and

[34] At the most, 64 of the poem's 1,334 lines can be called relevant to the hunt. (References are to Chaucer, *Works*, pp. 267–279.) From "Me thought I herde an hunte blowe / T'assay hys horn" (345–46), to "the hunte wonder faste / blew a forloyn at the laste" (386) constitutes 42 lines. From "Ther cam by me a whelp" (389) to "I hym folwed" (397) adds 9 lines. There are 8 lines describing the beasts of the forest (427–34); 3 lines are added by "this game is done . . . the huntes konne hym nowher see" (539–41), and 2 more (1312–13) with "They gan to strake forth."
Among the suggested sources of Chaucer's inspiration for the hunting passages are those which Étienne Sandras (*Étude sur G. Chaucer considéré comme imitateur des Trouvères* [Paris, 1859], pp. 92, 296–97) tentatively put forth. The texts from which he quotes, not alway accurately, have subsequently been edited by Tilander (*Cynegetica* 7 [Stockholm, 1960], lines 223–24, 245–46); Åke Blomqvist (*Le Roman des Deduis de Gace de la Buigne* [Karlshamn, 1951], lines 8131 ff.). John Livingston Lowes, in *PMLA* 19 (1904): 647 ff., drew attention to the passages in Froissart's *Paradys d'Amours* (ed. August Schéler [Brussels, 1870], 1: lines 916 ff.) in which the god of love, his limerers, and his company take pleasure in "l'amoureuse chace. (945)" O. F. Emerson, "Chaucer and Medieval Hunting," *Romanic Review* 13 (1922): 115–50, assumes Chaucer's independence, but compares his account with material in the much later *Master of Game*. This English treatise was, of course, a translation of the *Chasse* of Gaston Phoebus, itself dependent upon the *Livres du roy Modus*, a fourteenth-century book written during Chaucer's lifetime.

death—love defined and perfected by death, death itself illuminated, made stately, its terror muted by the husband's love, and
both love and death embraced within the Poet's vision. With a
formalized dignity, the chase in the forest discloses to us by the
merging of two near-homonyms, the death of the stag, the *hert*,
and of the beloved, the husband's *herte swete*. Chaucer's word-
play upon the pursued stag and the death-captured *heart-hart*
(these words having their many possible meanings, both in the
poem and in Middle English generally[35]) keeps us aware of the

[35] There are in the *Book of the Duchess*, 41 occurrences of all forms of
the word: *herte* and *hertes*.

Among those scholars who have commented on the likelihood of an
intended pun (although not necessarily concurring in its significance for
the poem as a whole), are Helge Kökeritz *PMLA* 69 (1954): 951; Paull
F. Baum, *PMLA* 71 (1956): 239; Donald C. Baker, *Studia Neophilologica*
30 (1958): 23; Joseph E. Grennen, *Modern Language Quarterly* 25 (1964):
131 f.; Bernard F. Huppé and D. W. Robertson, Jr., *Fruyt and Chaf:
Studies in Chaucer's Allegories* (Princeton, 1963), 49 f.; Beryl Rowland,
Neuphilologische Mitteilungen 66 (1965): 158 f.

The frequent repetition of *hert-herte* serves to sustain the essential
connection between the Knight's love-suffering and Octovien's hunting.
Its commonest meaning in the *Book of the Duchess* is the heart; secondly
it signifies the hunted stag; and thirdly the past tense of the verb "hurt":
it was White that *herte* the beholder with her lovely glance, though
because of her innocence it affected her *herte* but little (883–84). The
herte occurs first in Alcyone's story: her *herte began to erme* (grieve), she
vows her fidelity to Juno, "wille, body, *herte*, and al"; she is to Seys,
"myn goode swete *herte*." The *hert* of the chase (between 351–381) next
captures our attention and recurs in the words of the Poet to the Knight,
"I holde that this *hert* be goon" (540) and again to his audience, "al was
doon / For that tyme, the hert-huntyng" (1312–13). Once the hart as the
quarry of the chase has been introduced the *heart* continues to resound
in the words of the Knight's lament, and in the Poet's observation of his
emotional state. When the Knight finishes his first *complaynte* in the
form of a song, his heart suffers physically: it faints, the blood flies to
warm it, for it seems to feel harm, and sorrows seem to lie cold upon it.
The Poet hopes the Knight's heart may be eased by disclosing the cause
of his woe. The Knight hopes he may have pity from the heart of another, indeed, the Poet's own heart endures anguish just to listen to this
story (713).

In the Knight's account of his love service to White and his winning
her, he speaks of his heart as his whole being and will which he dedicated
to the god of Love. When he declares that she *syt so* in his *herte*, heart

double theme. Octovien conducts his imperial mortal chase for the *hert* in the distance, while in the foreground the Knight mourns his *herte*'s loss: the meanings and fate of each, hart and heart, reflect upon the other.

As a structural device the same chase directs the sleeping Poet to the scene of his principal revelation, the loss of "faire White" and the husband's lament, giving him the subject of his poem. Thus the chase composes a frame or enclosure about the sorrowing figure of the Man in Black. In this respect the *chase* forms a parallel to the *book*, the "romaunce" that leads the waking Poet in the narrative's first part to his discovery of Seys and Alcyone and encompasses their legend in the same type of frame.

Opening with an account of the Poet's wakefulness, the *Book of the Duchess* closes swiftly with his awakening. Within this symmetrical setting, the Poet is drawn into two scenes of un-equal length—these being joined by the reminder (the "fether-bed" invocation to Morpheus) that he remains yet in his bed. The two scenes are parallel: the first bookish, brief, paradigmatic, establishes the themes of love and death, while the second is a rich, allegedly personal expansion of a love-and-death episode, informed by lyric conventions. Awake, the Poet is conducted by means of his book to a glimpse of the lives of Seys and Alcyone, a pair of pagan lovers whom he sees that death will separate. Theirs is a tale comparatively swiftly recounted (62–220), the

---

signifies the mind and the imagination. The heart is the seat of joy (1173, 1175), but it can be identified too with the lover's vulnerability to sorrow: "me thoughte myn *herte* brast atweyn" (1193); "with sorowful *herte* and woundes dede" (1210–1211). When his heart seems to change body, so that "she had the *herte*" (1153), it metonymically represents the Knight's whole being and affections. Finally she *is* his *"herte* swete" and the two unite so that "our *hertes* wern so even a payre, / that never nas that oon contrayre." With the framework of the hart hunt, and the varying meanings that arise from *heart* with respect to Blanche and the Knight, the final force of "al was doon / for that tyme, the hert-huntyng" becomes importantly equivocal: it suggests not only the literal pursuing of the quarry, but the Knight's longing for the vanished beloved, and death's hunt for the soul.

intensity of their love-suffering evoked both by direct statement
and by Alcyone's grief-filled utterances. The elements, the sea
and the tempest, have destroyed their bliss. Chaucer strips away
Ovid's description of the storm as he does other details—the
lovers' mythical antecedents and destinies. Ceyx, *siderius* in
Ovid's account, was Lucifer's son; Alcyone was the daughter of
Aeolus: Deschamps' *Balade* recalls her relationship to *"le dieu
des vens."*[36] Gone, too, from Chaucer's retelling is their happier
transformation as birds, which Machaut included in his version
in *La Fontaine Amoureuse.*[37] By excluding from the narrative the
vision of these two lovers, once born of the stars and wind, now
shedding their human bodies and soaring together over the sea
that had divided them—by sweeping away their mythic natures
and moving transfiguration, Chaucer gives us only the un-
alleviated spectacle of their human wretchedness, which they
acknowledge to each other in Alcyone's dream. This starker
presentation of the fortunes of the first pair of lovers becomes,
to the Black Knight's sumptuous lament, what the dumb show
may be to the play. Chaucer deprives the Seys-Alcyone episode
of its meteorological and aviary allusions, and by keeping this
first episode spare he can reserve in the second episode the rich
solar and venatic images, the sun and the slain hart, to the
Knight's lost beloved.

Once the Poet has learned of the pitiful Seys and Alcyone,
his repeated "I . . . red thys tale" (224–5, 228, 231) completes
its enclosing bracket, stresses its legendary (in the literal sense)
quality and brings us back to the Poet sleepless in his chamber.
In this attitude he invokes Morpheus, who figured in the first
vision, to carry him to the condition in which he may witness
the second. Asleep now, and dreaming, he is conducted by a
chase to the grief-stricken knowledge—"hyt dyde myn herte so

---

[36] *Metamorphoses* 12. 445 ff.; Deschamps, "Balade de Ceix et Alcyone,"
Œuvres Complètes, ed. le Marquis de Queux de St.-Hilaire (Paris, 1878),
1: 118–119.
[37] *Œuvres de Guillaume de Machaut*, ed. Ernest Hoepffner (Paris, 1921),
3., lines 691–92.

moche woo"—of a second unhappy love story. The sounds of
the chase (with its horn echoing that summons of Juno's messenger to Morpheus when he "blew his horn ryght in here
eere," 182) cause the Poet to rise, as it seems to him, out of his
bed.

> And as I lay thus, wonder lowde
> Me thoght I herde an hunte blowe
> T'assay hys horn, and for to knowe
> Whether hyt were clere or hors of soun.
> And I herde goynge, bothe up and doun,
> Men, hors, houndes, and other thyng;
> And al men speken of huntyng,
> How they wolde slee the hert with strengthe,
> And how the hert had, upon lengthe,
> So muche embosed, y not now what.
>   Anoon ryght, whan I herde that,
> How that they wolde on-huntynge goon,
> I was ryght glad, and up anoon
> Took my hors, and forth I wente
> Out of my chambre. [344–358]

Just as the book he read had led the Poet to the revelation about
Ceyx and Alcyone, bracketing that part of Chaucer's poem, the
chase is the conductor to the second part, the revelation about
White and the Man in Black. On horseback he rides to the field
where he overtakes "a gret route / Of huntes and eke of fores-
teres, / With many relayes and lymeres." A limerer leads him
further on to the "forest syde" where he accompanies or at least
observes the party until the scene fragments: the stag "rused,
and staal away"; stag and hunter lose each other; a dog separates
from the rest and boundingly draws the Poet to wander through
a flowery green, through groves of game, until he finds the
"man in black," his back against an oak tree.

Death's hunting party guides the poet to this, the subject of
his poem; the hunt that has deprived the man in black of his
beloved sends forth a little emissary, the whelp, to bring the

Poet and his theme together. The "chase of the story" is one of the sub-types of the figurative chase. Gottfried von Strassburg had written with scornful punning of the "finders of wild stories, huntsmen of stories"; Wolfram in *Parzival* stressed the importance of the flying course of narrative, like a well-shot arrow from the bow; and much later Cervantes gives us that arch-huntress in green, the sly Duchess who, having discovered in the wood a fully-fledged pair of characters out of a published book, Don Quixote and Sancho Panza, captures them to contrive extravagant fresh plots for them to enact. Chaucer too "chases the story" in his Clerk's Tale. Here, a frolicsome hound leads the Poet to his theme and its human subjects.

It is the Poet who is most conscious of the chase, however. He catches glimpses of it in the distance, but the knight refuses to give his attention to it. The Poet remarks on the hunt several times. The knight, wrapped in his woe, remains oblivious of its progress: "My thought ys thereon never a del" (543). Neither does he see nor hear the hunters sounding their horns on the homeward march. Refusing to recognize Death's chase, the knight concentrates upon his grief and his praise of love. Pensive, withdrawn, he indulges luxuriantly in a lament which, though formalized like the activity of the chase around him, expresses ardor and anguish. We must become aware at this point of the three planes of action in this poem: each of the parties engages in a game. The hunt is the game that Death plays, in the guise of Octovien. Beyond the knight's notice the emperor and his company range over the wood crowded with the mortal quarry that awaits their bows:

> And many an hert and many an hynde
> Was both before me and behynde.
> Of founes, sowres, bukkes, does
> Was ful the woode, and many roes,
> And many sqwirelles, that sete
> Ful high upon the trees. [427–432]

The movement of the hunt casts into relief the knight's stillness,

their action, his passion. The hunters engage in pure, ritualized
act; they exert power over the life in the forest; the quarry they
seek may ruse but finally must yield. The knight, in contrast,
remains motionless, "overcome," eloquent. By his own definition the man in black is a lover. Love's thrall from youth,
he affirms: "I ches love to my first craft; Therefore hit ys with
me laft." [Therefore, it has remained with me.] The game
lovers play is with Fortune, and the knight defines his loss as
that of one who has been forced to relinquish his *fers* to Fortune
in a game of chess. Chaucer's most famous lover, Troilus, it
will be remembered, was also one to see himself "spilt" by
Fortune, confessing that he had honored her "above the goddes
alle." But the Poet's game is poetry. Chess and tables have no
charms for him compared to the "beter play" of an old romance.
And his imminent business will be to compose the elegy for
Blanche.

What Chaucer will do to serve the man in black in his grief
is to observe and listen intently, say very little that is intelligent
though it seems to be courteous and well-meant, and to write
this elegy. Chaucer's developing role as the servant of love's
servants will, in the future, be distinguished by a remarkable
degree of irony, sophistication, and self-consciousness. Here he
is initiating that role: an uncertain, somewhat reticent observer,
withdrawn, too, from the searing immediacy of experience,
notably of love, he has been granted nevertheless an unusual
view of the whole of that experience, together with the capacity
to complete its meaning through his art. This poet's perspective
is often denied to those who merely love intensely and painfully,
and who write conventional verses about their love. Chaucer is
both less and more than the man in black: he is less in that he
is ignorant—his slow-dawning understanding of the situation
simply emphasizes his position as an outsider of love. But he is
more in his power of vision that enables him to see the mortal
chase and to be impelled by it to put love into death's perspective. He sees what the lover does not see; he sees, with its
diverse elements, the final poem.

The man in black now proceeds to compose his own story, using the conventional materials at his disposal. Once again it is instructive to compare the man in black to Troilus, who is a well-read lover. Troilus writes Petrarchan and Boethian songs, blots with tears the letters which he has written by the book, and then one day, wandering disconsolately through Troy, where he recognizes places of importance to him, he sees the love affair in its entirety:

> "Lo, yonder saugh ich last my lady daunce;
> . . . . .
> And yonder have I herd full lustyly
> My dere herte laugh; and yonder pleye
> Saugh ich hire ones ek ful blisfully." [5. 565, 568–70]

> "And at that corner, in the yonder hous,
> Herde I myn alderlevest lady deere
> So wommanly, with vois melodious,
> Syngen so wel, so goodly, and so clere,
> That in my soule yet me thynketh ich here
> The blisful sown; and in that yonder place
> My lady first me took unto hire grace." [5. 575–581]

Suddenly he sees the possibilities of all this: "Men myght a book make of it, lik a storie" (5. 585). Yet what a strangely reduced story! Troilus is far less skillful at this than Chaucer. Troilus's version of *The book of Troilus* reads like a collection of mournful jottings, very little like the story we have been told of him by Chaucer. It takes Chaucer to write Troilus's splendid lines for him, and finally to put his love affair into a perspective that death and history affords, giving his hero at the last the briefest glimpse of that perspective.

While Chaucer in 1370 is certainly more diffidently respectful of the poetry of the man in black, considering the occasion, among other things, than he needed to be of Troilus in 1385, the earlier and the later work have this in common: The lover in the poem writes conventionally of his love affair; his view of his experience is limited by the intensity of feeling in which he is immersed; the Poet has the larger view and the capacity to seize it and record it in his poetry.

When the Poet listens to the man in black, he hears a highly-wrought, literate complaint from this knight, a contemporary, a noble and a Christian. All that Chaucer did not allow to the legend of Seys and Alcyone, he now allows to knight's lament. In the lament, steeped as it is in traditions of rhetoric, various conventional elements converge, among them amatory lyric, *planh*, and glorifications also associated with the Virgin.[38] The knight's praise and elegy for his lady rise to a peak. He re-creates their enamorment and the happiness which brought him to life out of the death he had endured before he won her mercy: "As helpe me God, I was as blyve / reysed, as fro deth to lyve — / of al happes the alderbest,— / the gladdest, and the moste at reste." He celebrates their perfect unanimity (1277–90). Images of radiance gather about the idealized White. While her inky-suited knight, weary of life at the beginning of his lament, might well think himself in hell like "Cesiphus" or "Tantale," he conceives his lady as whiteness and light. She resembles the very sun that illumines the sky:

> as the someres sonne bryght
> Ys fairer, clerer, and hath more lyght
> Than any other planete in heven,
> the moone, or the sterres seven,
> for al the world so hadde she
> surmounted hem alle . . . . [821–25]

It is worth recalling in what context the sun was introduced in its only other appearance in the poem. It had burst into the Poet's dream just before he rode off to the chase. "With bryghte bemes / with many glade gilde stremes" (337 f.) the sun pours through the painted windows, lighting in all their colors de-picted images of lovers of antiquity, as well as "text and glose"

[38] Stephen Manning, "Chaucer's Good Fair White: Woman and Symbol," *Comparative Literature* 10 (1958): 104; James I. Wimsatt, "The Apotheosis of Blanche in *The Book of the Duchess*," *Journal of English and Germanic Philology* 66 (1967): 26 ff.

from the *Roman de la Rose*. This second mention of the sun in the lines just quoted compares it to White, who outshines all the rout of ladies as sun outshines stars, moon, planets. The dazzling, golden-haired White in her solar brightness illumines, like the sun shining through the painted glass, those dead lovers of antiquity, Seys and Alcyone, making vivid clarity of their plight, as their deaths have been made somberly to foreshadow hers. Chaucer, having struck out the brightness of the starborn Seys from his narrative, as well as the transfiguring conclusion, attributes all the poem's celestial radiance to White. In fact as his poetic energies dwell on the legend of Seys and Alcyone, upon the "derke valeye," dark as hell, the effect of the contrast is to stress the shaded hopelessness of the pagan tale, in which Death triumphs over love, against the luminous descriptions of White whose love, immortalized in the poem, is as strong as death because of her light.

Yet she is dead. While her remembered living brilliance shows forth in the knight's praise of her solar attributes, her mortal passage is enacted by the distantly perceived hunt. As the immortal beloved she is as glorious as the sun. But the word play upon *herte* and *hert* directs us to her earthly aspect, and with this play we are never totally unmindful of the manifestation of White as the quarry of the august pursuer.

Are we to recognize Octovien as an emperor of Roman antiquity, as the hero of a Middle English Romance, or a King of the Other World, an "Octavian" of British history, rendered Eudaf in Welsh myth, who appears in the *Mabinogion* in an ivory chair carving chesspieces?[39] Whatever model Chaucer drew upon for his distant hunting lord, he has tactfully avoided

[39] Mother Angela Carson, "The Sovereignty of Octovyen in *The Book of the Duchess*," *Annuale Medievale* 8 (1967): 46–57, investigates Chaucer's Octovyen as a "composite figure" that draws its life from Welsh and British history, a hunter like Arawn, and a king in a four-cornered (chessboard?) other-world like Eudaf. The author makes the interesting observation that this other-world king, Eudaf, busies himself with the pieces from a board-game called Gwyddbwyll, which is a venatic rather than a military form of chess (p. 50).

casting him as a Prince of the Christian hereafter whose hunting is analogous to the desire of God or Christ for the soul of man. It is noticeable that the Poet proffers no explicit Christian consolation on the loss of Blanche. Had he done so it would hardly have been appropriate for the knight to ignore these; yet, it would have done slight honor to Blanche's memory to have concluded the elegy with a resigned and comforted knight. To the end he sorrows. In our parting view of him, "he wax as ded as stoon / and seyde 'Allas that I was bore . . . I have lost more than thow wenest'" (1300 ff.). The Poet's last words to him, "Be God hyt ys routhe," do not contradict Seys's last words to Alcyone, "to lytel while oure blysse lasteth." The knight acknowledges that God may well have desired the heart-hart in the board-game (680–682), but he shows no sign of conforming his will, like the mourner of *Pearl*, to his "princes paye." Neither must Chaucer enact the quest for the hart in any grim or terrifying way, suggestive of Death's ghoulish stalking. With Octovien he strikes a non-Christian, classical neutrality. Virtually invisible in the *Book of the Duchess*, "th'emperour Octovyen" proves exotic enough not to be confused with any Christian divinity or to be already burdened with symbolic associations, yet suggestive enough to convey the sense of majesty, authority, remoteness in time and place. He seems a worthy pursuer for so noble a hart. The hunt takes place in the distance, a frieze depicting the desired hart's flight and pursuit. It is the universal and ineluctable power of death. The knight's eyes turn from it. Insulated in his reverie from any consciousness of the hunt he reads his own fate in terms of a different game which false Fortune controls: his gaze bends, figuratively, to the chessboard, in whose unalterable black and white squares are reflected the poem's dual themes: White and the man in black, love and death, joy and sorrow, radiance and darkness.

To the Poet is granted the overview. Sympathetically he observes and shares the grief of the man before him; at the same time he rests aware, as the sufferer refuses to be, of the great chase in the distance. The chase has both defined and perfected the love of the noble pair, as it has guided the Poet to his themes. The Poet, moreover, as a reader of books and a student of *auctores*, has discovered the tale of Seys and Alcyone, a protracted exemplum to the plight of the lovers before him. All these elements, granted to him through book and vision, he has embraced in his work. The pattern of longing repeats itself in the elegy: Alcyone longs for Seys; the knight longs for his lady; the hunter longs for the quarry. Only the last is fulfilled, since death has greater material certainty than earthly love. Yet, death has indeed been palliated, its grandeur remaining positive but distanced. How? By the adoring and radiant transformation of the dead woman in the knight's utterances, which in turn have been caught within the Poet's vision and given point and meaning by their juxtaposition with the old pagan romance that permitted him the vision. Blanche as a living beloved may never again be held, but as a symbol, White, she is captured within the poem's permanence, even as the mortal *hert* has been captured by the hunter.[40]

What has enabled the poet to behold, understand, and record

[40] How does the hunt end? Are we to understand, as some readers have claimed, that the hart has eluded the hunters finally since, in lines 381 and 540-1, it has rused? There is nothing in Chaucer's narrative to support this conclusion. It was normal for the hart to ruse; its rusing, or doubling upon its traces, could always be counted on in the course of any chase. Neither does the sounding of the *forloyn* on the horn mean that Octovien was not finally successful.

Riding homeward, the hunters *strake forth*. The verb *strake* meant to sound the horn, either repeatedly or in prolongued notes, sometimes distinguished from the sounding of a single long note. (Tilander, "Nouveaux essais d'étymologie cynégétique," *Cynegetica* 4 [Lund, 1957]: 229-233.)

To turn to the text that Tilander quotes from first, *The Master of Game*, p. 110 and ff., we learn that there were different manners of *strakyng*: one would be performed on the homeward march after the stag had been slain, while another would indicate that the king wished to hunt no longer. It is *how* the notes are sounded, not the mere fact of "stroking" that conveys whether the hunters have well sped or not. Either Chaucer is noncommittal, discreetly refraining from stating why "al was doon, / for that tyme, the hert-huntyng," or else he assumes we know the stroking to mean the Death.

the totality of these various elements is the vision that has come to him, his *sweven*. For we must refrain from taking Chaucer's insomnia all too literally. His thirst for sleep must be understood to include the poet's need for dreams, the visions that are divinely bestowed. The vision serves as the medieval poet's muse. What will become a humorously conceived search for subjects and "tidyinges" in the *House of Fame* is here a serious consideration. Visions are granted to poets like Chaucer through the reading of books. Authors of the past—"clerkes" of "olde tyme"—provide subject matter, but in dreams the subject is clarified, takes on perspective and enables the poet to create meaningfully. The poem completes and perfects the poet's vision of love and death, as death itself completes, and in the case of the man in black, perfects love. Chaucer's concluding determination refers to his poet's craft: "be processe of tyme" he may be able to put his dream and learning into poetry. His last words "now hit ys doon" emphasize the completion of his *sweven* through *ryme*.

One thing Chaucer does not do is to permit his Poet's larger view to become the vantage point for a philosophical resolution such as that of a Theseus in the Knight's Tale or a Troilus from the eighth sphere, beyond love, yet forever immersed in love. To do so would have been presumptuous (even if he had the philosophical materials in his library at the time) in a poem whose aim is elegiac and consolatory. Instead the themes of love and death and their accompanying themes of joy and grief, supported by the imagery of light and darkness, and the sun and the hart, remain locked in suspension. Each penetrates the other: death may have dominion over lovers while love endures beyond death. Yet both death and ideal love remain stark, autonomous, and indomitable. Chaucer will not attempt to state a resolution. But the three symbols by which the dead lady is remembered contain the paradox: the stag the symbol of her mortality, the solar figures of her immortality, and of both, the phoenix of the knight's song, a creature subject to death but endlessly vital through its brightly burning fire.

The Instructive Chase Transformed: Love as the Latter End
of Knowledge. *Tristan.*

Like *Sir Gawain and the Green Knight*, Gottfried's *Tristan*
is a romance containing a remarkable profusion of hunting
detail, conspicuously and strategically placed to reveal or prefigure some aspect of the hero's experience. Gottfried von
Strassburg, well-acquainted with the hunt as a practical activity,
and alert to its possibilities as a literary symbol (he must, as his
literary passages show, have known Heinrich von Veldeke's *Eneit*)
exploits in addition its medieval status as a formalized branch
of knowledge and execution. His Tristan arrives on the Cornish
scene expert in the chase, and demonstrates what he knows.
While we have already been told that Tristan is adept at all
courtly forms of learning and behavior, and he is soon to manifest
other signs of this at Marke's court—through music, languages,
and poetry—the most dramatically realized introduction we have
to him occurs in the scene in which Tristan breaks the stag and
instructs others in the ritual.[41] It is a scene so particularized in its
technical information that the reader may well wonder whether
Gottfried gives us more than is strictly necessary. Is this an
occasion for the poet to elaborate meticulously a procedure that
especially interested him, a *tour de force* to delight his audience
—perhaps imitated from an existing rule book—or does it
achieve some end integral to the romance? How, if at all, does
this noticeable exploitation of his hunting knowledge cast light
upon the life of a youth whose significant career will be one of
love? What is the relation between this initial scene, centering
upon the undoing of the stag, and that other major hunt scene
that forms a balance to it, late in the hero's development, where
Marke his enemy pursues a white stag's traces to the cave where
Tristan and Isôt are dwelling? What of the images associated
with trapping and hunting that recur so frequently between

[41] The whole episode of breaking the stag and the return to Tintagel
occurs between lines 2759 and 3326. References are to Friedrich Ranke
(ed.), *Tristan und Isold* (Zürich, 1930; rev. and rpt. 1967).

these two large scenes of the chase, as well as just before and
soon after these scenes, images showing Tristan caught up in
various kinds of hunting activity, both actual and metaphorical?
Let us pause for a moment to survey the instances in which
Tristan's hunting characterizes him in literary contexts both
before Gottfried and after. The notion of a hunting Tristan
persists especially in English literature. Arthur's court is to
welcome Sir Tristram as "the man of moste worship. For of
alle maner of huntynge thou bereste the pryce, and of all mesures
of blowynge, thou arte the begynnynge, of alle the termys of
huntyng and haukyng ye are the begynner." The fifteenth
century *Boke of St. Albans* invokes his name for the pupil: "My
dere chylde, take hede how Tristram dooth you tell, How many
maner beestys of venery ther were."[42] Earlier versions of the
Tristan romance also stress Tristan's engagement in hunting
activities. In the *Tristramssaga* (1226) and the English *Sir
Tristrem*, late in the thirteenth century, the hero demonstrates
his skill when he undoes a stag for Marke's huntsmen. Especially
interesting in *Sir Tristrem* is the comparison to Manerius, in-
dicating a measure of renown, beyond the Latin poem, of the
Manerius legend:

> On hunting oft he ʒede,
> To swiche a law he drewe
> Al þus;
> More he couþe of veneri
> þan couþe Manerious.[43]

Earlier than Gottfried, in Béroul's romance and in Eilhart's,[44]

[42] On Tristan in English, see François Rémigereau, "Tristan 'Maître
de Vénerie' dans la Tradition Anglaise et dans le roman de Thomas,"
Romania 58 (1932): 218–37; Malory, *Works*, "The Book of Sir Tristram
de Lyones," p. 427; Julians Barnes, *Boke of Huntyng*, ed. Tilander,
Cynegetica 11 (Karlshamn, 1964): 22, lines 2–3.

[43] Eugen Kölbing (ed.), "Sir Tristrem," lines 293–297, in *Die nordische
und die englische Version der Tristan-Sage* (Heilbronn, 1878–82).

[44] Béroul, *Tristan*, ed. Ernest Muret; rev. ed. L. M. Dufourques
(Paris, 1967); Eilhart von Oberge, *Tristrant und Isalde*, ed. Franz
Lichtenstein (Strassburg, 1877).

we see a less courtly Tristran [Tristrant], living close to life's exigencies. In these works he appears as a desperate outlaw; himself the wretched object of repeated manhunts, he relies upon his knack for hunting to keep alive. Hiding in the wilderness with Yseut [Isalde] he catches game for food. In danger of being tracked down by his own dog, Husdent, who mourns his master and eagerly gives tongue on his scent (the king and court following close behind), Béroul's Tristran, exclaiming "My lady, we are being hunted!" swiftly considers killing the hound (1563), although he instead teaches it to hunt its prey in silence, thus earning his reputation as a trainer of hounds.[45] Eilhart has the fugitive lovers flee further into the wilderness to evade the noise of the baying hound, while Kurnevâl runs to seize Ûtant, as the dog is here called. Then with Ûtant's aid, Kurnevâl finds his way back to the lovers, following Tristrant's *slauwe*.[46] Eilhart develops the suggestion that Ûtant is in fact hunting his master: the dog goes after "tame quarry that is man and woman" (*dô vûr der hunt sêre / nâch eime wilde daz was zam: / daz was [beide] wîp unde man*, 4488-90). Further emphasizing the hunted animal's plight of his hero, Eilhart adds the cruelty of the wolf-trap that a ferocious Marke sets by his wife's bed to cut her lover; Tristrant, when he returns to his own bed, bursts his bandage and bleeds like a swine (*der hêre . . . / . . . begunde blûten als ein swîn*, 5349). When Gottfried works this detail into his poem, he describes the bloodstains as those of Love's (Minne's) guilty tracks, caused by a harried animal.

The changing role of Tristan from hunter to quarry emerges in Gottfried's romance both by way of the two principal hunt episodes and through the thickly scattered images.[47] Tristan, in

---

[45] This event is also recorded in the Oxford *Folie Tristan* (*Les deux poèmes de la Folie Tristan*, ed. Joseph Bédier [Paris, 1907], lines 873 ff.; and is referred to in Eilhart, *Tristrant*, lines 4541–45).

[46] See Dalby, *Lexicon*, s.v. *slâ*. This is the track of the quarry, usually with the sense of being bloodstained.

[47] John S. Anson, "The Hunt of Love: Gottfried von Strassburg's *Tristan* as Tragedy," *Speculum* 45 (1970): 594–607, has intelligently discussed the importance of the hunt in *Tristan* and observes the trans-

all the confidence of his youth, presents himself at the outset to
Marke's astonished and grateful huntsmen. He is self-reliant,
canny, graciously at ease with every manner of man. He shows
himself in command of the codes and behavior of the court,
even as they must be performed in the wilderness. Gottfried
abbreviates the pursuit and death (compared to the *Saga* version)
that precede the breaking of the deer, though he describes how,
on a later occasion, the King and his new-made *jegermeister* do
conduct a stag chase (3427 ff.). What concerns the poet here,
however, is to dwell with affectionate care on the quarry. Under
Tristan's direction, the men divide the carcass and reassemble
it in a "stag's shape" for the homeward march, to present
(*prisanten*, 3056) at Tintagel. Tristan, the linguist, corrects their
terms as well as their work. One doesn't flay off the deer's hide
in a random manner (*enthiuten*—"unhide" it), but strips its
"bark" (*entbasten*).[48] With all the emphasis on ceremony and art,
we are in the presence of a concrete, a practical business. One
parcels out the stag's body for a purpose. The venatic work is
uncompromisingly literal, firmly located in the limbs and entrails
of the animal. These various portions have their specific uses: the
chine goes to the poor, chosen tidbits are the dogs', other morsels
are speared on the *furkîe*; the main pieces make up the "stag's
shape." In many respects the *bast*, the breaking of the stag, is like
a handbook set-piece.[49] Tristan removes first the hide, then the
hindquarters (*hufbein*), forequarters (*büegen, buocbein*), breast
(*brust*), chine or spine (*rucke*), ribs (*rippe, riebe*), rump (*cimbere*,
2905; later, 2944, with the sense of the animal's pizzle, see Dalby,

---

formation of Tristan from master huntsman to the object of a court
hunt. He has however ignored the very considerable investigations of
Dalby; in fact, he does not mention the *Lexicon* at all, and thus misses
the linguistic richness supporting the imagery.

[48] See Dalby, *Lexicon*, s.v. *bast*.

[49] Tilander (*Cynegetica* 8 [1961]: 47) finds Tristan's Quarry similar to
that in the fourteenth century French handbook, *Les Livres du roy Modus*,
chaps. 28 and 29. One of the differences is in Tristan's reserving the
liver for his forked stick, to present at court, instead of feeding it to the
dogs.

s. v. *zimbere*), loins (*lanken*), tail (*ende*), paunch (*panze*), and stops short of the large intestine (*pas*) so as not to sully his hands. His sense of the purpose of each portion is clear. On the hide go the dogs' portions: spleen (*milz*), lungs (*lungen*), the large intestine, the paunch, or "tripe," the heart, quartered, which he removes from the "pluck-string" or windpipe (*ric*, or *herzeric*, to which heart, lungs, and liver cling). Then he proceeds to the forked branch (*furke* and *furkie*) to be reserved for the march and presentation: the liver (*leber*), pizzle (*cimbere*), the "net" (*netz*),[50] and the kidneys with their surrounding flesh (*lumbel*).

What can this anatomization signify for the romance and what does it tell us of Tristan? For one thing it gives us an understanding of his disciplined "knowing," his meticulous sense of a craft that he executes with passionate, unquestioning observance of its rules. No detail is too small for his scrupulous attention. He has a clearly defined idea of how a task in a courtly context should be done with decorum. He knows what a king's due is and how his rights should be presented to him. He demonstrates, in short, an absolute devotion to a narrowly conventional ideal of performance. These personal characteristics of Tristan's which the hunt scene serves to elicit, these symptoms of his courtly orientation, look toward future events of the romance, both in straightforward anticipation and with ironic contrast. His sense of homage to a king he has never yet beheld will radically alter: the spell of love will render Tristan incapable of abiding by *any* obligation to Marke, his kinsman and liege lord. His youthful commitment to courtly ritual and behavior will yield to a repudiation of the ways of the court, with its customs of spying and reporting, its accepted mechanical modes of determining and executing justice, its demands of duty to a weak king. His fervor with respect to conventional decorum here will become supplanted by his embracing a love wholly in conflict with what the court expects of him.

Tristan's eventual roles as teacher and as artist are already

[50] See Dalby, *Lexicon*, s.v. *netz*: the filaments connecting the liver and spleen to the abdominal viscera.

implicit in this hunt scene as well. Both functions are locked in
his fate with Isôt. Well-taught, he is fit to instruct others, as he
proves to the huntsmen. But he will never be a ruler of men, since
he will have renounced his kingdom and inherited title in favor
of service to Marke. And it is this service that thrusts him in the
position of Isôt's tutor, forming the relationship that culminates
in their love. This early alliance of teacher and pupil also anticipates the lovers' collaboration as artists when in the wilderness
they compose and sing lays of love wrought out of their own
pains and joys, with all the craft of music and poetry that Tristan
had long ago taught Isôt. Again, Tristan's expression of creative
power as a composer of love poetry is prefigured in the initial
hunt scene in a manner humorously betraying the novice: here
Tristan is already the confident (though immature) artist,
reassembling from the anatomized portions of the quarry a
grotesque deer of fantasy.

Above all the initial hunt scene serves as a conductor directly
to Marke and Marke's authority, and indirectly to Isôt.[51] Versed
in *höfische jegerîe*, Tristan rides homeward—not realizing that
Tintagel is ancestrally and henceforward his home—in the train
of the undone stag. So does he unwittingly offer himself to
Marke, destined to be undone like the stag he has broken. From
now on he will be Marke's man, himself abetting in his sub-
jection. As he has stripped and unpieced the quarry, so will he
divest himself of lands and worldly possessions, preparing for
his new investiture in Marke's service. Being in Marke's control
steers him toward Minne's fearful dominion as well: the wound
he earns serving Marke carries him for its cure to Isôt's mother
and Isôt. And being under Minne's control will, in turn, force
Tristan ever more ineluctably into the position of Marke's prey—
until that chase in which Marke's hunting leads directly to the
door of Tristan's grotto.

[51] Tristan's route to Isôt in the train of the homeward-bound hunting
party is circuitous, yet as inevitable as the more conventionally guided
journey in Eilhart's poem, where the quarry of the chase leads the party
directly to Isalde.

Tristan's fresh assurance here in the wilderness, his assertion of power and authority over the stag's slain body, which culminates in his being named "master of the chase," is to clash with exquisite irony against his eventual change to a condition of hunted quarry. Here as yet he is ignorant of the hunted course (revealed through Gottfried's imagery) which his life will take. From his present command over this practical, meticulously organized and conventional sphere of learning, Tristan travels to an experience of love in which the poet will cast him metaphorically in the quarry's role; he exchanges his knowledge of the chase for the incipient victim's helpless awareness when he first struggles in the "snare." Eventually all his intellectual and physical efforts will be transferred from the exercise of conventional courtly accomplishments for their own sake to the service of his love. Tristan's formidable cynegetic knowledge brings him into Marke's, then Minne's power; and Minne forces him to unlearn every commitment to courtly ritual that that knowledge symbolizes.

Let us examine the working of Gottfried's imagery, as Tristan moves with inescapable certainty along his life's course, from the position of the dazzling boy teaching venery to Marke's men, to that of the stalked victim of Minne, of the equally preyed upon Isôt, of Marke, and of his flunkeys at the court. The first glimmering of the plight that is to constitute Tristan's principal and consuming experience, his love shared with Isôt, is accompanied by a cluster of hunting and trapping images. He drinks, she drinks, and he begins to sense danger; the image is that of a snared creature:

"Nein" dahter allez wider sich
"la stan, Tristan, versinne dich
niemer genim es keine war."
          . . . . .
der gevangene man
versuohtez in dem stricke
ofte unde dicke
und was des lange staete. [11745–55]

"No," he kept thinking to himself "let it be, Tristan, collect yourself, do not take notice of it." The caught man strove in the snare continually and with effort, and was long bent on this.

Soon afterward, the two turn to each other as trappers, *wildenære*—that is, huntsmen in another's employ. Not their own masters, it is to serve Minne that they set their snares for each other:

> der minnen wildenaere
> leiten ein ander dicke
> ir netze unde ir stricke,
> ir warte unde ir lage
> mit antwürte und mit vrage:
> si triben vil maere under in. [11930–35]

Minne's huntsmen, they laid for each other, over and over, their nets and their snares; they arranged their relay stations and their trapping places with answers and with questions: they pursued much private talk.

With their love's consummation, on board ship, the image of the net recurs to conclude this section of narrative:

> Minne diu strickaerinne
> diu stricte zwei herze an in zwein
> mit dem stricke ir süeze in ein
> mit also grozer meisterschaft,
> mit also wunderlicher craft,
> dazs unreloeset waren
> in allen ir jaren. [12176–82]

Minne the ensnarer bound their two hearts together with the knots of her sweetness with such great skill, with such wonderful strength, that the bond was never loosed in all their years.

The captured condition of both lovers, in which each is predator and each is caught, finds expression, too, in allusions to the limed bird. These images, as A. T. Hatto has shown, are related to that of Isôt as "Minne's falcon," since she both behaves as predator and becomes herself caught upon "Minne's limed twig."[52] It may be pointed out, furthermore, that the initial cause of Tristan's separation from his home had been his eagerness for falcons: the promise of hunting birds of many kinds for him and his half-brothers drew him to the Norwegians' ship. A falcon first lures Tristan; Isôt as love's falcon will make him love's prey.

When Isôt first appears before us in the Irish court procession (on which occasion the churlish steward will press his marriage claims), her elegance and ravishing grace emerge through the falcon motif. She is as beautifully made as if Minne had shaped her to be her own falcon (*als si diu Minne draete | ir selber zeinem vederspil*, 10896-97). Although she is as yet untramelled by love, the fact that Minne uses her for an end of which Isôt, in her proud innocence and splendid youth, is unaware, indicates her lack of freedom. She is not really her own woman, though she may think so. Isôt's brilliant eyes first seize our attention:

> Feather-lined ravenous glances—
> snow-thick they flew,
> plundering this way and that—
> I think that Isôt robbed
> many a man of himself.

> Like a falcon on a branch,
> neither too softly nor too firmly
> her eyes took their prey. [10997-99]

Gottfried had already remarked upon the frank and eager eyes of Isôt, when in the women's quarters she had studied Tristan with interest, even devoutness, scrutinizing his face, his limbs,

---

[52] This figure has been analysed in detail by Hatto in "Der minnen vederspil Isot," *Euphorion* 57 (1957): 302–307; In my discussion I draw with appreciation upon the author's findings.

Both the limed twig and the snares of Minne already appeared as images in the Rivalin-Blanscheflur episode. Rivalin can no more disentangle himself from love than can the bird from the limed twig. Struggling to fly, the bird simply defeats itself through its own efforts until it lies enlimed upon the twig (*und gelimet an dem zwige liget*, 858). Rivalin, overcome by Minne, is caught in her snares (839).

his whole body immoderately (*uzer maze*, 9993). Then, after she has been quelled by the love drink, a limed and snared creature, she once again turns upon him with her plundering but secret and amorous gaze. And once again we are reminded—when she has tasted the potion and love—that Isôt is Minne's falcon: *der Minnen vederspil Isôt* (11985). We recall the account of her beauty before her capture, when, still an unwitting predator, she was upright and candid as a sparrowhawk, sleek as a parakeet— when love's image had lain in wait under her cloak.

Isôt is aware of her capture: she recognizes the lime of the spell-casting and alluring Minne:

> do si den lim erkande
> der gespenstegen minne[53]

Struggling, she becomes more and more enlimed (11789, 11814), until in tears she finally confesses her *nôt*: "*l'ameir*." Gottfried has added a wryly appropriate detail in anticipation of this conceit of Isôt, consummate though inadvertant predator that she is for Tristan. The disgruntled *truchsaeze*, the steward, blind to women's virtues and incapable of love, disparages Isôt and all women as "poor hunters," and somehow misses again by using the figure of stalking with a hound, rather than the image of a bird, which would be Isôt's true motif: "You [women] treat a

---

[53] Dalby's comments (*Lexicon*, s.v. *spen*) on the adjective *gespensteg*, modifying *minne* in l. 11793, are worth remarking. *Spen* is a decoy. Isôt recognizes that "enticing Minne" has lured her to a lime-spread branch, and there is a delicate implication of something false and cruel about the lure. The adjective, moreover, has been anticipated in the Rivalin-Blanscheflur episode, as were the images of bird and snare. Blanscheflur, aware that she has conceived Rivalin's child and that her lover is shortly to sail back to his country, apostrophizes Minne in despair over "your [the goddess's] alluring trickery" (*din gespenstigiu trügeheit*, 1410).

We may further note that when Marke bends over Tristan and Isôt asleep in their love cave, vacillating between a judgment of guilty or not, Minne with her "decoying" (*gespenstikeite*, 17554) lured him (*spuon*, 17597) to such a passionate adoration of her beauty that he believed in her innocence. The deceptive connotation is of course explicit here.

straight trail as crooked and a crooked trail as straight; you have fastened to your leash an unreliable [hound]" (9876-9879). Once the lovers have been enmeshed by Minne and each other, they become prey for the king and courtiers who try to "entrap" them. In a remarkable clustering of trapping images, Marke and Isôt engage in night-hunting as they lie in bed together. First he spreads and arranges cleverly a snare for the queen, and catches her in it:

er rihtete unde leite
mit einer kündekeite
einen stric der küniginne
und vienc si ouch dar inne. [13679-13682]

Pretending he is to go off on a pilgrimage, Marke tricks Isôt into naming Tristan an her chosen guardian. Thus he arranges his places for traps and relay-stations (*sine lage und sine warte*, 13702) and prepares his nets (*den stric, den er ir rihtete*, 13861). Temporarily Isôt evades her husband with her pretences, but again he spreads nets and traps with questions (*er leite ir aber mit vrage | sine stricke und sine lage*, 14029-14030). Finally she closes the episode, though only for the time being, by gathering him in her arms, pressing him to her breasts and "setting the word traps" (*vahen* has the sense of "trapping to kill"). She allays his doubts:

und begunde aber do vahen
wider an ir wortlage
mit antwürte und mit vrage. [14162-64]

This temporary victory gives way very shortly to the husband's setting a new trap. Marke announces a hunting party, whose real object will be to catch the lovers. While he prepares for the chase, Melot, the dwarf, "sets traps" (*lage leite*, 14368) for Tristan and Isôt. Tristan, pleading illness, abstains from Marke's hunt, "a sick hunter" longing instead for "his own preserve." Sick for love, however, and also, less hunter now and increasingly quarry, Tristan nearly falls. When Marke and Melot creep back into the orchard, however, and Tristan catches sight of their shadows in the tree, he prays for deliverance from *"dise lage"* (14639).[54]

On a night when Tristan had already gone to visit the Queen, the language of the hunt in which the incident was expressed implicitly identified the type of quarry he is:

> der minnaere Tristan
> der stal sich tougenliche dan
> an sine strichweide
> ze manegem herzeleide
> im selben unde der künigin.
> dor unvermeldet wande sin
> und sicher siner dinge,
> do haetim misselinge
> ir stricke, ir melde, ir arbeit
> an den selben pfat geleit. [13485–94]

Tristan the lover stole secretly to his grazing place to the abundant anguish of himself and of the queen. Though he thought himself unchallenged [i.e., by "hounds"] and certain of what he was doing, yet had ill-luck set her snares, her baying hounds, and exerted her hunting labors on his very path.

In an analysis of this passage, David Dalby (s.v., *strichweide*) has shown that its language depends upon the stag chase: *melde* is the hounds' baying or challenge; *stricke* the huntsman's nets, *arbeit*, his efforts. The noun *strichweide*, pasture or grazing place of deer, indicates that Gottfried pictures his hero as an animal stealing to pasture. Marjodo, the steward, creeping after Tristan to spy on him, follows his trail (*spor*, 13564) across grass and snow. Later, (15100-01) Tristan describes Marjodo and Melot as "dog" and "serpent"—traditional enemies of the stag—when,

---

[54] Beyond this episode, there are two further occurrences of the net figure: When the lovers return to court from the Minne cave, Marke exhorts them to avoid the sweet tangling nets of their inner glances: *die vil süezen stricke / ir inneclichen blicke / vermiten* (17717–19). The last time Gottfried uses the net, it is to express wavering Tristan's quandary, burning for the blond Isôt, yet drawn to the new Isôt who attempts to ensnare his thoughts and quicken his love (*die gedanke stricket*, 19107).

together, they continue to go on their hunting course after him,
and lay traps for the lovers. While the author, moreover, portrays Tristan as a deer, a graceful, gentle quarry, Marjodo dreams
of him in the guise of his boar emblem and fancies he sees him
fouling the king's linen with foam from his mouth.[55]
The metaphorical image of Tristan as a grazing deer bears a
relation to the way the banished lovers are conceived in the
Minnegrotte episode, with its allusions in the love chase, its
quarry, and the culminating pursuit of the strange white stag in
the cave's environs. At court Tristan has clearly become a misfit
because of his love for the queen; stalked by invidious spies he
has grown as alien to the ways of the court as the wilderness
creature Gottfried evokes. In the forest, however, dwelling in
Corinaeus's cave, Tristan and Isôt find themselves in accord with
their surroundings; the magic of the cave is such that it seems
meant for them alone. In perfect unanimity with the life of the
forest, they glide together like deer (see Dalby's comment, s.v.
slichen); the birds greet them as companions; their very footprints are indistinguishable to the court huntsman from those of
the white stag he has raised and followed to the door of the
fossiure. The cave that they dwell in as creatures of the wood is
compared to the lair of a hunted, but unattainable, animal; entry
to that cave becomes symbolically the attainment of a perfect
earthly love. At the cave's threshold the track of true love (*diu
waren spor der minne*, 17124) might have been discernible had
not the marble been so green and self-renewing. The poet
himself claims that he has not been able to cross that threshold;
his efforts and labors in love's chase have not brought him
results (17108-09), despite his pursuit of quarry (*bast*) to its
entrance.

Besides these implied comparisons of the lovers with innocent,
charmed creatures of the forest, their own hunting is mentioned.
But this is as different as can be from the ritualized, practical
chase early in the romance. The poet stresses that the lovers find

[55] Dalby makes this observation about Tristan, seen as two types of
quarry, *Lexicon*, s.v. *strichweide*.

sufficiency in contemplating each other. Freed from the need to consume earthly food, Tristan and Isôt hunt only for pleasure. Their hunting is the true noble diversion, the "bele chose" that extant French hunting manuals of over a century later would praise. Not impelled by need, it is joyously shared play, like their composing songs of love. As their former trials become transmuted into poetry, so their pains as the objects of so many "snares" and "traps" become neutralized by their present idyllic hunting and their mysterious connection to the white stag.

That Tristan and Isôt have, in the past, been made the quarry of Minne and of the court spies and Marke, that they here become one with the life of the forest, and that their cave is the object, figuratively, of a pursuit to which many lovers aspire but to which few attain, constitute the details of a love chase that is crowned by the figure of the strange white stag (*der vremede hirz*). Its horns trim and undeveloped, it surpasses the normal not only in its whiteness but in its maned head. Its association with the *fossiure* is hinted at.[56] Gottfried tells us that the stag disappears in the direction—that of the cave—from which it had come.

The *hirz* functions conventionally, moreover, in that it acts as a conductor for Marke, bringing him to the discovery of the lovers in their grotto. Marke hunts for solace, an Ovidian stroke absent from the *Saga* (which has him hunting in his wonted way). His huntsman and a hound find the way to the lovers by following first the white stag's traces, then the lovers'. Can the white stag's connection with the lovers be established? Gruenter identifies the stag with Isôt. Marke's ineffectualness, his lack of resolution, evident throughout the romance, are here indicated

---

[56] This episode has been dealt with by Rainer Gruenter, "Der Vremede Hirz," *Zeitschrift für deutsches Altertum* 86 (1955–56): 231–37; and Julius Rathofer, "Der 'wunderbare Hirsch' der Minnegrotte," *Zeitschrift für deutsches Altertum* 95 (1966): 27–42. Ann Snow, in *"Wilt, wilde, Wildenaere:* a study in the interpretation of Gottfried's *Tristan,"* *Euphorion* 62 (1968): 365–77, has treated the subject of Tristan's "wildness," his intimate identification with the wilderness, and, to an extent, his hunting rôle.

by his ineptitude as a hunter. His need for another to act for him (as Tristan had to act in rescuing the Queen from Gandin) becomes reaffirmed here, where his huntsman is more capable of "finding the way" than he is. His failure as a hunter expresses in sum his failure as lover and husband. The white stag, an unattainable and splendid oddity, remains as alien to him as Isôt. Rathofer enlarges this view, drawing Tristan into his discussion and suggesting that the white stag includes both the lovers in its meaning. Pointing to the text I have quoted earlier, in which the "hound," Marjodo, creeps after Tristan who glides deer-like toward his pasture, Rathofer proposes that the deer-Tristan, about whom Gottfried often uses the adjective *vremede*, finds a deliberate echo in the *vremede hirz*. From the mysterious uniqueness of the stag, its hybrid nature, its elusiveness, emerges the sense of the unique love, the mystical union of Tristan and Isôt.

Certainly the stag is a stag of love, as unreachable for ordinary mortals, such as Marke, as is the cave of love; it is untouchable as the lovers themselves have suddenly become. In the cave an immunity hedges them: they, the cave, the stag seem charmed. Something about the cave makes the huntsman start back, frightened as if in the presence of some wild thing (*etswaz von wilden dingen*, 17451). Marke, passionately moved and in tears, becomes himself captured by the wild thing, decoyed (*diu spuon im sine sinne*, 17597) by the seductive radiance of the sleeping Isôt and all that it falsely tells him of her innocence. As he is unable to capture the stag, he is unable to penetrate either the lovers' seclusion or their secret. He leads his party away from the grotto, unwilling to have others gaze on the sight within. In the marvelous stag's invulnerability, transferred now to the sleeping pair, there lies a reply to that first hunting scene of the romance. There, the mercilessly unpieced stag, reduced to its bodily portions, then grotesquely reassembled as Tristan's offering to Marke, along with himself, signified the beginning of Tristan's bondage. Now a stag appears, as if miraculously brought to life out of the agonies and subterfuges of the lovers, in a new body,

white, immortal, elusive forever from the earthly hands of the
king. But Tristan is asleep. He does not see the stag, nor does he
ever know of it and what it may tell others of his love, as he once
knew so intimately its slain counterpart. Tristan's knowledge of
Minne is welded to the specific knowledge of its pains and joys,
as his knowledge of venery had long ago been manifestly related
to the body of the quarry. That knowledge of the slain stag's
body was his first circuitous conductor to this wilderness in
which he lies, where now the enchanted white stag courses. But
Tristan has moved beyond the worldly, courtly, knowledge of
venery to the new mystical unknowing of love. A vision of the
magnificent, transcendent stag that frequents the area of his cave
eludes him, finally, as well.

IV

Medieval Allegories
of the Love Chase

France: The Sanguinary Stag

While Chrétien, Gottfried, and Chaucer—their work ranging over the later twelfth, early thirteenth, and late fourteenth centuries—could fuse the love chase imaginatively with other types of symbolic hunt and thereby enrich the texture of their narratives, obscure writers were developing the chase as a single theme in love allegory. It is among such writers that a hunt provides the line of the narrative, and the varied activities of the chase are filled with amatory meaning. Either this meaning is made plain by the author, who may tell us outright that "the hunt is like pursuing a woman," or it emerges from the way he designates abstractions: a wood called *jonece* in which *Amours* seeks quarry, hounds named *desirs* and *pensers*, a deer's antlers named to signify a woman's *biautés* and *noblece*. That the great poets were able to refer allusively to the figures and themes of the love chase, working them into their poetry in an individual manner, indicates that such themes were being perpetuated by the allegorists (as they also were by medieval imitators of Ovid): writers less gifted, less fluent, less renowned than those whose names endure, who continued in their writing to equate hunting methods with stages of enamorment or the schooling of a lover's heart. It is to these minor literary craftsmen that we may turn for a grasp of the medieval love chase in its fully elaborated and most detailed expression.

The earliest of these hunt allegories appear in France. Three are especially noteworthy. *Li dis dou cerf amoreus*,[1] an artless mid-thirteenth century poem, is, so far as I have been able to discover, the first allegorical poem of the love chase in a vernacular. *L'amoureuse prise*,[2] a more ambitious composition, reflecting the probable influence of court writers such as Froissart and Machaut in its alternating lyric forms with narrative, is dated April 1332 by its author, Jean Acart de Hesdin. *Le dit du cerf blanc*, contained in a manuscript of the poems of Machaut, may be a late fourteenth century work.[3] As we shall see, the authors deal diversely with the love chase. But they very interestingly have one feature in common: all three arrive at a climactic vision of the enamored stag in its agony, bleeding. In the earliest, the *cers amoreus* represents the woman whose thoughts and desires so harry her that at last *Amours* the hunter is able to bring her to her knees and force her, as the dying stag, to accept love. The *Amoureuse prise* gives the converse of this situation: here the quarry is the man, the narrator, writing in the first person of a

[1] See my edition, "An Unpublished Allegory of the Hunt of Love: *Li dis dou cerf amoreus*," *Studies in Philology* 62 (1965): 531–545, based upon the two mss.; and *Histoire Littéraire de la France, ouvrage commencé par des religieux Bénédictins de la Congrégation de Saint-Maur* 23 (1856), 290 ff. Passages cited in this discussion are from the principal ms., BN ms. fr. 25566.

[2] Ernest Hoepffner, ed., *La Prise Amoureuse von Jean Acart* (*Gesellschaft für romanische Literatur*, Vol. 22 [Dresden, 1910]; additional ms. variants appear in Hoepffner, "Zur 'Prise amoureuse' von Jehan Acart de Hesdin," *Zeitschrift für romanische Philologie* 38 (1917): 513–527.

On the poem, see P. Weingärtner, *Quellenverhältnis und Allegorie in der Prise Amoureuse* (Würzburg, 1926), which analyzes in detail the poet's considerable dependency upon the *Roman de la Rose*; and Antoine Thomas, "Frère Jean Acart, Poète Français," *Histoire Littéraire de la France*, 37, fasc. 2 (Paris, 1938), 412–418.

[3] *Le dit dou cerf blanc* is No. 25 in Arsenal 5203, a ms. containing *Le dit du vergier, Le dit de la Fontaine amoureuse, Le chastel d'amours* and other works of Machaut. Ernest Hoepffner (*Œuvres de Guillaume de Machault* [Paris, 1908], 1, 44) assigns the ms. to the fourteenth century. Ms. Arsenal 5203 appears to contain the only text of *Le dit du cerf blanc*. It consists of 161 leaves of parchment, with thirty-five illuminations. *Le dit du cerf blanc*, which itself has ten illuminations, is the last work in the ms. book, beginning on 155 r⁰ and concluding on 161 v⁰.

desperate chase of which he is the object. Driven to the point of death by the beauties of the woman he loves, and by his own desires, he lies at last mangled and pleading for mercy. *Le dit du cerf blanc* stands apart from these earlier poems. While hounds of the chase are glancingly mentioned as a potential danger to the stag, no conventional hunt takes place. The narrator, who is the lover, tells of his "pursuit" of his white stag in a protective effort to keep it from harm. Anxiously he watches over the stag's blisses and torments. Torments come not from hunters, but first from a horde of flies that cruelly bite the stag, and next from its exiled, painful straying through a desert of thorns and stones. While the cause and significance of the stag's suffering differ from one poem to the next, all three authors concur that the bleeding body of the stag represents the appropriate condition for lovers. Here are the focal scenes in which the sanguinary stag is depicted in the three poems. The poet of *Li dis dou cerf amoreus* defends the treatment of the stag:

> *Love* leaps—he hasn't hesitated—then quickly bends the stag to his will. The dogs are so worthy and watch so closely that as soon as *Love* strikes the stag they drink its blood and dip themselves in it. *Love* does not restrain them, since indeed he has subdued the stag in order to feed the hounds. [292–300]

Jean Acart in the *Amoureuse Prise* becomes painfully elaborate in his dramatization of a lover's ardent plight:

> Now I was taken; the hunt was finished. *Love* by good fortune had conquered me . . . and divided me, the spoil, into three parts as if it had been after a chase. . . . Thus my body remained in *Love*'s possession, and it seems to me he will not stir from it. . . .
>
> Afterwards, just as it was proper to feed the dogs after a hunt, so *Love* gave them the intestines and other matter woven about the entrails to devour. And he gave them my blood to drink. Now no one could imagine how I was used when each of the hounds was led forth for the strewed feast that I was. I could do nothing to avenge myself, but suffered like a martyr. What a sight to behold —each of the dogs dividing up the inward part of my body to lay waste to it, *pleasure* sipping my heart, and drawing and sucking

the blood, and *will* too, without menace, tearing at it by himself with his teeth! There was nothing left within my body that had not served to feed them.

Thought, without being the least tired, had already drawn nearly all my blood. If *hope* had not given me remedy it would have been bad for me; but I had cherished him so that he did no more than lick me.

When the dogs were sated, *Love* cut out my heart and my will and gave this entirely to the gentle good and perfect one by whose hounds this capture was effected. [1751-1799]

Finally, the author of *Le dit du cerf blanc* introduces the new, non-cynegetic element in his account of the wounded stag:

And evil flies ate and devoured its flanks and sides, more than ever; yet so long had the stag remained standing there that he thought himself still to be feeling great pleasure. But now does he feel afflicted with a torment so agonizing, so diffused over his whole body, so evil, so violent, that no one has ever seen anything so painful. For he is so bitten everywhere by flies that the bright blood could be seen on his neck, sides and flanks, striping his white skin. [158 v°]

Can the sufferings of martyrs, as popular devotion dwelt on them, have influenced such spectacles of the bleeding victim? Unlike episodes in earlier love hunts, these scenes evoke the harsh pangs of the afflicted or fallen quarry. Gottfried, while he had given an explicit account of the breaking of the quarry anticipating symbolically the condition in which Tristan was to find himself, did not suggest what the stag felt.

Both the *Cerf amoreus* and the *Amoureuse prise* reflect an awareness of the figure of the "martyred lover" that had been developed by amatory lyric poets of Provence and was current in French sources likely to have been known to the authors of allegory.[4] The man in the *Amoureuse prise* senses his martyrdom

[4] E.g., in the poetry of the troubadour Gavaudan, "For Gavaudan cannot end either his lament or the pain that makes a martyr of him" (ed. Alfred Jeanroy, *Romania* 34 [1904]: 507); or again, Arnaut de Mareuil writes to ask his lady for an assenting reply to his entreaties,

at the moment of being lacerated by the hounds: *ains sueffre comme fait martir* (1780). For him, the martyred state expresses the intensity of his love-longing as he thirsts for the beneficent healing powers of the mistress who will conduct him to happiness. As for the lady who is the *cers amoreus*, her acknowledgment of martyrdom comes with the first assault of the dog, *pensers*: *Je ne sai cause ne raison | que souffrir doie tel martire* (144-45). In this poem the woman feels her martyrdom as she offers resistance to the hound, *thought*; whereas the stag's eventually yielding body and blood to the thirsty pack is allegorized as her moment of bliss, her *boine eure* (324). In both poems the commonplace of love's martyr implies the appropriateness of lovers' suffering, with the religious echoes of "martyr" remaining faintly perceptible. Such echoes are far clearer in the *Cerf blanc*, where the flies' attack upon the stag, as he joyfully gazes upon a luxuriant rosebush, recalls the infestations of flies and lice in Exodus 8 : 21 ff. These tended to be moralized as the pangs of fleshly desire, the longings of the body;[5] they are the "blodi flehen of stinkinde þohtes" that lie about the devil, "tes dogge of helle," against whose "deaðes bite" the *Ancrene Wisse*

"so that the desires I have for your lovely body and an anguished martyrdom do not strangle [my heart]." Yet, he continues in the same lyric, "pleasant and sweet, and *without* martyrdom do these sufferings seem, because of the good I expect of them." (Poem 10, pp. 60, 62.)

The "pleasant martyrdom" of love also recurs in Poem 16, p. 96 (ed. R. C. Johnston, *Les poésies lyriques du troubadour Arnaut de Mareuil* [Paris 1935]).

In the *Roman de la Rose*, the god of love tells the lover of those who willingly give up their bodies to a martyrdom, sustained by hope of greater joys to come. (Felix Lecoy [ed.], *Le Roman de la Rose* [Paris, 1965], 1. 2602-12; and cf. 2633-34).

[5] The *Glossa Ordinaria* (*PL* 113, col. 208) gives: *Quarto loco Ægyptus muscis percutitur,* ... *in qua insolentes curae carnalium desideriorum figurantur. Ægyptus vero muscis percutitur, quia corda eorum qui saeculum diligunt, desideriorum inquietudinibus feriuntur* ... *cynomyiam, id est, muscam caninam, posuerunt: per quam canini mores significantur, in quibus humanae mentis voluptas, et libido carnis arguitur.* Isidore's *Etymologies* are the probable source, 12. 8, 11 ff. Cf. Bede, *PL* 93, cols. 368-69; and Jerome, *PL* 26, cols. 1115 and 1207, on Psalms 77 and 104 respectively, which refer to the plagues of Exodus.

warns.[6] In *Le dit du cerf blanc*, the poet's reiterated *paines, dolours, tourments*, endured by the stag because of the flies and the desert to which they drive him, signify the purifying process through which a lover must pass to be worthy of acceptance. Here as so often in the love poetry of twelfth and thirteenth century Europe, virtues that had long been ordered to a religious end are integrated into the world of earthly love.

Li dis dou cerf amoreus: The Stag of Love

How do these three poems lead to their differing climactic spectacles of the sanguinary stag? *Li dis dou cerf amoreus* opens with an eighteen-line prologue on the value of poetry, following which the poet tells us briefly that while lingering in a wood he observed a hunter and his hounds chasing a stag. He describes how he waited until the chase was ended, the stag captured and broken, the hounds fed on the blood, the carcass sent by the hunter to a friend. This episode, only 22 lines of the whole poem (which has 326 lines in the manuscript, fr. 25566), caused him to ponder, his reflections giving rise to a pleasant melancholy that continues to stir his heart. The outcome of this state is an illumination: hunting and taking the stag, he has perceived, resemble the pursuit and capture of a woman: "And I thought, as a result of this event, that woman is of such a nature—that she is just as fine to hunt in such a way that one can pursue her love. Thus, whoever loves with a heartfelt love the lady who is the stag of love, he must wait and suffer" (53-59). The author virtually dismisses the lover from the active pursuit: mournful, attendant, he hopes for solace: "He often signs and laments, for he thinks he may never win such quarry. For the more he prays and the more humbly he behaves, the more the stag flees and ruses. Such is the lady who pays no attention to his pleading except to trifle with him. So, he dares not beg her anymore, nor has he the power to do even so much as make her turn her face towards him" (104-112).

[6] *Ancrene Wisse*, ed. J. R. R. Tolkien, *EETS* (1962), 249:149.

Love pursues the Stag of Love while lovers in the audience look on from above. Illumination in *Li dis dou cerf amoreus*, ms. 25566, folio 220 v°, full page. Bibliothèque Nationale, Département des Manuscrits.

It is not the lover who hunts the woman, the *ciers amoureus* (58), but *Amours*, the inexorable hunter that stirs, hounds, slays the stag. The poem focuses upon the woman, whose resistance and yielding to love it traces in the stages of a hunt. In this the poet is conscious of a formal procedure: perhaps the appearance in this century of hunting books in French, together with codifications, both earlier and contemporary, of rules of love,[7] account for his sense that there is a right way of going about it: "Whoever undertakes to hunt such a stag—it is most fitting for him to know all that pertains to the chase, and nonetheless to love too: the stag, the hunt, the capture" (91-95). Discernible in the *Cerf amoreus* are three stages in which different hounds perform their functions: two scenting dogs unharbor the game, that is, drive it from its couch and start it running; the coursing hounds, or hounds of the pack, conduct the main pursuit; and two more are brought in at the end, as if the poet thought of them as relays to assist the flagging pack. At the formal hunt's final stage the pack rallied for the decisive onslaught and the Death: this is in fact what the last four hounds of *Amours* do.

Amours' first hound is *boine amours*, the lead-hound (*meneres*) that quests for the food needed by the other dogs. So far they have fed upon *regars* and *contenances*. The other hounds work in pairs: *pensers* and *souvenirs*, *volentés* and *desirs*,[8] and finally *pitiés* and *humilités*. The way these work upon the stag to force its surrender—together with the almost passive role of the lover— indicate that the author's chief interest is to explore the stages of feminine enamorment. The hounds represent attributes of the woman who is ineluctably vulnerable to love;[9] the chase signifies

[7] Knowing what steps to take in pursuing a woman had its corresponding topos in the "five stages of love," stemming from Ovid, *de Amore* 1. 6, and imitated by vernacular authors. A summary of its development is given in Peter Dronke. Cf., above p. 107n.

[8] Raimond Van Marle, *Iconographie de l'art profane, du moyen-âge à la Renaissance* (The Hague, 1931); fig. 125, p. 108, shows a stag pursued by the dogs *désio* and *pensier*, with the hunter present.

[9] While the hounds are the woman's faculties that drive her to yield to her lover, the stag's twelve antlers represent qualities that make her

her agony as she struggles against the onset of her own thoughts and passions.

The stag hides in the thicket of *pride* (*buisson d'orguel*). Its unharbouring is begun by *thought* (*pensers*), who tugs, gnaws, and drags, assisted by *memory* (*souvenirs*), who now keeps her in the grip of *pensers* and who later will recall to the lady *les amistés | les honnourables privautés*, (271-72) that she ought to keep in her heart. These two intellectual faculties operate, moreover, by forcing her to reflect on the merit of the man who has long loved her.[10]

In the second stage, the two hounds of longing, *desirs* and *volentés*, run leashed together, but *volentés* breaks the restraining cord and badly frightens the stag. He runs, now torn and hard-pressed by these dogs, with premonitions of his death. When *pensers* and *souvenirs* join with *desirs* and *volentés*, the lady (explains the author) begins to fear gossips who murmur and spoil all. So the stag rushes through the wood in search of a brook in which to cool himself and turn the hounds off his track. *Amours*, however, who has been hallooing and urging the hounds throughout, produces the last two, *pitiés* and *humilités*,[11] which

---

lovable to the man: these are *bontés, sens, honneurs, biautés, vaillance, contenance, noblece, simplece, maintiens, boins los, humilités, tres parfaite carités* (81-88).

[10] In analyzing the processes by which a proud and chaste woman may be passionately aroused, the poet has put into allegorical form what had already been narrated in romance. While the medieval *Énéas* omits the Virgilian image of Didon as a stricken hind (save for the brief "*amor ki molt l'asalt,*" 1418), the author does choose to linger over the stages of Didon's torment as she tosses throughout a sleepless night (1219 ff.), clasping her pilow and weeping before confiding to Anna in the morning. Chrétien de Troyes perhaps had this in mind when, in *Le Chevalier au Lion*, he allows Laudine to engage in a nocturnal dialogue with an imagined Yvain, only to persuade herself "not to hate him," as a bush is kindled to flames by breathing on it (1729-1782). Then, like Didon, the lady proceeds to address her *confidante*. *Énéas*, ed. J.-J. Salverda de Grave, 2 vols. (Paris, 1925); and *Le Chevalier au Lion*, ed. Mario Roques (Paris, 1965).

[11] The meaning of *humilités* in an amatory context has been treated by Dronke in an excursus, "The Concept *umiltà*," *MLRELL*, 1:158 ff.

drive the stag down to its death. The hounds' feasting concludes the alimentary references scattered throughout the work, the first literal, the rest figurative: *boire le sanc* (40), *noureture* (66), *pourveances* (68), *alaitent* (297), *alaitier* (299). Such a cynegetic feast of love is notably absent from the love chase among classical authors, where the hunt expresses mainly the harshness and necessity of desire, never the nourishment of lovers. As for the poem's lover, though he is said to be part of the triad, *Amours*, beloved, and lover, his participation in the feast is not accounted for. Instead of the gratification of lover and beloved, the poet has described love's consummation—that is, the hounds being fed on the stag's body and blood—as a fulfillment of the lady's own affects and sensibilities when she renders up her body. The striking down of the stag, its death and breaking, dramatize the woman's relinquishment of her separate alien identity, enabling her to enter a new condition: the death of the stag signifies the birth of the woman to happiness, driven thither by love:

> A boine eure fu dame nee
> Quant ensi est d'amour menee.
> Car n'est dechute ne souprise. [323–25]

Far from being lamentable, like the stricken Dido, the spectacle of the bleeding stag serves to praise the power and joy of *Amours*. "It is a foolish man who questions whether *Love* can hunt nobly," declares the poet.

L'Amoureuse Prise: Love's Capture

Reversing the roles of lover and mistress as they appear in *Li dis dou cerf amoreus*, (a poem which he undoubtedly knew, as a comparison of rhymes reveals) Jean Acart gives us a love chase in which *Amours* tracks down the lover as quarry until he lies

---

where the author demonstrates that the sense "is quite distinct from that of the traditional theological virtue. In the language of *courtoisie* a lady's *umiltà* . . . is an active virtue: it is the lady's power of mercy, her capacity to condescend to her lover and to show him grace."

broken, eviscerated, pleading for his lady's mercy.[12] As in the

[12] Among the medieval precedents for this motif of the love-smitten man as the hunted and captured stag, there is a passage in a song by Rigaut de Berbizilh:

> aissi co.l sers, que, cant a faig son cors,
> torna morir al crit dels cassadors,
> aissi torn eu, domn' en vostra merce,
> mas vos non cal, si d'amor no.us sove. [Alberto Varvaro, ed., Rigaut
>   de Berbezilh: *Liriche* (Bari, 1960), p. 124, lines 52–55.]

In *The Song of Lovers*, by the poet called 'Irāqī, the story goes that a man who was forever "stoking the body's furnace" wandered out into a field where a beautiful young woman came riding. She was one in whose soft hair "a hundred thousand hearts, / weary with pain, were snared and fettered fast." Of the lady,

> Intent upon the chase, intoxicate,
> with arrow poised in bow, and bow in hand,
> thou mightest say that with a single glance
> she would have pierced the hearts of lovers all.

When he beheld this lady riding to the chase, the man was stunned and he followed after, shedding scalding tears from the heart.

> The princess soon espied him, from afar
> scenting the breath of love that from his heart
> came wafting: in amazement at his case
> she loosed the horse's reins, and swift as wind
> fled to the chase.

The lady would not yet hunt the sighing lover, whom she "scented" as if he were an animal, then rode away from him in quest of actual game. But the lover fell to the ground, nonetheless, his soul pierced with "the fatal dart / of parting." In his anguish he ran wild with the savage beasts, becoming "lost in the pathless wilderness of passion." Hearing, however, that she was to come hunting once again, he put on a slaughtered deer's hide and had himself pursued by her. So he received the lady's shaft in his heart. This portion of the story ends:

> . . . upon the path
> where his beloved passed he slept in blood
> and, as he died these verses he declaimed.

The dying lover then sings to his lady, declaring to her in the third and last verse of his song:

> When thou art hunting, lovers all
> yield gladly up their lives to thee:
> I do not fear thy shaft may fall
> but only yearn thy face to see.

earlier work, *thought* (both in the form of *pensers*, a hound, and *cuidier*, the avenue on which the lover finally falls) plays a prominent part in effecting the capture. Eighteen lyric poems, alternating *balades* and *rondeaux*, account for 307 of the poem's 1914 lines.[13] Like the utterances of a choric voice, these lyrics interrupt the narrative at intervals to express the lover's hope, anxiety, prayer, and praise. The voice of the allegory is personal rather than public: the author addresses himself to the beloved woman in an opening *balade* that acknowledges the delight of his captive state, and he follows this with a declaration of his intention—to reveal how the capture came about. Jean himself provides the title *L'amoureuse prise*.[14] He asks patience, furthermore, for his speaking figuratively—*par mistere*—since he wants to achieve a more pleasing expression:

The bleeding wound of her "prey," as he calls himself, excites the lady's pitying attentions. The verse that follows generalizes that ladies will bestow their love only after having slain their lovers. (Fakhru 'd-Din Ibrāhīm ibn Shahriyār of Hamadān, called 'Irāqī, *The Song of Lovers*, ed. and trans. A. J. Arberry [Oxford, 1939], p. 33 ff.). Readers will recognize the similarity between the lover's disguising himself in a deer's hide and Peire Vidal's confession, a century earlier, how he had during a period of love-madness, put on the skin of a wolf and had himself hunted by men with greyhounds and mastiffs. (Peire Vidal, "Razos di V," 18–35, in *Poesie*, ed. d'Arco Silvio Avalle, 2 vols. [Milan, 1960], 1:54–56).

[13] Ernest Hoepffner's later article in *Zeitschrift für romanische Philologie* revises the number of lines (see note 2 above).

One of the mss., Arras 897, contains only the final ballade. Were the ballades an afterthought, interpolated, as Ernest Langlois suggests (*Les Manuscrits du Roman de la Rose* [Lille, 1910], p. 114), or did a scribe suppress the lyrics in order to allow the allegory to move without interruption? On the problem, see Antoine Thomas, *Histoire Littéraire de la France*, 37, p. 414; Gaston Raynaud, *Romania* 40 (1911): 129–31 Ballades 6 and 7, and Rondeaux 8, 9, 10, have been anthologized by Nigel Wilkins, *One Hundred Ballades, Rondeaux and Virelais from the Late Middle Ages* (Cambridge, 1969).

[14] I have followed Thomas' proposal (Ibid., p. 413) that the proper title may be taken from the author's own designation:

Et pour ce *l'Amoureuse Prise*
Ara par droit cilz dis a non.

Hoepffner entitles *La Prise Amoureuse* after the ms. incipit.

Et se je parol par mistere,
N'en soit vers moi meüe d'ire,
Car c'est pour plus plaisamment dire. [64–66]

This prologue is succeeded by the first *rondel*, whose theme is the sweetness of being ensnared by *Amours*. Then with a spring description Jean establishes his landscape of love. Here he affords a dimension to the poem which is absent from that of his predecessor in the *Cerf amoreus*: the scene of the chase is a *carte du Tendre* through which a heroine of Mlle. de Scudéry might delicately have maneuvered. Here, various parts of the forest indicate changes in time, condition, or attitude. Four great routes cut through this *bois de jonece*, where love hunts by preference: *leëce* (*bliss*), *compaignie* (*companionship*), *cointise* (*elegance*), and *fol cuidier* (*foolish thought*). These roads over which love's hounds will chase their quarry have their smooth and rough stretches, their birds, blossoms, weeds and confusing sidepaths, but the last is the most disastrous. *Fol cuidier*, running between a plain and a hanging cliff, eventually gives out where the forest grows cold and the trees thin, deprived by painful age of the "fruit, leaf, blood and strength" (266-267).

The narrator describes his pleasant diversion along the highroad of *leëce*, a first sally it would appear, since he admits that previously he has passed his life hidden in the *thicket of childhood* (*buisson d'enfance*). There his senses lay dormant.[15] From his secure hiding-place, he had already observed how *Amours* takes its beasts in the forest of *jonece*, and he knows that some victims yield easily to love, whereas others struggle against the capture. But the narrator recognizes that his time of invulnerability is past. *Amours*, with his huntsman *desirier* (438), sets out to pursue him. At the beginning of his flight, the narrator is able to retreat from time to time the safety of the *buisson d'enfance*, to forget for the moment his troublingly unfamiliar sensations of love. However,

---

[15] The five senses, *regars*, *oïr*, *touchier*, *gouster*, and *oudourer*—besides *cuers*—remain attributes of the narrator's that respond independently, and in this order, to the assaults of the hounds, with the exception of *oudourer* which doesn't function in the allegory.

at a certain point he finds that he can no longer go back, and the chase becomes inevitable. Thus the allegory deals not with enamorment alone, but with the turmoil of youthful sexual awakening, where even pleasure lacerates the lover and joy and calm are things of the past.

Amours begins by leashing up a pack of hounds and posting relays upon the four routes of the wood.[16] The type of quarry he is out to capture is not plainly identified; near the poem's conclusion the author speaks of himself to his lady as "*vostre serf de valoir*" (1855); perhaps, inasmuch as *serf* is an alternate spelling for *cerf*,[17] he intends a pun. The hounds are the victim's principal assailants, as they are in *Li dis dou cerf amoreus*. Here there are twenty-eight, "well trained to dislodge any kind of game" (*bons et bien ordenés pour voir, / a toutez bestes esmouvoir*, 402-403). The hounds are not *Amours'* own, but belong to his people— *N'erent pas sien, mes a sa gent*—presumably, men and women who love or are loved; the god only borrows them for the occasion of his hunting. As allegorical figures the hounds fall into three types: those designating the woman's qualities (the largest group); those designating the man's, and two that reflect the opinions of others who talk about women, though these two, *los* and *renon* (whose music rivals that of David and Orpheus) might also be regarded as attributes of the woman herself. Hounds that represent the woman initiate the chase by flairing out their quarry, and so indicate, somewhat paradoxically, that such a woman is not merely passively attractive, but preys by the very reason of her desirability. Doing the work of tracking and un-harbouring are *biautés, bontés, sens, simplece, maintiens, courtoisie,*

---

[16] The hounds *los* and *renon* (praise, reputation) are placed as relays, as it were, on the road of *compaignie*; *cortoisie* and *maniere* upon *cointise*; *espoirs* and *semblance* are sent to the road of *fol cuidier*; and *voloirs* and *plaisance* to *leëce*, in this order. These hounds attack the quarry in turn as he reaches their respective roads.

[17] As in line 338 of *La chace du cerf*. See also the example given in Tobler, s.v. *Cerf: Altfranzösisches Wörterbuch* (Wiesbaden, 1956): "Ensi com le serf corrant / Grieve soif et maistroie, / Me vait s'amor destraignant." The source is a song of Gautier d'Epinal.

larguece, doucours, gentillece, maniere, faitiscece, honestés pleniere, biaus parlers, riquece, avenance, franchise, atraiant contenance (406 ff). Later, close to the moment of capture, *atrait* (1593) joins in, possibly a variation of *atraiant contenance*.[18] None of these hounds, qualities that emanate from the woman, ever injures or bites; only *biautés* "tugs" at the lover's gaze, but gently and pleasantly. In addition, the victim finds himself continually pursued by prudent considerations, forces lying outside the allegory. Not hunting hounds, these appear to be the voices of the lover's humanity counselling him to save himself. *Avis* (reason), for instance, warns *regars* against the hound *plaisance*:

> For he is too terrible a hound; his baying is too dangerous. Whoever is—even with propriety—bitten by him, he is put, as if sleeping, to death. Now it seems to those who cherish him that he does no more than lick; so they rejoice and wait for him and take no warning against the fact that *plaisance*, in licking them, goes to suck the blood out of their body. For in licking with his sweet licking he maddens the licked one, who remains even like one asleep since he has placed himself in love's power. This is the amorous lethargy, this is the joyful malady that leads, singing to the death, those whom Love holds in his dominion. [606–623]

At a more advanced stage of the pursuit, *biautés* becomes a fountain (1313) at which the panting quarry seeks to quench its thirst:

> And when *regars* (the lover's *gaze*) has seen *biautés* his thirst has grown so strong that he cannot refrain from amorous glancing. So delightfully is he held there that he has become hydroptic and altogether lost his self-restraint: yet the hydroptic one loses nothing of the thirst that torments him by drinking. Thus when *biautés* is before him, *regars* is not relieved of his thirst, and instead becomes thirstier as he becomes more drunken; he drinks continuously as he gazes all the more; in sucking he drank in

[18] Of these hounds seven appear also in the *Cerf amoreus*, as the antlers of the stag: [bon] *los, biautés, bontés, sens, simplece, maintiens, contenance*.

delight. And the more he drinks the drier he becomes. It is drunkenness that he incessantly licks at; biting himself inwardly he goes on licking, and in drinking he gets drier. That's the amorous hydropsy, the yearning drunkenness that brings joy and pain. [1282–1302]

The stag's quest for water, when he is hard pressed by the dogs, here becomes converted to "love's hydropsy."[19] Like "love's lethargy" this is a traditional image of the pathology of love, in which the afflicted seems caught in a hopeless cycle of drunkenness and unslakable thirst—a malady that causes the heart to "fry and cook" (*qui fait le cuer frire et larder*, 1306). Thus the poet has the suffering lover figuratively engaging in an ardent quaffing, anticipating the hounds in the climactic "martyred" scene when they will just as eagerly drink at him.

While the beloved's hounds, led by *biautés*, begin the chase and drive the lover from the route of *leëce* to that of *compaignie*, the other hounds, that prevent him ever from returning to his comfortable thicket, and that perform the cruel nipping and disemboweling, are the tireless thoughts and affects of the lover himself. These tormentors are *voloirs, espoirs, plaisance, delis, pensers, souvenirs*, and *dous samblans*.[20] With two of these, *pensers* and *souvenirs*, *Amours* engages in night hunting, attacking the lover in his bed.[21] The scene changes from the forest to the bedchamber. This onset effects a turning point in the interior action that "dislodges" the victim—in the hunt's terms—and

---

[19] Troilus sings this way of his new affliction (1. 406): "For ay thurst I, the more that ich it drynke." E. R. von Curtius, *European Literature and the Latin Middle Ages*, p. 280, has assembled other examples of the hydropsy topos.

[20] This last hound, not an aspect of the lady, as in the *Roman de la Rose*, signifies the way in which appearances present themselves to the lover; coupled with the hound *espoirs* and posted on the road *cuidier*, *samblans*—"qui change vil chose pour chiere" (474)—suggests the lover's precariously founded optimism.

[21] The unharboring of the hounds *pensers* and *souvenirs* to torment the lover at night corresponds to the scene in the *Cerf amoreus*, where these same hounds serve to "dislodge" the lady by forcing her to reflect upon her lover's merits.

propels him toward the *prise*, the capture. *Souvenirs* forces the sleepless lover to reflect upon his lady's charms *"membre a membre"* (905 ff). While the poet follows a rhetorically prescribed order in his evocation, many of the details—the lady's slitted eyes, brown and sparkling as topaz set in pearl, the endearing mole between her arching brows, the blond coils of hair fair by nature and not by art, that flank her ears—seem to be individually perceived. Routed from peaceful sleep the lover begins, like game, to run in earnest, moving from the road of *compaignie* to *cointise*. The hounds lying in ambush assault him there, like relays assisting the hounds of the pack. The hydroptic fountain of beauty appears as the victim is rushing along *cointise*, and he becomes drawn to it, to his lady's beauty, like a butterfly to the candle (*com papeillons a la chandeille*, 1322). Finally on the route to *cuidier* (as *fol cuidier* now is called), the last onslaught takes place. The poet has *Amours* intervene, however, despite the extent to which the god has permitted the hounds to tear and feast upon the quarry. *Amours* strikes, but prevents total destruction—*sans plus blecier . . . sans manecier* (1587 ff.). Whereas the death of the stag in *Li dis dou cerf amoreus*, the lady's surrender of her wholeness, paralleled her rebirth to *boine eure*, the hounds' attack of their victim in *L'amoureuse prise*, leaving the body broken in passion's torments, means not fulfillment but the threat of permanent lovesick despair which only the beloved can heal. The lover begs the lady to relieve his illness. The overwrought effect of the climactic scenes in which the quarry lies bleeding has been, however, controlled and deliberate. The death and distribution of the quarry complete the fantasy of the lover's total relinquishment of self to Love and to the beloved. At the close this is metaphorically seen from a more composed perspective: the Death, which is the lover's surrender, shows only his absolute dependence on his mistress; the "portions" she receives, his heart and will, show his faculties dedicated to her love-service. The poet reiterates, conventionally, his plea for pity and closes with a *balade* whose first stanza restores a formalized note of calm:

Gens cors, en biauté parfais,
    Et par fais
Sus toutes dames parfaite,
Or sui je pris et atrais
    Par les trais
De vostre amoureuse atraite,
Si vuelliés de moi curer
    Et curer
Celui qu'en vous tout a mis,
Mort ou vie, comme amis. [1885-1894]

Le dit du cerf blanc: The White Stag

While the *Cerf amoreus* and the *Amoureuse prise* may be taken
as companion pieces, showing in contrasting but complementary
fashion the roles of the man and the woman in a love chase, the
poem I wish to consider together with them, *Le dit du cerf blanc*,
presents an altered situation. A chase is implied only distantly:
it is spoken of by the Queen of lovers as a lure that encourages
an eager young stag to break out of its enclosure and run into
danger. In its simplicity and its pleasure-seeking, the stag will
be stirred by the sweet sound of the dogs and pause to listen,
risking surprise and capture:

> For the stag is innocent and full of gaiety; he seeks his grazing in
> many different kinds of places. His aim and concern is to do as
> he likes without there being the slightest wickedness in him, nor
> any base vice. Anyone can see that, however simple-minded one
> may be. If the stag is hunted, so that he has to abandon his pasture
> when he hears the hounds, he emerges from the thickets. But
> out of innocence and a free spirit, and following his inclination,
> he gets into so desperate a position that when he perceives no
> respite from the hounds he willingly stops and waits for them.
> [156 v^a and ^b]

However, the personage *Amours* is no huntress but the Queen of
lovers, to whom the narrator "confesses," that is, he recounts
the adventures of his precious white stag, over whose frolics he
has been watching with an anxious eye, especially since the stag

The lover, the queen of love, and the white stag. Miniature in *Le dit du cerf blanc*, fourteenth century, ms. 5203, folio 156 v°. Bibliothèque de l'Arsenal.

has become enamored of a Rosebush. He now asks the Queen for counsels and reassurances. The stag's adventures plot its journey from a state of artless curiosity, a love of freedom, and an innocent lasciviousness—if that is what its enraptured admiration of the Rosebush is—to a submissive and purified condition, where it will be content to dwell by the Rose, tethered to it with a chain of gold. The narrator's pursuit of this amorous stag is a vigilant one as it wanders happily, confusedly, and then painfully, from place to place; not a truly hunted stag, the *cerf blanc* dramatizes the patience and endurance of a lover throughout a testing period.

At the opening of the poem, the narrator recounts his walking out on a spring morning, and elaborates upon the sweetness of the season. Earth is full of colors. Nature recovers her beauty after winter's deprivations. Birds sing in their language. Nightingales scold backbiters, who have caused pain to true lovers. Finding himself in a pretty orchard, preoccupied with how he may give pleasure and homage to his beloved, the narrator is surprised by the appearance of a lovely lady, robed like a princess in white and riding a white palfrey. She identifies herself as the Queen and affirms her power as "root of joy and sorrow." When the young man begs her to hear his story and grant him her help, she graciously assents; dismounting, she gives him her hand, and they sit together on the grass. He begins:

> Then I said to her, "Gracious lady, the truth is that I have in my retreat a park that I love, and it is right that I should, for my treasure lies therein. It is the chamber of my body; in it I have stored grievous sorrow that I've known—whether it was right or wrong—and I have devoted my reflection, thought, and feeling to its being well closed in upon every side. Now for a long time I have held a white stag captive there; he was so fine, so exuberant, and joyous, that to be near him was all my joy; because of this I had a mind to keep him. But he went from me and he'll tell you why: for he was so desirous of finding diversion that would be to his liking, that in no harness or control would he remain. Nor was he content with the good things in the park that had nourished him, nor did he long for anything except to leave my park."
> [156 r⁰]

Here at the outset the poet makes the allegory nearly explicit. Dwelling within that park which is his body's chamber, the white stag may represent the heart, the will, or the desire— whichever of the lover's faculties is to undergo a process of refinement in order to become worthy of the beloved.

When this innocent and playful creature broke out of his enclosure, continues the narrator, he himself recaptured and bound the white stag by a golden chain,[22] hoping to keep him

---

[22] The figure of the richly collared or gold-chained white hind is found in Petrarch's sonnet 190: In *Una candida cerva sopra l'erba* the dazed poet beholds at sunrise a white hind with horns of gold. Written in diamonds about the hind's collar appear the words "Nessun mi tocchi . . . libera farmi al mio Cesare parve."

In the *Decameron* (4th day, 6th story) Gabriotto dreams that he holds to his breast a snowy hind. A chain of gold is fastened to the hind so

within the park and close to him. But the stag, still too eager to be free, again bounded forth to seek his amusement in the fields. This time he broke the golden chain. The young man then followed the white stag until together they came upon a flowing river beside a beautiful garden, *li lieux joieux*. Paradise, in which Adam and Eve were placed, was not more beautiful nor better provided with pleasures. The stag, desiring to enter this fragrant garden of delights, searched until he found the opening, concealed by tall trees and hedges. Inside all was resplendent with brilliant blooms, with color and light; but the noblest of plants found there was a Rosebush bearing a single vermilion flower. The narrator now tells the Queen how he observed his stag who, fascinated by the bloom, approached the *rosier*. There the stag paused, overcome with confusion, doing nothing more than gazing at the Rosebush. It is at this moment of lost and transfixed pleasure that the horde of flies descends without warning upon the *cerf blanc*. At first he appeared able to ignore their stinging, persisting in his steadfast contemplation of the Rose, and enduring the shedding of his blood and the loss of his great beauty. At length, however, in pain he ran out of the lovely garden and found himself in a desert, wide and wild, planted not with foliage, but with rocks. There, his flesh torn by thorns, himself unable to find any rest, the white stag leapt high and low in his agony. Now desperate,

> Entra mes cers, qui tant de grant meschance,
> De grief, poverte,
>
> D'aspre dolour, de grant paine ot sofferte. . . . [159 v^b]

Eventually, he made his way once again into the garden. The

---

that it will not leave him. But in the dream a coal-black hound springs upon Gabriotto, gnaws at his bosom, and tearing his heart out of his body, runs off with it. Immediately after Gabriotto tells his dream to his beloved, Andreuola, he suddenly falls ill and dies. Does the author intend the hind to signify, as with the *Dit du cerf blanc*, the heart or soul of the man, or is it his beloved, or a fusion of both?

narrator tells of his following to see what the stag would do: he saw him return to the Rose, which he now regarded with lowered gaze, humbly chastened. As he did so his beauty was restored. Since the stag appeared content to remain motionless beside the *rosier*, his owner succeeded in drawing near and attaching him to the *rosier* by means of a gold chain.

The lover's consternation at finding his white stag stung by flies. Miniature in *Le dit du cerf blanc*, fourteenth century, ms. 5203, folio 159 r°. Bibliothèque de l'Arsenal.

His tale concluded, the narrator turns to the Queen of lovers, seeking her word that the stag will not again break loose. She consoles him: the stag is now bound by a chain which she herself has forged. The *rosier* to which the stag is fastened draws its sustenance from a strong and noble root. Firmly fastened, he will receive harm neither from chain nor rose but will remain evermore in the lover's control. With such assurances and a last injunction to him always to be mindful of her, the Queen vanishes. The narrator praises her, *"ma dame Amour."* Now, returning to the *lieux joieux*, the lover—for so he must be—finds all in order there: his white stag makes no effort to break the chain that binds him to the Rosebush. Placid, beautiful, happy, and humble the stag regards the Rose. The lover goes on to sing the praise of the Rose which confers honor upon any human creature who unswervingly bends his gaze to it. He praises also the unbreakable chain, and closes with an expression of joy and a final apostrophe of the Rose for whom he has rimed this *dit:*

> . . . toujours lié et joiant,
> Car nulz amans n'ot onc honneur si grant
> com j'oy de vous; or m'en vueil taire atant. [161 v^a]

> Explicit le dit du cerf blanc.   [161 v^b]

The motifs from two literary traditions join in *Le dit du cerf blanc:* there is the *rosier* in its earthly paradisal setting derived from the sphere of the *Roman de la Rose*, and there is the vulnerable *cerf blanc* of the amatory hunt tradition. The poet has developed his theme of the worthy lover's necessary purification through the further incorporation of references that reflect a significant use of Scripture. The biting flies of sensual thoughts show an imaginative use of commentaries upon Exodus 8, as well as Psalms 78 and 105 which allude to the plague of Exodus that the Lord visited upon the Egyptians. Moreover, the stag's punishment and departure from the *lieux joyeux*—a place said to rival in ornament and delight that Paradise in which Adam and Eve were placed—because of his excessive joy in the *rosier* recall the expulsion of the first man and woman from Eden because of their fatally uncontrolled longing for the fruit of the Tree in their garden. After a period of suffering, however, in a barren landscape, the stag returns to a condition of bliss within the *lieux joyeux*. The poet has varied the love chase, and intensified the moral meaning of the true lover's rejection, castigation, and final acceptance, through a parallel with the sinning, fall, punishment, and regeneration of spiritual man.

Germany: The Elusive Quarry

Before Hadamar von Laber: Burkart von Hohenvels, Mechthild von Magdeburg, Wolfram von Eschenbach, Albrecht von Scharfenberg

Probably Gottfried's *Tristan* is the most celebrated of German medieval poems in which the hunt, developing in this instance from motifs of the lovers as courtly quarry in Béroul and Eilhart, unfolds intelligibly and intensively as a hunt of love. It is also the earliest of such hunts of love in German.[23] A little over a century later, the massive amatory *Jagd* of Hadamar von Laber appears on the literary scene: it is a work little known today and

[23] David Dalby, *Lexicon of the Mediaeval German Hunt* (xxii and n.), lists eight passages in which the chase is a metaphor of love, or the quest for *Saelde* or *Êre*, in other works. Does the poem known as the "Königsberger" *Jagdallegorie* (ms. Universitätsbibliothek zu Königsberg 898) precede Hadamar's *Jagd*? Its editors, Karl Stejskal (*ZfdA* 24 [1880]: 254–68) and Fritz Schulz (*Festschrift zum siebzigsten Geburtstage Oskar Schade* [1896], 233–37) consider it a thirteenth century poem known to Hadamar, and regarded the fourteenth century ms. as a copy of an earlier original. Gustav Ehrismann (*Geschichte der deutschen Literatur bis zum Ausgang des Mittelalters*, 2.2.2.: *Die Mittelhochdeutsche Literatur* [Munich, 1935], 499, 501) and Heinrich Niewöhner (Wolfgang Stammler, *Verfasserlexikon*, 2:564) think it may be dated after Hadamar. A summary of the arguments on both sides is found in Walter Blank, *Die deutsche Minneallegorie: Gestaltung und Funktion einer spätmittelalterlichen Dichtungsform* (Stuttgart, 1970), 187–194. Dalby (xxii–xxiii) summarizes some of the arguments, although his own reason that the "Königsberger" poet's smaller pack of hounds indicates an earlier date cannot be accepted. *All* hunt allegories *after* Hadamar have reduced the numbers of hunting dogs. My own view is that the "Königsberger" was composed later than Hadamar, and I discuss it together with other later minor poems of the love chase, with which it has much in common. The crafty cynicism of the first part of the poem, the poacher's subsequent remorse and moralizing, the poet's expressed antipathy throughout to courtly service and self-denying love make it an unlikely model for Hadamar, whose affinities are with the lyric poets and with Wolfram. I suspect that like Hadamar's other imitators, the "Königsberger" poet selected features of the *Jagd*— the unprincipled hunter, the debate over hunting methods, the love judgment—for closer treatment.

one that merits considerable attention for its sensitive if fantastic exploitation of the chase. Between these two, the *Tristan* early in the thirteenth century and the *Jagd* near the middle of the fourteenth, four poets—two writing lyrics, two writing romances—may here be examined for their contributions to the love chase in German literature. Of the lyric poets, Burkart von Hohenvels and Mechthild von Magdeburg contrast in their respective commitments to the spheres of earthly and heavenly love. In romance, Wolfram von Eschenbach and Albrecht von Scharfenberg give shape, through the figures of the hunt, to two ways of love: Wolfram's is devoted to an ideal of human and earthly good, Albrecht's to a moral, Christian principle.

Dissimilar in style, sensibility, and intent, Burkart and Mechthild enlarge the possibilities of the hunting metaphor within the compression of lyric form. Burkart's song is careful and anguished, an elaborately constructed lyric in the tradition of secular Minnesang, and it is the first literary work to compose an allegory of the hounds as the passions and condition of the wooer. Mechthild is ecstatically direct; cultivating the sense of joy through pain, her love language is bound by none of the restraints, precisely because of its divine scope, of her worldly contemporaries.

Let us turn first to Burkart. In the opening stanza of a lyric[24] of five ten-line stanzas, the poet establishes his beloved as the game, his mind, spirit, and thought as hunting dogs, and his heart as the hunter:

> Mîn herze hāt mînen sin
> wilt ze jagen ūz gesant.
> der vert nāch mit mînem muote.
> vil gedanke vert vor in.
> den ist daz vil wol bekant,
> daz daz wilt stēt in der huote
> bî der, der ich dienstes bin bereit.
> ir sin, ir muot, ir gedenken

[24] Olive Sayce, ed., *Poets of the Minnesang* (Oxford, 1967), 157–159; notes on 267–268.

kan vor in mit künst wenken:
wol bedorfte ich fuhses kündekeit.

My *heart* has sent my *mind* out hunting for game. He courses
in pursuit with my *spirit*, and *great thought* leads the chase. Well
they know that the game dwells in a park beside her whom I am
ready to serve. Her own *mind*, *spirit*, and *thought* can artfully
evade them. I would need the cleverness of a fox.

In a delicate analysis of this lyric, Olive Sayce has noted the
"threefold arrangement of keywords"; for instance, the *sin, muot,
gedenken* of strophe i recur in strophe ii, along with another series
of three—the beloved's qualities. She is *snel* (swift), *wîs* (prudent),
starc (strong). In each of the five strophes, the editor remarks
an analogous group, or pair of groups of three such nouns or
adjectives.

There are, in addition, three principal metaphors: hunting,
seagoing, and painting. Seemingly unrelated, these activities yield
images which the poet uses to produce a twofold emotional effect
throughout the lyric, of oppression and loss. In stanza 1, Burkart
already hints at the victim's role the lover will have to assume, by
introducing the fox—usually a hunted rather than a pursuing
animal. Further harsh animal images are bred in the second and
third stanzas, which describe the beloved's power. She is the
proud game (*wilt*); she has the strength of spirit that dwells in
the lion; her bonds are so fast that a griffin's claw could not pry
them loose.

The poet praises his mistress, as the *wilt*, for her swiftness,
prudence, and strength. Now each of these qualities is made to
refer to her *gedenken, sin* and *muot:*

> *snel gedenken* vert vor winde,
> *wiser sin* bī menschen spilt,
> *sterke* in leuwen sich ie barc:
> der gelīch ir muot ich vinde.

> *Swift thought* outruns the wind; a *prudent mind* shines out among
> men; *strength* has always dwelt in lions—I find her spirit like that
> strength.

These qualities themselves become nouns, capable of exerting dominion:

> ir *snelheit* mir wenket hōhe enbor,
> ir *wīsheit* mich überwindet,
> mit ir *sterke* sī mich bindet.

Her *swiftness* hovers high above me; her *prudence* is my master; with her *strength* she binds me.

Having launched his poem with a chase, Burkart permits the original attributes of the *wilt* to multiply at an alarming rate, until it becomes certain that the quarry rules the hunter. He in fact no longer seems to be tracking *her*. It is she who, with her beauty, casts a net[25] about the one whose thought *she* would capture:

> ir schoenè diu leit den stric
> der gedanke vâhen wil.

The initial hunt and animal images serve to direct us not only to the lover's subjugation, but to his sense of loss. These themes continue to echo in the poem, though not always in images of the chase. Stanza i describes the man's separation from his own faculties (pursuant hounds), and shows the fleetness of the beloved. Then the hunter must endure being estranged from his senses, from high spirit (*hôher muot*), from consolation (*trôst*). The hunting metaphor returns in the final stanza, with Minne now as the huntress:

> Minne vert wil wilden strich
> unde suochet triuwen spor.
> von dem gewinne
> scheiden muoz, swer triuwe nie gewan.

Minne courses upon many an animal's path and follows the tracks of *faithfulness*. He must give up hopes of winning a portion, who has never acquired *faithfulness*.

[25] Snaring game in nets might describe either hunting *or* fowling. But in the poet's image of thoughts that soar upward toward the beloved (*swes gedenken gegen ir swinget*, line 38), *swingen* indicates the flight of a bird to be snared by the beauty of the beloved.

Minne joins lovers in their pursuits, but gives no assurance of their winning a portion. The poem's closing lines indicate the dubiousness of success.

The disparate images of the beloved's portrait locked and sealed in the lover's heart, and grief's anchor, also sunk within his heart, reinforce the sense of the binding strength of the beloved as proud game. The "sail of joy" that moves away from him parallels both the beloved quarry's evasiveness and the lover's privations. Just as the hunter falls at the mercy of the quarry, so the whole lyric continues to play upon the lady's daunting power and the lover's helplessness. Burkart's images are conventional, but he has joined them together so that the subsidiary images carry out the intent of the principal one of the chase.

The lyric passages which Mechthild von Magdeburg has left us must be set in contrast to Burkart's tortuous and suspended poem. Mechthild, a mid-thirteenth century mystic, exploits the metaphor of the chase in a manner that is concise and exultant. The throes of the pursuit arise in a dialogue between God and Soul: the Lord asks his laboring huntsman, Soul, for an account of the quarry, love.

Du jagest sere in der minne;
Sage mir, was bringest du mir,
min küniginne.[26]

Sorely you hunt after love; tell me what you are bringing to me, my queen.

But in a rapturous exchange between Soul and Love, Soul's

[26] P. G. Morel, ed., *Offenbarungen der Schwester Mechthild von Magdeburg, oder das fliessende Licht der Gottheit* (Regensburg, 1869), p. 18.
In a lyric of Mechthild's contemporary, the *béguine* Hadewijch of Brabant, is the image of a rider in search of true love. Having despaired in the face of temptations to pursue alien pleasures, she now addresses God: "My love, when you come to me you will raise me up with new solace, and so with high spirit I ride on" (Edward Rombauts and N. de Paepe, eds., *Hadewijch, Strofische Gedichten* [Zwolle, 1961], p. 90, lines 38–40).

suffering, as the quarry, is penetrated with delight. *Sele* acknowledges that *Minne* has hunted, caught, and bound her, dealing deep wounds that will never mend, and clubbed her with blows. "Shall I at last recover from you?"

Minne replies with the compelling anaphora:

> Das ich dich jagete, das luste mich;
> Das ich dich vieng, des gerte ich;
> Das ich dich bant, des frôwete ich mich,
> Do ich dich wundete, do wurde du mit mir vereinet,
> Do ich dir kuline schlege gibe, so wirde ich din gewaltig.

> That I hunted you was for my delight;
> That I caught you was for my desire;
> That I bound you was for my joy.
> When I wounded you, you became one with me.
> When I gave you blows with a club, I ravished you.

From features of the chase, Mechthild has wrought a fantasy rich in erotic associations; the union of hunter and hunted, the victim's projection of his own pleasure onto the imagined conqueror, Love. Her daring to revel in the completed hunt as a deeply joyful event—for her, the consummation of divine love—is not quite matched by poets of secular love. The soaring imagination of the mystic, for whom her beloved is her own creation, was never subject to the kinds of anxious repressiveness that could pervade the songs of the secular love lyricists. The persona of Burkart's poem acknowledges his jeopardy to the lady on whose account he suffers in flesh and spirit. Mechthild's liberation from the body's love enables her to envision a boundless divine love in the body's terms.

Burkart and Mechthild draw upon the connotations of the hunt in all its physical reality. Turning to the usages to be found within one of the romances we have selected for investigation, we may observe that Wolfram's "hunt" is sometimes explicit, sometimes attenuated. Take for instance his *jagen* and *bejagen* in *Parzival*. Its metaphorical sense of "hunt" or "hunt down" usually appears quite effaced. What Wolfram means by these verbs is "seek," "impel," "incur," "achieve," or "attain." His most frequent formula is *prîs bejagen*—to quest for or attain excellence or reputation (or its converse *unprîs*).[27] In three instances he associates *bejagen* with the Grail adventure: Sigûne tells Parzival that his unasked question would have "attained" him his reward (441.25); Feirefiz would "attain" to the company of those who see the Grail (813.20). Just once is the Grail itself made the object of the verb. Trevrizent tells Parzival:

> No man can achieve the Grail (*jā enmac den grāl niemen bejagen*) unless he is so renowned in heaven that he is called to the Grail.

Elsewhere in *Parzival* the verb *bejagen* refers to the winning of love, as it does in one of Wolfram's lyric poems in which the petitioning lover wonders beseechingly whether his long yearning may "hunt down" the favor of his lady's love (*ein liebez ende an dir bejagen mîn langer gern*?)[28] Of course, the translation of *bejagen* as "hunt down" must be a guarded one. Of the lovers in *Parzival*, Gramoflanz declares he never could win the love of Orgeluse: "*Ich enkunde ir minne nie bejagen!*" (606. 13), while in the same terms Meljacanz "wins" his loves by force (343. 28), and Parzival "wins" for Jeschûte her husband's loving greeting (263. 24-25). Similarly Wolfram expresses love's drive or impulse with the verb *jagen*. Obie's thoughts "impel" her toward Meljanz: *dar*

---

[27] In *Parzival* the verb *bejagen* occurs 63 times; among its objects are *âventiure, vreude, gunst, ungunst, roum, laster*, in addition to *prîs*. We may compare the frequent *prîs bejagen* formula to the line in a manuscript of the *Ancrene Riwle* (Corpus Christi 402) cited in the *MED*: *Ha hunteð efter pris & kecheð lastunge* [shame].

Horses or armor are occasionally the literal objects of *bejagen*, and in one instance it is the cures of medicines like those sought by Anfortas' physicians (481. 14). *Jagen* appears 23 times.

References to *Parzival* and *Titurel* aref rom Leitzmann, ed., *Parzival* (7th ed., 3 vols. [Tübingen: 1961, 1963, 1965]); Lachmann, ed., *Titurel* (6th ed. [Berlin, 1926]).

[28] Wolfram von Eschenbach, *Lieder*, ed. Leitzmann (*Altdeutsche Textbibliothek* [Halle, 1950]), 6: 19–20, p. 190. The use of *ende* (consummation) is worth remarking, since it will become one of the crucial hounds in Hadamar's *Jagd*.

jagent mich herzen sinne (365. 30), as do Gâwân's toward Orgeluse (591. 20), and Minne "drives" knights from distant countries to vie for the love of Herzeloyde: *uz verrem lande nû hie sint | ritter die diu minne jaget* (65. 26-7). It is worth noticing that Wolfram describes Parzival's yearning in the same terms; the youth, however, strives not toward a worldly love but in the direction of the Grail: *mich jaget des endes mîn gedanc* (329. 28)—"my thoughts drive me to that goal [to behold the Grail]." In this, he unconsciously echoes his father Gahmuret who, years before, had parted from his brother despairing of his own restlessness, his objectless striving: *ouwê war jaget mich mîn gelust?* (9. 26), "Alas, where is my desire driving me?" Father and son share a common eagerness of spirit, but a worthy object appears only to the knight of the second generation.

As he describes his hero's circuitous route to the Grail, Wolfram makes us aware of the path, or track (*slâ*, which has especially the sense of a trail fresh with blood), along which Parzival is conducted toward or diverted from his destiny. In guiding some of his wanderings, the penitent Sigûne plays a role. Marion E. Gibbs has demonstrated that "Sigûne's directions, even when they are misleading or negative, can be used as the basis for a new direction."[29] Judging, for instance, that Parzival may not be ready for the path that could lead to his death, Sigûne indicates a wrong one, wide and well-trampled. Later, a fresh trail (*slâ*, 256. 11) leads him to the place where he can atone for his wrongs to Jeschûte. On another occasion Sigûne is more encouraging, when she tells Parzival that with God's help he may find a track (*ein slâ*, 442. 12) to Munsalvaesche. But *ungeverte*, "pathlessness"—with the additional sense of "misfortune"— keep him from following the Grail messenger. Once again he misses the track (*slâ*, 442. 28) to the Grail.

That Wolfram had in mind the cynegetic sense of *slâ* becomes evident. When Parzival grows a little "warmer" in his quest, he finds a significant trail, and other hunting allusions appear. The

[29] "Wrong Paths in 'Parzival,'" *MLR* 63 (1968): 872–876.

good old knight Kahenîs, riding on God's trail (*gotes vart* 446. 29), exhorts Parzival to follow the "scent" (*spor*, 448. 21) with him and the other pilgrims.

Instead, Parzival loosens his reins for God to guide him, and thus rides upon the fresh track that leads him to Trevrizent (*er rîtet nû ûf die niuwen slâ | die gein im kom der ritter grâ*, 455. 23). This trail leads him beside the place where he had formerly rectified his wrong to Jeschûte. Perhaps Wolfram means this recollection of an earlier atonement as a token that his hero is on the right path, for the path takes him immediately to the hermit Trevrizent, with whom he passes a fortnight of instruction and penance. When he finds Trevrizent, Parzival tells him of the encounter with Kahenîs: "I rode his track and found you" (*ich reit sîn slâ unz ich iuch vant* (457. 10). The old pilgrim has been an inadvertent conductor to Trevrizent as sacred animals were the conductors of heros, a discreet parallel which the language makes. We may contrast these instances of a sacred trail, that Parzival continually loses and finds, to a reference in Gâwân's more worldly adventures. Gâwân comes upon a track (*slâ*) all bloodied as if a stag had been shot on it. (507. 25 ff.) The track leads him to his adored and haughty mistress, Orgeluse!

Apart from these allusions to the tracks that knights pursue, Wolfram reserves a special place for two literal and revealing hunting episodes. He begins with the child Parzival as he performs cruel acts in ignorance. These are resonant acts, however, and they echo afterwards in tones that define the meaning of the earlier event. The boy brought woe to wild animals when he slew them with his uncourtly javelot (*gabilôt*), then, in a manner that would have been regarded as unhuntsmanlike, hauled the carcasses home in one piece (120. 2-10). Still with a hunter's eye he admiringly compares the armor of the first knights he sees to a stag's pelt, the armor appearing more resistant to his *gabilôt* (124. 12-13). These incidents anticipate his crude slaying of Îther, whose armor he does not know how to undo (155. 21 ff.), any more than he could undo a stag. Kay's uncaring remark that dogs (meaning the lives of such as Parzival and Îther) must be sacrificed to win the boar's head (150. 22) clarifies the parallel between Parzival's wanton slaying both of beasts and of the man. Like quarry, Îther is cut down, a victim of Parzival's thoughtless prowess. However, Parzival's uncomprehending tears as a child over the birds he has shot with his bow (118. 6) prefigure the deeper anguish of Minne into which he later falls (281. 23 ff). The occasion is when a falcon escapes King Arthur's falconers and strikes one of a resting flock of geese, causing three drops of blood to stain the snow. It is no longer the death of birds that moves Parzival, but the blood as a token of the bird's former life, through which he suddenly perceives the beauty of Kondwîrâmûrs and his nearly forgotten love for her. Thus Wolfram causes Parzival's childish hunting experiences to foreshadow his two conventional knightly enterprises—battle-strife and Minne.

In *Parzival*, the chase images are sporadic.[30] Equivocal words like *jagen* and *bejagen* are often used colorlessly. Yet they are words that always remain potentially alive to the development of a fuller metaphorical treatment, when this is apt to the poet's purpose. Conscious of how he might use hunting images and episodes to express his hero's growth, to suggest the quest of love or even of the Grail, Wolfram did not here choose to allow the chase to dominate. Perhaps he did not wish to put too strongly the idea that the Grail could be the object—"quarry"—of a hunt with all a hunt's frenetic haste. What must matter is the blessed *way* to that place (*die saelde vart*, 470. 26), for Parzival, a laborious and error-fraught route which he is forced to travel as he becomes slowly wise.

Wolfram does, however, give a first hint in *Parzival* of the full, intricate love chase he will develop in the sylvan episode of his *Titurel*. The lady Sigûne of *Parzival* has appeared as a grieving penitent for having denied herself to her beloved Schîonatulander

[30] On the place of falconry, as distinct from the chase, in *Parzival* and *Willehalm*, there is an account in A. T. Hatto, "Poetry and the Hunt in Medieval Germany" *AUMLA* (*Journal of the Australasian Universities Language and Literature Association*) 25 (1966): 47 ff.

and then sent him on a chase, a lover's chore, that terminated in his death. She tells Parzival:

> In serving us both, he hunted down (*bejaget*) death for himself, and for me, sorrowful longing for his love. [141. 17–19]

Here a literal translation of *bejagen* is justified (while it also means "won"), for it expresses Schîonatulander's actual pursuit along a path reddened with quarry's blood, a path on which (by a nexus of events that Wolfram leaves dark in both *Parzival* and *Titurel*) he finds his death. The history of the two lovers now unfolds in the *Titurel* (so called for the old Grail King whose name appears at the beginning) fragments, where the hunt works both literally and figuratively. As children together Sigûne and Schîonatulander come to confide their love to Herzeloyde and Gahmuret, respectively, in whose protection they have grown up. There are the occasional metaphors: Gahmuret, himself having been "hunted to the death" by Minne (74. 4) is able to "scent out" the traces of Minne upon Schîonatulander (95. 1).

These brief suggestions of a love chase are to crystallize in an explicit symbolic event. The second *Titurel* fragment opens upon the forest idyll of Sigûne and Schîonatulander living chastely in their tent. Schîonatulander has been fishing, when their calm is broken by the sudden appearance of a hound trailing a sumptuous jewelled leash. The hound has its own story. It had, together with the leash, been the gift of a countess, Clauditte, to the Duke Ehkunaht. The hound and leash constituted a pledge of her love, and her choice of him as husband and ruler of her kingdom. The hound, escaped from Ehkunaht, has been coursing in full cry upon a trail freshly red with the blood of game. Schîonatulander leaps up to seize the hound for Sigûne's sake, acknowledging at once that he is prepared to suffer because of this. The hound's rich collar bears a jewelled legend which is continued on the brilliant fashioned leash. In part, it relates the story of Clauditte and Ehkunaht, but the rest is a counsel of intense importance for true lovers: *Gardevîaz!* This is the hound's name as well, representing the German "*Hüete der verte*," or "Watch the paths!"[31] The leash unfolds the meaning of this injunction, which also continues to deepen in relevance as the episode progresses.

Sigûne's fever of interest in the leash, now fastened to their tent pole, causes her to untie it, for the knot hides the conclusion. Once again *Gardevîaz* escapes. The fragment ends with Sigûne's sending her knight, who has long been pleading for her love, upon a chase for the hound. This chase will inexplicably cost Schîonatulander his life. Watching her paths, that is, protecting Schîonatulander and guarding the course of their love, is just what Sigûne blindly does not do. (Is this why she so conscientiously guards Parzival's paths in her later life?) Instead, she yields to an insatiable curiosity to know the end of the story inscribed on the leash, no matter what the cost: she causes Schîonatulander to run upon the hunting path, promising him her love when he finally returns with *Gardevîaz.*

Let us examine the workings of the two charged and nearly inextricable symbols that figure together in this love chase: the hound's leash, or *brackenseil*, and the path, the *vart.*

The *brackenseil*: The Hound's Leash

Wolfram clearly indicates that the hound's name, its actions, and the legend on the leash prescribe the conduct not only of lovers but of all good men and women. *Gardevîaz* watches its own trail as a hound must (153. 2-3). Attention to the trail, emphasized in books about hunting, acquires here a larger meaning. Clauditte and Ehkunaht, acknowledged patterns of excellence, conscientiously "watched their paths" (as in 151. 4 and 153. 4). All men and women who "watch their paths" well will enjoy the world's favor now, and gain heavenly bliss hereafter (144. 2-4). And the collar goes on, introducing a commercial metaphor that will subtly point up Sigûne's later actions:

[31] Bernhard Rahn concludes his summary of the possible color and lapidary symbolism of the leash, endorsing a suggestion that Wolfram may have modelled the name *Gardevîaz* upon *Scivias,* the mystical treatise of Hildegard of Bingen (*Wolframs Sigunendichtung: Eine Interpretation der "Titurelfragmente"* [Zürich, 1958], 70-76).

"His worth will never be for sale, who 'watches well his paths,' for worth dwells and grows strong in a pure heart, so that no eye ever beholds it in the shifting, inconstant market place" (145. 2-4). It could not be plainer: the hound attending to its trail is a model for human excellence.

Hounds in the hunt allegories are projections, wholly or in some degree, of their masters. *Gardeviaz* expresses the conduct or fate of the person who owns him at the time; as the narrative continues, meanings of *Gardeviaz* amplify. The hound symbolizes Clauditte herself at the moment of her sending it to her beloved; its leash is the bond of love by which she offers to engage herself to Ehkunaht.[32] Hound and leash bestow worth on each other: "no leash was ever better furnished with hound; the hound, too, was excellently leashed" (142. 2-3). The jewelled leash is that blissful bond that joins the true man and woman, enslaving neither, but enabling both to move together along the path of their love, which both watch devotedly. The hound's correct role is to guide the man who holds the leash in his hand; by implication, the holder is the master, but the hound is the guardian of the moral inscription.

This vision of human being and hound joined by the precious chain of love is an ideal that is not achieved in *Titurel*; the opening gesture of Clauditte merely hints at this as the perfect fulfillment. As Sigûne reads about Clauditte and Ehkunaht on the leash, the poet allows the shadow of an alternative possibility to hover: it is the memory of Clauditte's older sister Flôrîe, who had set her lover an impossible task costing them both their lives (147-148). Flôrîe, the capricious and unwittingly destroying mistress, is the prototype for Sigûne, who will commit the same error.

The hound must leave Ehkunaht to be free to enter the sphere

---

[32] Wolfram has perhaps something like this in mind when, early in *Parzival*, he has Queen Amphlîse send Gahmuret a letter offering him her love and her crown:

dîn minne ist slôz unde bant
mîns herzen und des vreude. [76.26.]

Your love is the fetter and bond of my heart and its joy.

of the principal lovers in the narrative. Once Gardevîaz breaks away from Ehkunaht, the hound is no longer relevant to the Clauditte-Ehkunaht story. It simply contains this, along with its sister-alternative, the Flôrîe-Ilinôt romance, as two possible courses for Sigûne. *Gardevîaz*, drawn into the new context of Sigûne and Schîonatulander, is an object already laden, and must now take on yet another burden of significance, by reflecting Sigûne's action and her fate with Schîonatulander. Now that Sigûne has the hound and leash, what will she do with them? Which sister will she emulate? But all has been foreshadowed by the blood-red path upon which the hound had coursed.

First, Sigûne has the leash tied to a tent-pole, just as she has wrongly bound Schîonatulander, keeping him in servitude by withholding her love. It is this that she laments in *Parzival*, at a later moment of her story, long after her lover has died: "I was demented that I did not grant him love" (141. 20).[33] The knot of the leash, like bondage in love, prevents the full revelation of its legend, the "dénouement" of true love. Paradoxically, however, her loosening the knot only fetters Schîonatulander more tightly, for when the hound escapes this time Sigûne imposes a condition. Unlike Clauditte, who freely granted hound and leash to her love to keep, Sigûne will accord love to Schîonatulander only after he has performed a service. He will have to hunt for Sigûne's love in the shape of the hound: she has given nothing freely. Making love conditional upon her knight's service only reaffirms Sigûne's failure to "watch her paths," for it recalls the commercial metaphor on the hound's collar: the worth (*preis*) of those who watch their paths cannot be bought or sold.

[33] Here Wolfram's conception of Sigûne may owe something to the topos of the "cruel beauty" who is made to suffer for not having given her love at the appropriate time (cf. W. A. Neilson, "The Purgatory of Cruel Beauties," *Romania* 29 [1900]: 85–93). Cf. the story of Rosiphelee in Gower, *Confessio Amantis* 1: 335–340 (ed. G. C. Macaulay [London, 1900]): a lady tells how her change of impulse to love comes too late, and forever in the afterlife she regrets that she could not fulfill her love. The impulse, however, of true love is rewarded with—and symbolized by—a jewelled bridle.

Significantly, Schîonatulander's parting plea to Sigûne is: "Be gracious, sweet girl, do not hold my heart so long in your bonds" (*wis genaedec, süeziu maget, [unde] halt niht mîn herze sô lange in dînen banden*, 167. 4) The *brackenseil* is the glorious bond of love which, wrongly used, becomes a fetter to enslave. This symbol, as we shall see, is a central one with Hadamar. Wolfram has named this leash both in *Titurel* and in *Parzival* as the thing that destroyed Schîonatulander: "The hound's leash was for him the beginning of a time of joy's loss." (*Titurel*, 138. 4) And Sigûne tells Parzival: "*ein brackenseil gap im den pîn*" (*Parzival*, 141. 16) —"A hound's leash caused his suffering." Wolfram's stroke of paradox is to allow the leash to symbolize bondage and enslavement just when it is *loose* and idly trailing, for it dooms the man to stay on the path until death ends his chase. The recklessly running knight, the fugitive hound, the useless leash—that is, the desperate *Minne*-servant, the capricious and directionless woman, and her failure of commitment—offer a dismaying vision of love in disorder.

The *vart*: The Path

Just as Sigûne's mishandling of the *brackenseil* makes of it an instrument of woe, her failure to "watch the paths" turns their love's course into an avenue of death. Schîonatulander is fishing, recognized in the Middle Ages as a tranquil even virtuous variation of the hunt, when *Gardevîaz* escapes. Sudden confusion ensues as he throws down his fishing rod and leaps through brambles onto wrong paths that lead him astray (*den het im ungeverte alsô gevirret*, 160. 3), scratching his white feet and legs. The track made by his bare and bleeding feet becomes more discernible than that of the wounded quarry that had been fleeing there (161. 3). Now the two earlier allusions to the blood-red path gain relevance. The bleeding feet of Schîonatulander are a compelling sign both of his forced flight and of the suffering he will endure on his mistress's account. Sigûne, unconsciously cruel in her innocence and curiosity, drives Schîonatulander into the unnatural role of *Minne*-quarry. In this role he must course with feet that have been torn by *ungeverte* (false paths and misfortune), hunting a runaway hound. One is reminded of the Ovidian *adynaton:* sooner will the hound flee from the hares than will a woman refuse her love. Sigûne *has* refused her love; Schîonatulander, newly victimized, turns to pursue the hound which formerly had coursed in pursuit of a deer. The blood-red path has relevance both for Schîonatulander and the wounded quarry.

At various stages of the narrative, Wolfram has been preparing for this victimization of Schîonatulander. Early in the development of their love, Schîonatulander had tried to teach Sigûne of Minne, and had singled out the predatory Minne (unaware of the future implications of this for himself): Minne unfailingly transfixes whatever runs, creeps, flies or swims" (65. 4). Gahmuret, not long afterwards, identifies the *malaise* of Schîonatulander: "I sense love's traces upon you; her bloody trail is all too deeply marked" (*ich spür an dir di minne: alze grôz ist ir slâge*, 95. 1). It is as if, in this context, Schîonatulander is himself the path upon which Minne, a wounded animal, has left her traces—and this is the path that Sigûne has neglected to guard! Finally, there is an important ambiguity in the lines that occur at the beginning of the forest adventure, as David Dalby has observed:

> Sît in den wîten walt niht mohte gekêren
> daz vlühtege wilt, wan her vür den talfîn, daz wil sîn arbeit
> gemêren. [135, 1–2]

[The fact] that the fleeing deer did not wish to move into the wide forest, but rather [ran] here, before the dauphin [Schîonatulander]—this will increase his toil.

Arbeit can refer either to the exhaustion of a hunted animal, or to a hunter's labors to capture an animal; by its placing here, and the uncertainty of the antecedent of *sîn*, *arbeit* may be both Schîonatulander's and the quarry's.[34] Gradually, thus, an identifi-

---

[34] *Lexicon:* s.v. "*arbeit.*"

cation between Schîonatulander the hunter and Schîonatulander the victim will become fixed.

A lesser writer than Wolfram, Albrecht von Scharfenberg (*ca.* 1275), was to expand the *Titurel*. Albrecht's version of the *Titurel*[35] gives a good deal of attention to the image of the path and to the leash's injunction to "watch the paths." Before permitting the legend on the leash of *Gardivîas* to be revealed, Albrecht prepares his audience by a series of suspenseful delays. He repeatedly alludes to the inscription and to its power to astonish, impress, elate, and improve its hearers, without yet disclosing its contents. For instance:

> Whoever heard the inscription, his heart was gladdened. Before pain his spirit raised itself, indeed was exalted threefold. Sickness, injuries, all other pain, were made to vanish from the heart so that he grew oblivious of heart's pain. [1484]

Read at last, the inscription on the leash (1874-1927) tells initially of Clauditte and Ekunât (with no mention of Flôrîe and Ilinôt), dwelling upon Ekunât's superlative virtues. He is the well of honor, the blooms of excellence, and his fruits will profit the world. After having praised her beloved in these terms on the leash, Clauditte has inscribed the hound's name, *Gardivîas*. What follows is an extended series of definitions of *Gardivîas*, the appellative and rallying cry in which Clauditte had summed up all the glowing virtues of Ekunât. These definitions continue for the next 44 strophes, the last line of each strophe beginning with the ringing refrain, "nu hüete wol der verte!" The leash's inscription how exhorts all excellent men and women to *gotes minne*, both urging them to be mindful of salvation and heaven's crown and bidding them to guard against the shameful *verte* of earthly love's enticements. The Christian virtues of *gedulticheit* (patience), *diemüete* (humility), and *kiusche* (chastity) are praised;

---

[35] Werner Wolf, ed., *Albrechts von Scharfenberg Jüngerer Titurel* (*Deutsche Texte des Mittelalters* [Vols. 45, 55; Berlin, 1955, 1964]).

the *wâre minn* (true love) of God is to be preferred to the sweets of this world. The refrain *"nu hüete wol der verte!"* comes then to refer to the knight's obligations to the church and to the laity, towards widows and orphans, and to the strict maintenance of the *ritters orden*. Albrecht next varies his theme of vigilance with animal similes: one must be as watchful as the ostrich, alert as the lynx, bountiful and just as the eagle, stronghearted as the lion, and so on. Finally, he modulates from these bestiary comparisons to a flower allegory (1911-1925), enumerating the twelve flowers (*züht, kiusche, wîs, milt, triuwe, mâze, sorge, scham, bescheiden, staete, diemüete, gedulte,* and *minne*) to be borne in a garland by anyone who would take part in the "dance of honor."

Albrecht's version of the legend on the leash spells out a whole system of virtuous behavior, its emphasis more on Christian tenets than on a way of love. The contrast with Wolfram is striking: where for Wolfram the meaning of *Gardevîaz* was deepened by many implications latent in his narrative, for Albrecht everything is explicit and didactic. For Wolfram, the moral meaning is inseparable from a particular situation, Sigûne's transgression of an ideal of generous love; for Albrecht the message has become a general amalgam of current ethical notions.

The *Jagd* of Hadamar von Laber, which is the major allegory of the love chase in the fourteenth century, shows dependence upon both of these predecessors, Wolfram and Albrecht. While Hadamar is the innovator in Germany of the allegorically sustained love chase, he borrows three of the motifs figuring in Wolfram and Albrecht, which he incorporates in an individual manner in his own work, namely: the path, the injunction to "watch the paths," and the hound's leash. Like *Parzival* and the two *Titurels*, the *Jagd* uses such features of the hunt to express attitudes towards a course of action; with Hadamar, however, the action in which he interests himself is founded upon a specifically amatory ethic rather than one that is Christian, aristocratic, or humanely idealistic.

Hadamar von Laber: *Die Jagd*[36]

A century after Hadamar's death an admiring verse joined his name with that of Wolfram von Eschenbach: both were masters of learning: both sat high on the bench of poets.[37] Hadamar's circle of readers today must be considerably smaller than Wolfram's. Probably the *Jagd*, Hadamar's *Hunt*, has failed to draw an appreciative audience because of the difficulty of its language, its elaborate metaphors, and the abundance of hunting imagery and terminology, much of it long inaccessible. Hadamar is both repetitious and excursive: his proliferation of allegorical figures—nearly fifty hounds are introduced as needed, to express concepts familiar in courtly lyric and romance—[38] has undoubt-

[36] The two editions of the *Jagd* are J. A. Schmeller (*Bibliothek des literarischen Vereins in Stuttgart*, 1850, rpt. Amsterdam: Rodopi, 1968); and an eclectic one of Karl Stejskal (Vienna, 1880). I have founded my discussion upon Schmeller's text, which is based upon the fifteenth century Erlangen University manuscript.

Recent discussions of Hadamar's *Jagd* may be consulted in Tilo Brandis, *Mittelhochdeutsche, mittelniederdeutsche und mittelniederländische Minnereden. Verzeichnis der Handschriften und Drucke* (Munich, 1968), 201–203; Walter Blank, *Die deutsche Minneallegorie* 197–201; Ingeborg Glier, *Artes Amandi: Untersuchung zu Geschichte, Überlieferung und Typologie der deutschen Minnereden* (Munich, 1971), 156–178.

[37] *Die Unminne*, lines 36–40, ed. Gerhard Thiele, *Mittelhochdeutsche Minnereden*, 2 vols. (Berlin, 1919–1938) 2:63.

> Vonn Eschenbach der eine
> herr Wolffram ist genennet,
> vonn Labern nit der cleyne;
> der beyder kunst ich hann also erkennet
> an rümen, worten, silben wolgemessen.
> ir kunst ist meisterlichen,
> hoch uff gedichtes stul sind sie gesessenn.

[38] The hounds in the *Jagd* may be classified in the following way:
The man's attributes or possible attributes: herz (heart), fröude (joy), wille (desire), wunne (bliss), trôst (solace), staete (steadfastness), triuwe (faithfulness), lust (delight), lieb (love), leid (sorrow), harre (perseverance), muot (spirit), girde (longing), gedinge (expectation), twinge (pang), lîde (endurance), riuwe (regret), gedulde (patience), mâze (moderation), wâge (daring), irre (error), werre (confusion), gedanke (thought), troum (dream), sinne (understanding), swîge (silence), mîd (avoidance), sene (yearning).
The woman's attributes, or hoped for attitudes: genâde (grace), gruoz

edly made him less appealing to the tastes of our time than he must have been to his own.

Nevertheless, the *Jagd* is a work that commands notice. Dealing inventively with the metaphorics of the chase, perceptively with the subject of sexual love in terms of traditional styles and figures, Hadamar is concerned to record the interchanges between men and women, the nuances of feeling, especially the sufferings, defeats, fears, and gratifications of the stifled wooer, as he and his beloved engage in a long and painful game. He has devised a medieval *Clarissa*—though not with Richardson's *dénouement*. Often extravagant, contrived, and impulsive, ranging from a witty exploitation of conventional images to the blunt intrusion of a harsh, idiosyncratic one, Hadamar gives us an amatory poem that rewards our scrutiny for the energetic sensibility it betrays and for what it adds to our knowledge of imaginative conceptions of love in the Middle Ages.

Structurally, the *Jagd* is a sustained stag chase like the French allegories. Within this framework, Hadamar has adapted the practices and language of the formal chase to amatory attitudes already current in the literature of his compatriots. The known *persona* he projects, that of the lamenting Minne servant, now reappears as the hunter who in anguish chases the stag forever, determined never to capture it. Coming after the great moment of the Minnesänger, Hadamar reveals his intensive knowledge

---

(greeting), *heil* (reward—the hunter's portion), *triege* (deceit), *scham* ('pudeur').

Events shared by the man and the woman, or hoped for: blic (glance), *smutz* (kiss), *schrenke* (hug), *ende* (consummation).

Rivals: schalc (a base rogue), *göuden* (boastfulness), *untriuwe* (faithlessness), *wenkenwal* ([*wenc, wal* in Stejskal's ed.: fickleness, wavering] fickle wavering).

Friends and enemies of lovers: helfe (help), *rât* (counsel), *stiure* (support), *rüege* (accusation), *klaffe* (tattling, a "barker").

External forces: gelücke (luck), *gewalt* (power).

Non-allegorical hounds, of little use in this chase: holôr ("fetch"), *spitzmûl* ("sharp-muzzle").

The hound allegory is a conspicuous and extensively developed feature of the *Jagd*.

of lyric, whose unresolved "dialectic of Minne" he continues to
restate and explore. He incorporates within his narrative such
conventionalized tensions as are expressed in Minnesang. Not
only do the Minne hunter's complaints reverberate with the
paradoxical utterances of love lyric but his actions embody and
dramatize them. Hadamar's chase delineates a denied sexual
relationship: consummated (i.e., if the stag were slain), it would
be damaging to the woman and demoralizing to the man who
desires her. Unfulfilled, it turns the woman into a frivolous
destroyer, and becomes harrowing out of all proportion for the
man.

More explicitly than his predecessors, Hadamar recognizes
the sexual dissonances of which the chase image is capable. The
impasse he has created and his manner of expressing it depend
upon a realistic use of the language of the chase, of which his
knowledge was authentic and remarkably detailed.[39] He does,
however, wrench the hunt's principal reality—its aim of getting
quarry—so as to effect for his hero a pursuit with a touch of the
infernal wild chase about it: if the lover can hunt close to the
stag he will do it, though Hell gapes open for him (190). By his
own choice, the hunter allows the pursuit to be endless, with its
torments here and now, self-inflicted by his act of renunciation.

Hadamar's choice of framework, the protracted, inconclusive
chase, affords him space and time in which to explore his theme
of "the various aspects of Minne" (195), defined as "a broom
that sweeps shame from honor" (251), "a robber woman" (520),
"master of all the healing arts" (463), and, of course, one from

[39] At least four men named Hadamar von Laber occur in records
between 1218 and 1396. Heinrich Niewöhner (Stammler, *Verfasserlexikon* [Berlin and Leipzig, 1936], 2: col. 134) and Ingeborg Glier,
Artes Amandi, 157–158, judge Hadamar III, born in 1300, to have been
the author of the *Jagd*. This Hadamar, his brother Ulrich and their
father, Hadamar II, were vassals of Kaiser Ludwig of Bavaria. It has
been proposed that the poet's father, Hadamar II, may have been a hunt
official of Ludwig's, such as an *oberjägermeister*, inasmuch as an early
fourteenth century document grants specific hunting rights to him and
his sons. Perhaps it is sufficient to assume that hunting was a family
tradition of importance to these nobles. (See Glier, p. 158n.)

whose hunting none can escape (194). In addition to such
definitions and epithets, Hadamar incorporates brief love cases
and judgments, debates on hunting (that is, wooing) methods,
lyric laments, and disquisitions on various themes—*geselleschaft*
(companionship), *muot* (spirit), *sene* (longing), and *varwen* (love's
colors)—revealing his and his audience's intimate acquaintance
with the *Minnereden* conventions, as Glier suggests. Many of
the digressions from the hunting action occur in talks between
the Minne hunter and five counsellors or companions he meets
in the wood. A fragmentary sixth conversation takes place
without any introduction or conclusion. These men grant him
the benefit of their differing experiences by offering conflicting
advice. The progression from teacher to teacher is reminiscent of
the educating of Parzival, who receives directives from men and
women, old and young, until he finally joins the company at
Munsalvaesche. The *Jagd*'s hero meets a clever gamekeeper
(*klüg forstmeister*, 30-54), an old gray huntsman (*weideman vil
grîs*, 181-312), a young and brash hunting vassal (*knecht*,
348-360), a cynical hunter with unleashed hounds (411-421),
and a woodsman who interrupts this last debate to try to smooth
it over (422-27), and an apparently sympathetic listener to whom
the hero confesses how he has survived the rigors of the course
(487-493). The effect of listening to his voluble advisers is only
to intensify the Minne hunter's quandary. None offers him
advice he can follow, nor are prescribed courses of action replacements for the hunter's own experience. In contrast to these
knowing passers-by, most of them rich in experience and
counsels, the Minne-hunter himself maintains an air of despairing confusion. Hadamar has varied the *tumpheit* or foolish-
ness theme of Parzival with the *tôrheit*, the madness of his own
hero (e.g., 61, 192, 347). It is the madness of love, however,
rather than the folly of youth or ignorance. Thoughts of Minne
and of his lady deprive him continually of his senses. He eventually acquires *grîse*—grayness—without being cured of his love
madness, a state he willingly endures. "Grayness" and "gray
men" turn up in the *Jagd* as they do in *Parzival*. Herzeloyde had

exhorted her son to have respect for *"ein grâ wîse man"* (127, 21): several of his important guides or influences are such men— Kahenîs and Trevrizent, especially. The Minne hunter's passing from one counsellor to another resembles this initiatory feature of *Parzival*, but in his refusal to accept what the *grîse* of the poem proposes the hunter differs from Wolfram's hero. He neither covets nor wishes to emulate any "grayness." The Minne hunter's own gray hair, which comes upon him through sorrow, fills him with horror. He compares, for instance, his sensual longing to the hunger of the circling raven on whose cry, *"grâ grâ"* he puns: *"jâ, grâ trag ich mit leide!"* ("Yes, cawing, graying—these I endure with grief!" 529). Later he declares that not age but an external power (*gewalt*, a name given to one of the hounds), has forced him to grow prematurely gray (549).

The hunting action of the *Jagd* follows: The narrator sets forth (8 ff) one morning on the paths of game (*wildes genge*), having been instructed in this chase by Lady Minne. His sorrows here, he reflects, have been many. "And yet, Lady Minne taught me to hunt joyously, on a trail where often since then all my sense has failed": His scenting hound is *herz*, his own heart, an eager hound that will strain at the leash (74). To the relay stations (*warte*) the hunter dispatches *lust* (delight) and *gelücke* (luck), hopefully for future use, though the latter must be managed with caution for he may lead straight to the brook of *leckerîe* (discussed below, p. 194). Also posted along the expected route in *schalkeswald* (suitors' wood)[40] is *genâde* (grace). When the hunter sends his boy with *lieb* (love), he tells him he has to take *leid* (sorrow) as well, for these have always been inseparable—as in Minnesang. As for the hounds of the pack, the hunter chooses *fröude* (joy), *wille* (desire), *wunne* (bliss), *trôst* (solace), *staete* (steadfastness) and *triuwe* (faithfulness). With these whelps who

[40] *Schalkeswald* is the world of all those, regardless of rank, who hunt for feminine favors. The word *schalc* in its most general sense, that of a servant, meant more precisely a churl or menial, a fawning knave, a low fellow. Certainly Hadamar means *schalc* in an unfavorable sense: most of the suitors engaged in the great love chase are deceitful, bitterly competitive, dishonorable, bent on conquest by any means.

know the way but are in danger of being baffled by the rusing stag, the hunter sends the reliable old *harre* (perseverance). He is indispensable, for he has often confronted the stag at bay. With this pack to begin with, the Minne hunter has, as yet, no object. Before locating game, he engages in conversation with a shrewd old gamekeeper, the first of the seasoned counsellors he will meet. The gamekeeper quizzes him to determine his seriousness, instructs him in the use of hounds, and utters many warnings against wolves (spies and gossips), bogs, dark hedges, and deer that flee the light, that allow themselves to be hunted by too many (39) or that are at the point of death (52).

Armed with this preliminary advice, the hunter leaves his adviser and at once catches a glimpse of a stag's traces that causes him momentary paralysis and deprives him of his faculties (61). These are the beloved footprints for which he will embark upon his long and agonized pursuit. He acknowledges the fact that the footprints are indelibly struck on his heart, for the stag has stepped there. After losing, then regaining, the scent, he approaches the stag, but too closely: *herz* tears from its restraining leash and the stag wounds the hound (121). The stag escapes while the Minne hunter is left to groan and to attempt new combinations of hounds. This is an activity he renews throughout the *Jagd:* he may lose sight of *wunne* and *fröude*, for example, take up a new dog like *muot* (spirit), but count always upon *staete* and *triuwe*.

After this bruising encounter, the hunter tracks on foot, for his horse has lost a shoe. He enters a second conversation, this time with an ancient huntsman (181-312), the *weideman vil grîs*, who immediately recognizes his wounded heart. This gray-haired man, full of love's experience though now beyond love, first encourages the lover—his quest is worthwhile. However, he also attempts to prepare the young man for disappointments, for perfect mutual love is rare. The young man's question, whether he will grow gray in the chase, opens a discourse on the meanings of colors, with respect to lovers (242 ff.). As the conversation unfolds more of the possible sufferings in store for young lovers on this course, the old man eventually proposes that the hunter repair home from worldly vanity and pursue another path entirely, the one that leads to God. The familiar image of the Christ, the quarry, occurs: "Will you not turn your thoughts from the trail of this world—leash up *perseverance*, draw him back, and set him in pursuit [of game] whose hoof is stained with blood, for He ransomed us at so great a price" (268).[41] But as the young man cannot consider this redirection of his earthly aims, the *weideman* then speaks warningly of one Count Ludwig von Teck (293), one who is past love, and yet still addicted to it: "This will happen to you." Determined in his chase of the beloved deer, however, the young man leaves his adviser to hunt in *schalkeswald*.

Almost immediately he meets the stag for the second and only other time in the *Jagd*. *Blic* (glance), a swift-springing greyhound, represents the eye-force of enamorment that leaps from the lover to the lady and signals the possibility of their love. In terms of the chase, the stag is at bay (*bîl*) and turns pitifully to face the eagerly thronging hounds.[42] However, instead of the expected encounter between hounds and quarry—which would result in the animal's death—a struggle takes place between the hunter and his hounds, especially *ende*, the hound that would consummate the chase. The man turns upon the hound: I swiftly set upon him and dragged him far from the bay, I cast a

---

[41] Karl Stejskal's reading is "whose *track* is stained with blood," instead of "whose hoof is stained with blood." It is interesting that in this image, it is the foot of Christ, the stag, that is bloodied from its own suffering (or the track that is bloodied from the stag's foot, in Stejskal's edition), while the foot of the earthly mistress—as the stag—causes the wound in others. Thus, the *weideman* advises: hunt the stag that endures a wound, not one that inflicts it.

[42] E. E. Hese, *Die Jagd Hadamars von Laber* (Breslau, 1936), 31, n. 67, comments upon the active role of the beloved, as the stag at bay, for the stag appears prepared to yield (strophes 343.7; 344.3; 347.5). Summing up the action, Miss Hese writes: "The lady trustingly gives herself to her wooer (344.3); although the man is given the opportunity to abuse the trust and to exploit it in unchivalrous fashion, he nonetheless resists this temptation, heeding the woman's honor (344.4), and his own honor (355.1)" (Hese, 36–37).

leash around his neck—"Get away, you cursed scorpions, The wolves should gnaw your carcass evermore!" (345). But while the stag remains at bay, and the Minne hunter feels an onslaught of momentary madness, and is bereft of every sense, another hunter rides toward him abruptly. This is a young *knecht* who swiftly urges the slaying of the stag:

> er sprach: waz tût ir, meister,
> lât Enden hin ze einem bîle gâhen. [348]

> He said, "What are you doing, Master? Uncouple [the hound] *consummation*, send him to the bay."

As defined by the *Jagd*, this is an example of the unprincipled hunter, a slaughterer of game. The altercation between him and the lover dramatizes the lover's struggle against his desire. He argues: this act would dishonor the stag, for it would mean the severing of its foot. The allusion is to that practice in the formal chase which required the removal of the quarry's right forefoot to be presented to the most eminent person.[43] The hunter bursts out: "That I should lay it down careless of its honor, as if to cut it up, and were I to denude its foot of honor due, I had indeed contemplated this—" (350). Then he discloses in the very next utterance the truth of his hunger:

> waer ez im âne smerzen
> ich waen, ich wolt in ezzen ungebrâten. [350]

> if it weren't painful for the stag, I think I would devour it unroasted. [350]

Now the youth urges that they instead bind the stag and play: "He said, 'Let us tie it up, so we may then devise the way to peace, and find great disport and huntsmanlike matters. One could indeed play with this poppet just as children think up amusing tales to pass the time' " (351). Horrified, the hunter

---

[43] This ritual is described in *Modus et Ratio* 1.22; Jacques de Brézé, *Chasse*, st. 42.

would die before engaging in such a pastime. And hunting with *ende* would be tantamount to murder: "*solt ich ez danne morden?*" (355)

In the midst of this struggle, a new hound *smutz* (kiss) appears on the scene: "A little hound named *kiss*—Alas, that I heeded him—when he burns against anything—just as one who would plunge a glowing iron into a cold brook—he hisses. There would be much to say of this except that the betrayal of spies frightens me" (356). *Smutz* provokes the hunter to want to call for three more hounds: *schrenke* (hug), *lust* (delight), and *wunne* (bliss). But when the intruding *knecht* attempts to unleash *ende*, there is a fierce scuffle between the Minne hunter and this youth whom he threatens to blind and hang (359). While he upbraids the meddler, the stag breaks through the encircling hounds at bay: ".'The noble stag, affrighted, escapes the ring of hounds. I heard the hounds yelp in anguish so piteously as to break my heart" (361). This is a decisive point. The hunter, having already endured the mockery of the *knecht*, his own heart hacked down with fresh wounds, cannot bring himself now to possess the beloved—to slay the stag. He permits his quarry to slip away amid the hideous growls of the wolves, an ever-present menace. The *Jagd* is three-fifths over. The lover's decision to love his lady chastely, or in terms of the hunt, to pursue but not to capture the deer, will continue to provide Hadamar with material for more than 200 further strophes. He writes a penetrating strophe concerning the cost of this renunciation: "Towards *yearning* I drove *silence, thought*, and *dream*. Because of this my heart must sink and deny itself many joys. However the stag ruses by day, *dream* steals after it at night, until my heart wakes in terror" (371). The subduing of *ende* has driven forth more sinister hounds to torment the hunter, since he has let the deer run free. While he sleeps, the passions he has denied become replaced by a new hound, *dream*, that seems to continue to prowl after the stag—but the real victim is his heart.

The remainder of the *Jagd* is taken up with the hopeless quest that the hunter has chosen. There are renewed efforts to control and manipulate the pack. There is a noticeable rise in the number of lyric laments.[44] The hero exchanges words with a fellow huntsman whose hounds are gorged on wounded and exhausted quarry, and is chided for letting his own go unfed. But the Minne hunter reviles the other man for his sport, which is to murder game, and hotly accuses him: "Vile, misshapen you are in my opinion; the glazier has made eyes for you—let yourself smear them over![45] You allowed yourself with seeing eyes to grow blind" (420).

The *waldman* who intervenes to compose this debate also points out to the hero the brook of *leckerîe*, where deer splash and hunters founder. There is other treacherous terrain to be crossed or avoided: *rumelslîte* (gossips' hill), *affentâl* (foolsdale), the village of *tantenberc* (trifletown). Through this the stag runs—in other words, the lady is toying unmercifully with the lover's feeling. As the stag is never again to be brought to bay, the lyrical expressions of longing and grief, together with further theorizing about good and bad hunting and the management of one's hounds, now occupy the poet.

The *Jagd* closes with the hunter gray with grief, his jubilant hounds scattered. With old *harre* he persists on the track, determined to hunt forever, even after death.

For Hadamar to write of love's desire in the language of a chase—whose normal design is to drive dogs and pursuers headlong to the fulfillment of their purpose, the slaying of the quarry—and then to distort his metaphor so as to deny the hunt's obvious purpose, is to emphasize the unnaturalness of "ideal love" and to procure a maximum sense of tension in the narrative. Earlier writers of hunt allegories had assumed that the hunt's

---

[44] Hese (*Die Jagd Hadamars*, 15) makes a count of strophes which constitute lyric utterances of grief, and lists three times as many *after* 362, in which the decision is made to renounce the stag, as before.

[45] This is one of Hadamar's architectural images: eyes made by a glazier would be like the windows of a house. But as these neither let in "light" for this "blind man" nor reflect it, they must, like the walls of the house itself, be daubed with clay. The same image appears in strophe 293.

conclusion should be made to correspond to the union of the lovers, or to the "conquest" of one of the lovers, however cruel such a consummation might appear under the stress of the metaphor. Hadamar's decision to divert the hunt from its expected conclusion simply enhances the sense of the thwarted lover's torment.

Within this unusual concept of the chase as framework, patterns of imagery emerge, which also, in their vitality and their changes of meaning, manifest the strains and ambivalences accompanying the lover's dedication to such a demanding course. Hadamar bubbles with images of all sorts, from architecture, jousting, medicine, plant and animal life, as well as the chase.[46] In considering his contribution to the poetry of the love chase, however, I should like to concentrate upon an examination of four principal figures, together with two subsidiary ones, that typify Hadamar's unusual insight into the hunt's possibilities as a mode of erotic expression. There is the *vart*, or path, that carries the rider through time and through love's perilous landscape; occasionally it is identified with the beloved herself. Riddled with bogs and pitfalls, the path is nevertheless fresh with the scent and footprints of the stag. As the hunter presses forward with his hounds, he checks their impulsiveness and his own with the *seil, bant*, or leash. The leash operates as a repressive force and generates images of tying, binding, constriction and choking. Both the *vert* and the *seil* are received from Wolfram von Eschenbach and Albrecht von Scharfenberg, but Hadamar develops them more elaborately and concretely with respect to sexual love.

The beloved woman is the *wilt*, defined as a masculine animal by its highly praised antlers. As the stag recedes and in fact ultimately fades from view, the path lengthens, and still the hunter drives on, leashing and unleashing his hounds. The stag is generally replaced by a synecdochic image, the *vuoz*, the stag's

[46] Ernst Bethke (*Ueber den Stil Hadamars von Laber in seiner "Jagd"* [Berlin, 1892], 156–173) has given a good idea of Hadamar's range and variety.

footprint, while it is yet alive and the promise of its foot, a trophy of possession, if it should die. Moreover the slain quarry would offer the hunter and his hounds hope of *spîse*, nourishment, and so the *wilt* gives rise to a network of images based on hunger and food. Finally, the stag leads the hunting party to water, the brook of *leckerîe*. Because a deer generally took to water in the final stages of the chase, to assuage its thirst and cover its scent when utterly exhausted, the approach to *leckerîe* would seem to foretell the journey's end. Yet the *Jagd* makes *leckerîe* a false promise of refreshment to the hunter, a stream in which the quarry can play and float effortlessly while tormenting its pursuers. Because of the place *leckerîe* occupies in the hunter's progress—tantalizingly close to the hope of fulfillment of every kind—Hadamar contrives to evoke from this feature of the formal chase the suggestion, maddeningly misleading, of a promised crossing into a new realm of joyousness.

"Diu vart": Love's path

In the allegorical framework of a journey, where advances are plotted from stage to stage along a route, the path readily imparts a look of unity to the narrative: Hadamar's Minne hunter remains on the *vart* throughout the *Jagd*. In his continual allusions to the *vart*, however, the poet elicits a variety of meanings from it. Early in his adventures the hero is a vigorous, optimistic man with exuberant hounds like *fröude* and *wunne*. But the prologue sounds an initial warning that in love's pursuit a man may squander his years: "Whoever, for Minne, chooses a beloved for his delight, let him wait with care and watch, lest he lose his best years there [on the hunting course]" (4). The hunter reminds himself that he will grow gray on this journey (e.g., 109, 158) and that death itself will find him on the course (83). Even after death he may be engaged in hunting: "On earth, the body, the soul in the after-life, shall hunt eternally with *perseverance*, to what end no man can say" (568).

The *vart* is the course of a lifetime, but a life lived according to a single principle: it is the way of love and the traveler serves

Minne. Minne has indicated the path (8); the path can sweeten and embitter by turns (93, 266, etc.); it can console (257), and, because of the many trails crossing it, it can also bewilder (74).

The path of love runs through rugged landscapes, most of which, in ways not made explicit, emotionally evoke the hazards of the chase. Weather and landscape in the *Jagd* are chiefly of the sort to impede the lover. Here is no pleasance, no garden, but a harsh prospect reminiscent of the outer circle of Andreas Capellanus' afterlife of lovers, where fiery heat, desiccation, an earth-surface like an oven, and thorns punish those who did not grant love.[47] In *schalkeswald* one has to be wary of bottomless bogs (31), and dark and thorny hedges (41) into which quarry may creep. There are the brambles that scrape and thorns that wound before the hunter can reach the stag (93). There are the burnt-out places (*brande*, 130, 131, 508) where the dogs can seize no scent. The *vart* has teasing bends and twists (*bûge*, 452-3, *krumbe*, 406). The sun is hot and harsh, the weather intemperate (90, 446, 512). There is the brook of *leckerîe* in which good hounds drown. At the beginning of the chase, when the hunter is fresh, he observes the countryside sprinkled with flowers—and

---

[47] In the fifth dialogue, a nobleman tells a noblewoman of the torments in the afterlife of those who have rejected love on earth. He depicts a landscape to which *schalkeswald*, with its thorns and burning heat, bears some resemblance:

> The third and last part was called "Aridity," and with good reason for water was completely lacking, the whole place was arid, and the heat of the sun's rays was intense, almost like fire, and the surface of the earth was like the bottom of a heated oven. All about the place were innumerable bundles of thorns, each with a pole through the middle which stuck out a distance of two cubits at each end, and at either end of the pole stood a very strong man, holding the end of the pole in his hands. . . . There was a seat on a bundle of thorns prepared for each of the women [who had denied love], and the men assigned to each, as I mentioned, kept shaking the bundle so that the women were very severely torn by the sharp thorns; and their bare feet rested on the burning ground. [*The Art of Courtly Love*, tr. J. J. Parry (New York, 1941), 79–80].

the preserve full of hunters (28). These are his potential rivals. When he hears the birds' song, his eyes suffuse with tears, though like a child, he is unable to say why.[48] Nor is the landscape dangerous for the hunter alone: many a seemingly pretty field may in reality conceal a pit and a trap, covered over to catch the unsuspecting deer (216).

If the *vart* is the precarious way through lovers' country, it has nonetheless drawn a great many runners. The Minne hunter singles out the beloved's footprints from among the thousand there (340). The path is thoroughly trampled with coursing feet (104). There are indications that the path passing through *schalkeswald* is in some respects the world of the court, where one is crowded and jostled by toadies and meretricious seekers after favor. The hero fears those scoundrels who spoil good game by buying them, hanging gold around their throats (316, and cf. 344). In another instance, the poet interrupts the hunting action with an exclamation of pity for the poor, inexperienced lad who comes upon this course: "He is to be pitied; he must be deferential to the rude, sated ones. Whether dejected in spirit or afflicted by misfortune, how little a foolish, homespun boy ponders his harsh suffering" (507). We may recall Parzival's jostled reception when he first comes to Arthur's court. Hadamar may mean by this simply to convey love's bitterer realities—love bought, love scorned—but it is more likely that he intends to suggest the heady, ruinous atmosphere of a great court where knaves (*schalke*) sue for advantage. Certainly the Minne hunter feels angered and intimidated by his competitors who transact love, or whose methods are both unscrupulous and efficacious. In the hunt's terms, these cynical rivals strike down quarry which someone has already pursued and wounded, since they mean to feed their hounds at all costs. They lay traps and strangle deer, use poisoned arrows (46), poach, and break up quarry in out of the way places (546), roughly flay off hides (547), and

---

[48] Stejskal in his Introduction (xii), remarks upon the resemblance between this strophe (23) and *Parzival* 118.14–27, concerning the child's uncomprehending shedding of tears.

"swear false oaths" (213, 548). Does this figure, as Stejskal conjectures, refer to the luring call of the huntsman?[49]

Besides the possible meanings of the *vert* as the duration of love, the way of love, and a place where love is frequently met, the path is sometimes more narrowly identified with the beloved herself. The Minne hunter's first adviser, the shrewd gamekeeper, wishes him *ein edel fart* (a noble way), if he is to grow old with honor (53). He urges him not to hunt along a trail that someone else has begun, but to start a fresh one of his own (54). Right away *herz* is confounded and agitated by the sight of so many paths (55) until he discovers a special one apart from the rest. The hunter and *herz* are smitten with awe at the sight of this "path" (59, 60, 79). Later the old *weideman* inquires to make sure that the hunter has not stolen this path from anyone (200). But the Minne hunter has already turned away from paths upon which another hunter established his priority. How would he know this? According to the custom, as we have noted, the hunter strewed the path with broken branches (*brüche*)[50] to signal to others that he himself had unharbored the stag running there. The hero of the *Jagd* withdraws from paths so marked (*verbrochen*, 25), then eventually makes his own claim to a trail: "With a branch, quickly I strewed the path; in case any one should hurry there after me, I wanted to enjoy my hunter's rights there; whoever saw this branch would let me hunt further by myself" (69). The hunter's attention to his path, the *vart*, now in the sense of trail made by the chosen stag, becomes expressed through sight, touch and scent. What Hadamar may intend allegorically by these modes of observing the trail usual for a hunter, he does not make explicit. We are left to guess that a hunter scrutinizes his trail, as a lover studies his mistress' behavior and every gesture in an untiring effort to learn how she

---

[49] The practice is fully discussed in Dalby, *Lexicon*, s.v. *"blat,"* a term first recorded in *Parzival* 120. 13 to describe the child hunter's stratagem of whistling through a leaf to decoy his quarry. The word is not used by Hadamar.

[50] Dalby, *Lexicon*, s.v. *"verbrechen."* On the placing of these "brisïés" (OF), see Jacques de Brézé, *Chasse*, st. 5; *La chace dou cerf*, lines 164 f.

responds to him. Or, if the beloved's absence is significant, he may be assessing the signs and reports that inform him of her character and virtue. So, the hunter and his *herz* examine the path for "tokens" (MHG *zeichen*). There is the cry to watch the path: *hüete dîner ferte* (72), echoing Wolfram and Albrecht. More will be said about this below. What is too subtle for the eye must be felt with the hand. A hunter would place his hand in the footprints on the path, to judge their warmth, size, and depth; this technique was known as *greifen*. Hadamar has *"grîf in die fart,"* (42) as the hunter's instructions to his boy; he himself does this, as in 66, 77, 87, 340.[51] The identification of the *vart* with a person arises further from a remark of the old *weideman's:* St. Thomas had to touch the body of Christ (*er mit der hande | greif*, 256), a path full of tracks, in order to know that it was He. This is reminiscent of Wolfram's conceit—the body of Schîonatulander as a path in which Minne had left deep tracks—which may have been Hadamar's inspiration.

The most evanescent of tokens on the path is the scent that indicates whether or not the trail is the right one. A fresh scent (466) makes the pursuit easier; when the scent is cold the hounds become confused. Blood may freshen the scent, but no blood of this stag has been shed: the path is pure and clean: *wer sach ie fart sô reine?* 78). To get wind of the stag the dogs must flair out (*vervahen*) its presence: *"hâstu daz nicht verfangen?"* (80, and cf. 26, 84, 89, 610), the hunter asks his heart, and *"waz witert dich nû an, geselle?"* (57), "what do you scent?."

Perhaps the striking image of the freshening scent can be taken to signify the lady's granting encouragement to her lover, as in: "Now I hearkened to what *faithfulness* knew about my most beloved. The scent had freshened for him on the right track, and sweetly he gave tongue" (102). But the scent can also become a means of tormenting the hunter. Hadamar's Minne hunter groans repeatedly at the way the stag doubles on its traces, thus producing a strong scent that leads nowhere. We

[51] Compare *La chace dou cerf* (Tilander, ed., *Cynegetica* 7 [1960]: line 216) which describes this practice as "searching with fingers."

will recall the handbook accounts of how a stag would charac-
teristically turn and retrace its footsteps, then leap to the right or
left and disappear in the new direction.[52] Hounds in pursuit
would concentrate their efforts, mistakenly, on the doubled scent
which would, of course, suddenly stop short. The hunting party
thus would come to a temporary halt. The verb for the stag's
doubling at its normal pace was *widergân* (also appearing as a
noun, *widerganc*, in the *Jagd*, 80, 81, 87, 89, 266, 305, etc.).
When the stag doubled in flight, however—termed *widerloufen*—
it was said that he did so in a deliberate effort to mislead the
hounds (*Jagd*, 156, 202, 223, 314, 336, 406, etc.). These are the
"ruses" that madden the Minne hunter, and which Hadamar
compares to a woman's merciless teasing of her lover, when she
falsely "leads him on."

The hunter's attentiveness to the quarry's tokens conveys the
intensity of the lover's concern for the person of the beloved
woman. But he senses the need for controlling his eagerness.
Hastening along the course of his chosen love, the hunter engages in two conflicting actions: the one is the forward drive of
his chase; the other counters it with the forcible restraint he
imposes on his dogs, who are hungry. The pack's number and
unruliness[53] make it difficult for him to manipulate and direct
his hounds, especially since he is both urging them forward and
tugging them back by turns. So the hunter dramatizes the
dilemma of the lover, caught between desire and constraint.
Hadamar draws upon a fund of cynegetic verbs to tell of the
forward impetus and press both of hunter and hounds. There
are the verbs of pursuit, following the trail, or tracking down,
some with varying shades of meaning: *lâzen* (unleash), *jagen, ab-
jagen, ergahen, hengen* ("to follow the trail allowing the tracking

[52] The *ruses* (English, "doubling") of the stag are described in *Modus
et Ratio*, 1. chap. 22; Jacques de Brézé, *Chasse*, st. 26.
[53] This notion of the faculties out of control, the mind and soul in
agitation, Hadamar translated dramatically into the disunity among the
hunter's many hounds, who are perpetually scattering, being misled, or
else crowding and clustering. Compare the thronging multitudes that
squeeze through the gates in Prudentius' *Psychomachia* 665 f.

hound a free run at the end of his leash," according to Dalby),
hetzen (hunt or track down with the quarry in sight), *hinslahen*,
nachslahen, *vürslahen*, *vürgahen*, *vürgreifen* (to circle around in
a widening spiral in an effort to regain a lost scent). The hunter
engages in *blâsen*, *schrîen*, *ruofen*, and in imperative shouts to
stir his hounds forth: *lâ! hetzâ! hin! nâch! jagâ! jagâ nâch ime!
jû jû!*

Of the hounds themselves, Hadamar uses *suochen* (seek),
loufen (run), *abdreschen* (run upon, "thresh" a trail), *rinnen*
(swim), *vürgewinnen* (gain a lead from the other hounds), and
gives a vivid notion of their activity with *spüren* (scent), *snûrren*
(snuffle or wheeze while tracking), *denen* (strain at the leash),
kobern (run the trail in full cry), *klaffen* (bark excessively when
unsure of the scent), *ruogen* (grumble), *vervahen* (get wind of,
seize the scent), *wittern* (scent), *verniuwen* (find a fresh scent).
Gathering together such verbs in a serial line, Hadamar writes,
of the dog *herz:*

Ûfwerfen, schrîen, denen
mîn Herz aldâ begunde,
hinziehen[54] und anmenen. [57]

My heart then began to cast up its head, scenting the game, cry,
strain at the leash, pull away and lead toward the quarry.

and of the hunter:

Man sûche man lâzze, man henge,
man beize,[55] man iage, man schieze,
. . . . . .
daz lâ im guot swar in sîn wille wîse. [43]

However one may quest, unleash the hounds, follow the trail,
hawk, hunt, shoot, . . . let it content him wherever his will may
direct him.

[54] *Hinziehen* has the additional sense of "lying in the throes of death."
[55] Stejskal's reading: *man birs* (hunt with a bow) fits in the sequence
of the action better than does "hawking."

These and similar cynegetic verbs contribute to the sense of urgency impelling the lover toward his mistress.[56] On the other hand, the hunter exerts control with such verbs of strenuous attention as *luogen, hoeren, erblicken, wîsen, beschouwen,* and a variety of imperatives—*schônâ* ("soft"), *losâ! hoerâ,* and very frequently, *hüete!* Adapting the cry "Hüete der verte!" to his own use, Hadamar's hunter exhorts *herz* to watch the path and his, the lover's honor (72).[57] He twice determines to guard the stag's honor while sacrificing his own interests, and urges heart, the hound, to watch the beloved's honor (*hüet ir êren,* 97) above heart's own life. Later in the poem, the hunter makes it plain that protecting and "watching" the stag's honor means that he must turn *away* from the right path, hunting with the dog, moderation (*mâze*) and willingly paying the price (453). That "watchfulness" means the denial of sexual enjoyment, or at least a mistrust of it, emerges in several contexts. One who does not engage in hunting, the wily *forstmeister,* occupies himself in watching over deer so that big hounds will not harm them: "What is your means of diversion? Don't you hunt from time to time? 'No, I leave that alone; I guard the game against mastiffs' " [*ich hüet des wildes vor rüdischen hunden*] (45). Later, the memories of the woodsman make him pessimistic about the young hunter's prospects, and he urges the dogs to guard themselves against the destruction likely from the quarry: " 'Yes,' he said, 'it can cause grief; however beauty and steadfastness, intelligence and high birth may be combined, it's a sweet and poisonous gall that wounds many hearts: all of you young noble ones, guard

[56] Most of the cynegetic verbs do not seem to be assigned specific meanings in terms of the love allegory, except for *klaffen, schreien* (hounds' activities) and the like: these indicate a despicable boasting, or a failure to stifle murmurs of enthusiasm or despair when in the beloved's presence. Young *wille,* desire, cannot keep silent near the stag (63).

[57] Only in one instance does Hadamar make clear that the *vart* is the object of the verb *hüeten:* "Du hüete dîner ferte, / geselle, und mîner êren" (72). Otherwise he uses *hüeten* reflexively with a pronoun, as in "hüete dich" (70)—a usage like the French *gare à toi,* also addressed to the hounds (G. Tilander, "Nouveaux Mélanges d'Étymologie Cynégétique," *Cynegetica* 8 [Lund, 1961]: 161–164, 167).

yourselves before it' " [*iuch hüetet alle*] (225). An important prologue strophe, the one that introduced the hunting allegory, had already stated the danger of giving oneself over too impetuously to the joys of the pursuit, concluding with the warning of watchfulness: "How many hearts become hacked down in such a manner! A hunter must observe the path very frequently, lest he lose the trail while he tracks with his hounds; he has to be mindful of it. Therefore, you young ones, *watch!* (*hüetet!*) don't let your hearts run away too soon" (7). "Hüete" is in nearly all instances a restrictive motto: it is intended to hold the lover back from excessive joy or desire, both for the sake of his lady's chastity and his own well-being, lest he suffer punishment.

It is to the hounds, and especially *herz*, that the hunter bends with continual reminders of vigilance. Thus Hadamar's meaning of *hüeten* narrows, in contrast to Albrecht's, and even to Wolfram's usage. In their works the message on the hound's leash had addressed itself to the notice of good men and women at large, whom it instructed both in the morality of love and (in Albrecht) virtuous behavior in general. In the *Jagd*, it is only the hounds, the passions, who are so commanded. Even though Hadamar may have had in mind Wolfram's meaning and the wider moral significance contributed to the *hüete* cry by Albrecht von Scharfenberg, his use of it applies specifically to the lover's eagerness, and terror in the face of this eagerness, both for the beloved's sake and his own. When the stag eludes the hunter, or *herz* is impatient, the Minne hunter cries "*hüete dîn*" to the hound in order to be able to follow the path (62, 81, 89). Most of the time, however, the man anxiously schools his heart or other faculties, to silence and restraint. His caution is inspired by fear, both of external dangers and of the excesses his hounds may commit. For example, he urges watchfulness in the presence of spies and gossips (68, 72, 133); he warns the hounds not to let themselves be heard (70, 569); he is relieved that his unfed dogs can "watch" themselves in the stag's presence (112). *Hüete* also appears in conjunction with *êre*, and the meaning of honor is defined as sexual restraint in the *ende* strophes (see p. 191f above). An ideal pair of lovers would be *"ein mûtmacherinne / und ein êrenhüetaere"* (298)—the woman, a source of spirit, and the man, her guardian of honor.

Hadamar, in short, makes the theme of hunters' watchfulness applicable exclusively to love, usually sexual love, and does not seek to embrace within its possible meanings a whole code of ethical or religious behavior. Indeed, *Hüete* is a key word which is used to brake the hunt's perpetual forward-hurtling movement along the *vart*, the unfed eagerness of the hounds, and the hunter's passionate commitment to an irresistible course.

"Band, mîner staete riemen . . . .": Love's Leash

Significantly, *"hüete"* is the opening word of the *Jagd* in six of the mss., and it is this first strophe that also introduces the hound's leash. Hadamar does not say that the guiding principle, *"hüete,"* is inscribed upon the leash; perhaps he wished to make a clearer separation between the leash and the warning than had Wolfram and Albrecht.[58] Like the *"hüete"* warning, the hound's leash has frequently a restraining function. The leash's symbolic development, however, is richer and more various than is that of the commanding cry. Hadamar's opening strophes employ the leash in the two senses of the bond of love and the bond of control. Thereafter, he repeatedly comes back to his theme of the bond, diversifying it with questions of obligation, of bondage, of release, and with images of entanglement, constriction, and, finally, in an extreme and surprising form, of strangling. This last image recurs both in an impatient threat and as an expression of fear, involving everyone by turns—rivals, dogs, stag, hunter. Can we say with certainty that Hadamar intentionally makes his patterns of constrictive imagery dependent upon his initial strong apostrophe to the leash that holds his hound *heart*? Whether he wished his audience to recall the leash each time he wrote of binding or strangling is difficult to judge. Certainly the way was prepared for such an exaggerated development of the leash by

[58] Dalby (*Lexicon*, s.v. *"strange"*) has pointed out that *hüeten* is used just twice in a context with *strange:* strophes 1 and 62.

Wolfram's *brackenseil:* misused, it became a destroying fetter. And we should not forget that the language of binding in the lyric of Burkart von Hohenvels, discussed above (p. 168, f.), adumbrates the image of the huntress's net: "With her strength she binds me. . . . Her bonds [*diu bant*] have achieved a power that a griffin's claw could not pry loose. . . . Her beauty casts a net that means to capture [my] thought."

In the *Jagd*, the leash works to generate a pattern of images that ranges from the conventional *seil* to the curiously distorted replica of it which Hadamar has fashioned, the noose. To turn to the *Jagd*'s opening strophes:

"Hüet alweg dîn, geselle!"[59]
des wis ot staet gewarnet,
ez welle swar ez welle.
Vil manig lieb mit leide man erarnet.
Diu halse dich ûfhalte fur vergâhen,"
sprach ich ze minem Herzen,
dô ich ez an die strangen wolde fâhen. [1]

"Watch your path always, *mon amy!*" Be steadfastly attentive to it, wherever the stag may wish to be. Love most often is won with sorrow. Let your collar prevent you from going astray," I said to my *heart*, when I wanted to fasten him to this leash.

Band, mîner staete riemen,
ein sloz der mînen triuwen,
die mag enpinden niemen
in lieb, in leide, in fröuden noch in riuwen.
Ez ist gebunden und wirt nicht enpunden. [2]

Bond, harnesses of my steadfastness, a chain of my faithfulness, which no man can unfasten in love, in sorrow, joy or grief. It is bound and will not be unbound.

[59] I have used the ME custom of addressing the hounds hypocoristically with *amy* or *mon amy* to render *geselle*. See Tilander, *Cynegetica* 8 (1961): 136 f. For example William Twiti's *Craft of Venery* has: "ȝe shalle sey thus 'howȝe, amy, howȝe, venes y, moun amy'" (52), and the *Master of Game:* "He shalle say þus to hem here, How amy, how amy," (103).

How emphatic Hadamar is with his reiterations and lexical variations, determined that his audience shall catch his point!: the *halse* (collar, or neckband), *strange* (cord, and leash), *band* (leash, and bond), *riemen* (harnesses), *sloz* (chain, bolt); his verbs of restraint: *ûfhalten* (hold back), *fâhen* (leash); and finally the grammatical play upon *band, enpinden, gebunden, enpunden*. The hound's leash is first a means of disciplining his heart, keeping it in line, preventing it from committing errors, And secondly, strophe 2 enlarges the meaning of the disciplining leash to show that it is the bond of love, by which the lover's heart becomes willingly submissive to his mistress. The same bond engages his constancy and fidelity, qualities that are soon to feature as hounds in the chase.

Elsewhere in the poem, too, the leash is an instrument of discipline. When the inexperienced Minne hunter meets the *forstmeister*, his first adviser, he hastens to promise that he will unleash his hounds in so temperate a manner that his hunting will not violate any of the regulations of the game park or molest any quarry or any other hunter (44).

Significantly, when he meets one of the "bad" hunters, the hero is shocked to see him with his rapacious hounds all unleashed (*mit hunden abgelâzen*, 411). The hero shouts to him to couple his hounds so that he may hunt the abundant game properly: "*fâh ab, fâh ab dîn hunde!*" But the unscrupulous hunter with his unleashed hounds looks to seize upon quarry that is wounded or near the point of death, worn down by a predecessor!

Keeping his hounds well leashed in is one of the Minne hunter's perpetual concerns, especially *herz*, when he pulls with excitement. When *herz* becomes confused by the sight of different trails, he has to be recalled to the singleness of his devotion for the beloved woman to whom the hunter had, in the beginning, pledged his constancy with the leash: "My *heart* then began to snuffle after various paths. But I knew how to tug him back firmly by giving the leash a quick snap" (55). In this instance the leash becomes a corrective, even a chastening device. Not long after this, when *heart* eagerly presses after the stag,

having found the right track, all the poem's tension between
desire and restraint becomes momentarily absorbed by the leash:
"My heart on a taut leash strained upon the track" (74). In
agitation, when the quarry is near, *heart* casts off the restraining
leash: "A losing gain became my portion at this moment. My
heart tore away from the leash on which I had bound him fast;
I never more had power over him" (120). *Heart's* breaking from
the leash spells misfortune: "In order to leash up my heart, I
struck out after him on the course; the greater was my pain!"
(124); "Only wretchedness for the poor body who's not in
command of his own heart!" (125). *Heart's* crowning mishap,
once he has thrown off the leash, is that he is wounded by the
stag (121). The purpose of the repressive, disciplinary leash is
to preserve the virtue of the lady; breaking it calls forth the
infliction of a punishing "wound."

The leash may seem to tighten joyously around the lover in
a moment when he feels great emotion—deaf, sightless, lame,
and mute at a sight upon the path (61, 62). Yet in a despairing
mood, the lover conceives of the leash as an instrument to torture
Lucifer himself—the binding of Satan known from the apocry-
phal gospel of Nicodemus:

> unmût die sêle senket
> hin dâ Lucifer lît an dem seile. [135]

> dejection of spirit sinks the soul down to the place where Lucifer
> lies chained.

The lover's sense of painful enlacement becomes transferred to
a net so constricting that it seems to unman him and dry the
body's sap: "In a net of yearning [*in selenîchem netze*] / my heart
has become entangled. Will that now make my body void of green
sap, like a dry stump?" (375).

In an extreme form, the binding image gives way to thoughts
of hanging: this would be a preferable fate as the weary lover
declares, to harsh, life-long, unfulfilled yearning (149).

Even more acutely does this image become incorporated in a

terrible lament of the Minne hunter's soon after his dramatic renunciation of the stag, when he might have taken it with *ende:*

> Ich gib ouch nieman schulde
> dann mir und dem unheile.
> Swaz ich darumbe dulde
> daz ist billîch, wann mit einem seile
> solt man mich, ungelückes boten, henken,
> der sack ze wâpenkleide
> zaeme mir, darinne wol ein gaehes trenken. [366]

Also, I blame no one but myself and my unlucky portion. What I endure because of it is simply as if I—messenger of misfortune— were to be hanged on a leash cord; the sack [over my head] would suit me for armor; indeed, within it, a violent gulp [I'd drink]!

Here the poet puns on three hunting terms which can also apply to the plight of the hanging man: his *unheil*, ill-luck, refers as well to the hunter's lack of a portion; *seil* doubles for the hangman's rope and hunter's leash; and *sack* can be both the net used in the hunt and the sack covering the eyes of the dying man. In a characteristic interlocking of metaphors, Hadamar closes with the agonizing "draught" of a strangled man—the air for which he struggles inside the sack. As for the deathly drink, this motif will recur in the images of thirst and slaking, culminating in the perilous brook of *leckerîe.*

Non-metaphorical statements and queries about the bond of love occupy Hadamar from the beginning of the *Jagd*, at moments when the allegory is dropped. The lover, for example, calls his lady's attention to her part of the bond: their attachment: she is bound (*gebunden*) to guide him "graciously to grace" (172). The Minne hunter raises questions about the nature and dura- bility of the bond. Somewhat rhetorically he asks the gamekeeper (when the latter attempts slyly to direct him to easily capturable deer): "Where is love without sorrow? Where is the steadfast bond that never becomes undone? How are behavior, speech, and action shaped, when true love and constancy have knit up a true bond with fidelity?" (35). A similar question, whether a steadfast heart may ever free itself of love's bond, arises in the form of a love case: "Ladies, knights, squires, I ask you all together: may one [lover] rightly be free who cleanly broke away? Does this break release the bonds of the other one who was faithful? Who can unbind a steadfast heart from true love, and keep it from dying?" (522-526).

The bond of love is an image, in fact a theme, recurring generally throughout the *Jagd*. Inasmuch as this same image (both in its divinely ordained, and in its constricting, earthly senses) pervades the widely read and translated *Consolation of Philosophy* of Boethius, it is tempting to speculate that the Boethian image was as accessible to the literate Hadamar as it was to Chaucer in the next generation. Chaucer's almost obsessive use of the Boethian image of binding has been amply demonstrated,[60] though unlike Chaucer's, Hadamar's distinction between honorable and dishonorable bonds is, of course, related to the order of Minne rather than to marriage.

What Hadamar has done with the theme of the bond of love is to embody it in the equipment used by the hunter. The bond of love undergoes a significant transformation when conceived as a leash. Leashing in the *Jagd* means the controlling of sexual appetites. Hounds like *herz* and *ende* are leashed punitively, or become wounded, when they are too impetuous. Hunters who promiscuously slay quarry to glut their hounds hunt "unleashed," or advocate that the Minne hunter unleash his own crucial hound, *ende*, so that he can feed his pack. While the Minne hunter can actually punish his own hounds for their excesses, or see them punished, the only way he can deal with his rivals is to wish on them an utmost form of the leashing they failed to perform—strangling.

In reprisal for their continual harassment of the game in *schalkeswald*, the Minne hunter mutters curses and threats

---

[60] Thomas A. Van, "Imprisonment and Ensnarement in *Troilus* and *The Knight's Tale*," *Papers in Language and Literature* 7 (1971): 3–12. It may be added that the bond and snare images are not limited to these two works of Chaucer's.

against his rivals. Of the passing *knecht:* "I threatened repeatedly to hang him" (359); of a competitor loudly blowing his horn, hence interrupting the hero's pursuit: "Someone hunts with his horn. Let him hang for it!" (320); of those despoilers of quarry: "I thought, you murderers should be hanged" (317).

As for his own hounds, the virtuous, restraining leash placed around the neck of *herz* in the poem's opening strophe finds a strident echo in the leash flung with an imprecation around the throat of *ende*; it is the cord with which the hunter drags him from the prey: *ein seil warf ich im dô an sînen kragen* (345). As the hero later exclaims to a fellow hunter, concerning *ende:* "I would have hanged him sooner than allow myself maliciously to think of slaying the quarry with him" (417).

The Minne hunter himself is not immune from the threat of the cord. The bond of love may discipline the lover, but his declared devotion to the bond and the leash undergoes a series of changes. He begins to suffer thoughts of strangulation, of the drying of his body's sap; he transfers his own plight to the vision of Lucifer lying leashed in Hell. The poet has taken this symbol of love's fastness and continued to turn it over and over until it begins to deteriorate in positive value and reveal more sinister aspects of entanglement, constriction, and death.

Finally, the stag too becomes endangered by the cord. It is as if the lover's growing uneasiness and resentment toward the bond becomes transformed into an irresistible impulse—though it is expressed as a fear—to contemplate the stag in the same straits. For the beloved woman, after all, has been the cause of the agonizing bond. Thus the leash that enlaces the lover gives rise to a new image, even though not logically connected with it: the snare that confounds the quarry. Lascivious pursuers, themselves *un*bound by any code or scruple, are an ever-present threat to all quarry, which they would choke or strangle. The Minne hunter deplores those fawning courtiers who hang their gold around the good deer's throat, who take pains to sniff out where the game runs and discover who is choking it or driving it down (316). Evil hunters drive their quarry with mastiffs and seize them in nets (213). Others clandestinely lay traps in hedges they have prepared, where a noble deer may strangle[61] (321). Again, a perversely cruel mode of amusement is proposed by the young, interfering *knecht:* to tie up the stag to pass the time (*lât uns ez binden,* 351). The mortal danger of the *brackenseil* which in Hadamar's sources brought death to Schîonatulander and scars to the hands of his lady, here implicates every participant in the *Jagd:* hunter, rivals, hounds, stag.

A concluding strophe to the *Jagd* echoes Wolfram's episode of the *brackenseil,* whose end Sigûne sought to read and so untied:

> Ein ende diser strangen
> mit frâge nieman findet.
> Si sol dahin gelangen
> aldâ der tôd mîn leben underwindet.
> Alhie der lîb, diu sêle dort sol iagen
> mit Harren êwiclîchen,
> dâvon dem ende nieman kan gesagen. [568]

> No one finds an end to this leash by asking questions. It shall reach as far as the place where death overtakes my life. The body shall hunt here; in the hereafter the soul shall hunt eternally with perseverance. The end of it no man can tell.

The opening image of this strophe is that of a greatly lengthened leash cord, stretching from the present on into eternity. Does the poet want us to visualize the hunter bound to the leash, his heart fastened irrevocably to the other end of it? Are we to see it knotted in such a way that it can never be undone? Or is it a trailing leash that the Minne hunter, like Schîonatulander, must pursue until his death, thus signifying the endlessness of his love quest? Or again, is it a lifeline that he, like Theseus in the labyrinth, must grasp until it leads him out of this world and into the next, where the hunt must continue? The image is an

---

[61] Dalby, *Lexicon,* s.v. "*hecke,*" makes it clear that not all hunting authorities agree with Hadamar as to the ignobility of the *heckjäger's* methods—that is, setting snares within hedges that were artificially constructed for this purpose.

elusive one;[62] yet several meanings seem to emerge from it. The leash from the poem's beginning strophes signified both the lover's bond to his lady, and his decision to hold his impulsive heart in check; in other words, he engages himself in chaste submission to the beloved woman. Both the bond of love, and the terms on which it was first formed, then reaffirmed in the course of the poem, are now said to be perpetual. The impossibility of terminating the bond "with questions" is perhaps meant to remind us, too, of the simplicity of the formula in *Parzival:* a right question that would magically heal a wound and long years of malady is not, in this case, available.

A second meaning is possible, one that would hinge on the Sigûne episode in *Titurel:* it is the endless search for the "story's end." The leash end here, hidden from view (as it was from Sigûne), keeps the conclusion of the Minne hunter's story from ever being revealed. The love story will remain unsolved; it is unending like the leash, because of the lover's vow never to possess the beloved lady. Unconcluded, the narrative merely ceases on a note that reaffirms the bond of love while life shall last, and forecasts a mysterious, persevering chase for the soul in death. Perhaps, finally, in the recurrence of *ende* in the first and last lines, a somberly uncertain note is sounded, a dying reverberation of the consummation theme. Formerly a hound of love, *consummation* has been leashed, hence withheld forever. "No man can tell" what the end, the new consummation of that ghostly hunt will be when love's hunt is over.

The path and the leash were already laden with meaning for Hadamar because of his acquaintance with Wolfram and Albrecht. Hadamar both intensified and altered their meanings, adding enormously to the significant value of the *vart* and the *seil* with his profound technical sense of the hunt, so that both became capable of accentuating the complexity of "true love" and the deep tensions that divide the lover. A further group of

---

[62] Dalby, *Lexicon:* s.v. "*strange,*" proposes taking *strange* in this context to mean "riddle, allegory," but this interpretation does not take into account the extraordinary visual and sensory quality of the image.

images that merits scrutiny is one which depends upon the stag, its importance and behavior in the chase. Hadamar appears to have had no developed literary precedents for the images of *fuoz* (foot, also footprint), *spîse* (food), and for the brook of *leckerîe* (splashing), but to have spun these out in detail from the hunt directly and from his knowledge of its procedures.

"Daz wildeclîchez wild": The Elusive Stag

Why should it have seemed appropriate to the poet to represent a beloved woman as a male deer ?[63] One suggestive feature of the stag is its majestic head, and Hadamar, like the author of *Li dis dou cerf amoreus* before him, does not miss the opportunity to mention the antlers. The deer's antlers, MHG *prîs* (literally, "trophy"), and *krône*, the very top points, provide apt puns for the worth and crown of a lady:

> Für sîn gehürne schône
> [stêt im gar wirdeclîchen]
> ein goldes rîchiu krône
> treit ez. [85]

Above his lovely antlers—worthily it becomes him—he bears a gold and precious crown.

Hadamar goes further, wresting another conceit from hunting procedure. One of the first signs the hunter observes of his stag, as evidence of its nobility, are its "frayings" upon a tree—torn leaves, scraped bark, broken branches[64] at a height that indicates the stag's size and value:

[63] There are the symbolic possibilities of regality offered by the "head" or "attire" with its "crown" or "surroyal-top." I am, furthermore, indebted to Professor Maurice Valency for the suggestion that it perhaps would not appear strange to a medieval audience, any more than it did to those attending to Provençal lyrics, to hear "my lady" called "my lord": *midons*.

[64] The stag would rub away the "velvet" from the newly erupting antlers. See, for example, *Modus et Ratio* I, chap. 5 (*"freoirs"*); *La chace dou cerf*, lines 457 f. *Phoebus*, chaps. 28, 30; *Master of Game*, chap. 3: "þei fray here hornes to þe trees. . . ."

Ich tar nicht wol gesagen,
wann nieman mirz geloubet,
wie hôch ez hab geslagen
des hôher prîs ist immer unberoubet,
daz ist ein zeichen wîsen und den tôren.
Al nâch her, sicherlîchen,
ez tût kein hinde mit den iren ôren. [86]

I dare not say exactly, since no one believes me, how high the stag
has struck—never has it been divested of its lofty antlers; this is
a token [of excellence] to the wise and the foolish. Certainly no
hind could reach as high with its ears.

The stag's "lofty antlers" are also its "high worth." The hind
cannot aspire to the stag's heights, either physically or morally.
The distinction between hind and stag continues throughout the
Jagd, to the hind's disadvantage. In fact, in the *Jagd* and many
of the poems imitating it, the stag represents a splendid though
inaccessible woman, while the hind is game that can be captured.
The creature that the Minne hunter observes, limping, wounded,
much hunted, is a hind (426). Later in one of his self-revealing
asides, the hero confides that he could not have endured such
hardships on the hunting course and kept alive, if God had not
granted him a tame, compliant deer (490); then he goes on to say
that for diversion he would be glad to learn to make his way with
a shy hind, ignobly, like a *schalc:* "For sport I'd gladly learn to
ride with a shy hind in rogue's fashion" (491). Female of the red
deer are *huore* ("whore") and the colloquial *dinc* ("thing"),[65]
the latter a word which, in other contexts, has the added meaning
of "genitals". Although the recorded usage of these words,

[65] Dalby, *Lexicon:* s.v. *"huore," "tier."* Cf. the discussion below, pp. 234f.
The shameful aspect of the wounded *hind*, as distinct from the stag,
appears to be constant. The figure recurs in Spenser, perhaps intentionally to stress the disgrace of Duessa who feigns love for Christ,
referring to herself as:

A virgin widow whose deepe wounded mind
With love, long time did languish as the striken hind. [*Faerie Queene*,
1.2. 215–216]

referring to the hunt, is later than Hadamar's *Jagd*, the terms may have been known to him and provided him with the source of his distinction between stags and hinds.

"*Der zarte vuoz*": The Sweet Foot

Not only is the stag of the *Jagd* elusive: it is generally nowhere to be seen. Flight and evasion are its principal actions, and these actions preoccupy the hunter from the beginning of his quest. He soon connects the fleetness of the stag with his own state of mind. "Whither will the stag glide that would liberate us from longing cares?" (21). In a love poem in which the beloved is scarcely ever in view, the poet has devised images of the foot of the stag and the footprint it makes. The foot—*fuoz, schal, hand*—would be a trophy signifying sexual conquest of the lady. The Minne hunter expressed his unwillingness to denude the foot of honor (350), when he decided to hunt but never to capture the stag. He therefore can only long for the foot, which synecdochically represents the stag as the stag symbolizes the woman. Almost never seen, the foot, finally, is represented in turn by the footprints (also often *fuoz*, as well as *zeichen*, and *insigel*). The hunter now invests the footprint with a value that is almost fetishistic; it is an object of worship, and once it fades from sight, the hunter despairs: "This I lament to you, Lady Minne, sweet lady; Will I and my heart, my companion, still gaze upon a footprint that will indicate the right trail?" (537). Hadamar makes the footprint the most prized token on the *vart*, an eloquent sign of the lady's worth and uniqueness as well as of her various powers—to bless and gladden, even more, to inflict injury, and to secure her lover's devotion permanently. The Minne hunter acknowledges that he has singled out these footprints from among the thousand on the path (93, 340). He notices the sureness and nobility with which the deer must have stepped; if an emperor had wanted for his diversion to pursue this quarry the trail would always be plain and he would never lose it (64). The footprint is capable of bringing joy or woe. When first the hunter places his hand in the footprint on the path, he learns that here passed a creature that might enrich one's joy or impoverish it (66). He recognizes in a pathetic fallacy the bliss of the land on whose earth her [*diu liebe*] beloved foot rests: *saelig sî diu terre | alda ir lieber fûz die erde rüeret* (92).[66] But that same foot has a *schal* (hoof), and the hunter marvels, too, how finely this hoof can cut the path he watches so lovingly and so fearfully: "No leaf or grass blade is so delicate but it must be rent by the stag's hoof" (78). This prepares us for the manner in which the stag may affect the hunter's heart: "However the hard ground of misfortune and burning hot suns deprive me in my longing of the trail, even so I can recognize the footprint: it has imprinted itself in my heart" (90). "The stag has struck my heart and trod there, so that my mouth gapes wide" (91). A steel shaft releases itself from her foot (91): the foot of the stag has performed the function of the arrows of love! Small wonder that immediately thereafter *heart*, the hound, thinks the beloved's mouth might also injure and thinks it might be well to destroy the stag's teeth before attempting a kiss: "I wanted certainly to destroy his teeth because my mouth in kissing his hard to the bone had to draw back." With the treading of the stag in the lover's heart and *heart*'s fear of the stag's sharp teeth, the poet introduces the first of his trenchant, painful images expressive of love's pangs. The stag injures *heart* at the bay (*verwunden, verhouwen*, 121, 122) and the lover feels Minne's anchor sunk in his heart (123). Later when his weariness mounts he turns from this conventional image to a more vehement one: "the stag sticks like an axe in my heart!" (497). Then it is Minne's awl that pierces him through (539). With another hunter's term

[66] For this commonplace, of which there are many examples, see P. Dronke, *Medieval Latin and the Rise of the European Love-Lyric*, 1:173 and 178n., e.g.:

I envy you, fields: you will learn to love!
You happy beyond measure, blessed abundantly,
you on whom she'll leave the print of her snowy foot—[*Lydia*, from the *Appendix Vergiliana*]

or,

Happy the earth that you tread white-footed.[from *Anthologia Latina*]

for the footprint, *insigel*,[67] Hadamar can pun on "true love's seal" (*daz insigel staeter minne*, 36), and thereby achieve an image reminiscent of Burkart, when the hunter beholds a sight on the path that becomes painfully sealed upon his heart.

"Dîner güete spîse": The Food of Love

Cherished an feared, the footprint can wring emotion from the Minne hunter although it is merely a shadow of the foot, itself a trophy of conquest. Yet while the hunter appears resigned to worship the foot from a distance, he also has the whole stag urgently in mind as a source of nourishment for his hounds. Like the severing of the foot, feasting the hounds on the stag is another of Hadamar's metaphors of sexual possession. Rewarding the hounds was never the principal object of the chase; but the Quarry *was* performed as a matter of course, and according to medieval handbooks, and to Tristan of Parmenie, it was to be done correctly and with ceremony. Because the hero of the *Jagd* will never countenance the Quarry, the "bad" hunter exclaims somewhat justifiably that he is maltreating his hounds: "In my lord's country the master of the hunt would never engage you as his varlet" (418). To avoid the unreasonableness of declaring that good hunters do not capture game, Hadamar resorts to naming those hunters villains who poach, strangle quarry, and pursue "damaged" game all for the sole purpose of feeding their rude hounds. Food and feeding thus become an issue in the *Jagd*:[68] the hunter's hounds are hungry, but the thought of

[67] A full definition of *"insigel"* is the "imprint of a deer's foot in soft ground, with a lump of earth turned over in front of the imprint," (Dalby, *Lexicon*). The imprinted image as a feature of medieval love poetry is discussed in D. W. Robertson, Jr., *A Preface to Chaucer* (Princeton, 1963), 109.

[68] Once again, Hadamar adapts a widely used amatory commonplace, that of love's food, to the circumstances of the hunt. For example: "O Fotis, how trimly, how merrily, with shaking your hips you can stir the pot, and how sweet do you make the pottage. O happy and thrice happy is he to whom you give leave and licence to dip his finger therein." Then she, being likewise witty and merrily disposed, gave answer: "Depart, I say, wretch, from me; depart from my fire, for if the flame thereof do

devouring the beloved stag becomes another source of anxiety to the hero. When in *Li dis dou cerf amoreus*, the hounds were made to bathe in and feast upon the blood of the quelled stag, the poet could assert in a simple manner that *Amours* has been harrying the stag for the express purpose of feeding them (11. 298-300, see above, p. 153). But this expected climax of the love chase is for Hadamar the material for an image through which he can express the lover's need and his guilt—the food (*spîse*) the stag promises the hounds if ever it yields up its life. The hounds look forward to be fed (*geniezzen, neren*), but are destined to go hungry, as their master tells them, so long as the beloved—not the stag in these lines—withholds any nourishment more substantial than mere virtue: "You are, after all, unfed, unless her goodness alone feeds you" (82). *Heart*, the hound, longing for a kiss, would wish to nibble the stag's sweet muzzle forever (95). *Wille* runs tirelessly ahead of all the others; he

---

never so little blaze forth it will burn thee inwardly, and none can extinguish the heat thereof but I alone, who know well how with daintiest seasoning to stir both board and bed" (*The Golden Ass: The Metamorphoses of Lucius Apuleius*, tr. W. Adlington, rev. S. Gaselee [Cambridge, Mass., 1965], 60–61).

Chaucer tends to regard the erotic-culinary predilection with humor, as in Januarie's

"Bet is," quod he, "a pyk than a pykerel,
And bet than old boef is the tendre veel."

or, in a *Balade to Rosemounde:*

Nas never pyk walwed in galauntyne
As I in love am walwed and ywounde.

and Absolon's:

"I moorne as dooth a lamb after the tete."

Gower takes up the figure with the cooking pots "of love buillende on the fyr / With fantasie and with desir" over which reigns Thought, the cook (*Confessio Amantis*, ed. G. C. Macaulay, 2. 913 ff.).

Hadamar, on the other hand, seems entirely and painfully serious. His use of the commonplace may be illuminated by such discussions of the infantine or filial lover in medieval literature, as Maurice Valency, *In Praise of Love* (New York, 1961), 32, and Heinrich Möller, *Journal of American Folklore* 73 (1960): 39–52.

could be urged on, fed like the hounds in *Li dis dou cerf amoreus*, by a look: "Hey, how he would run again, were he nourished by a loving glance" (113). "He may feed yet if he runs up to *luck*'s relay station" (114).

When the hunt allegory is momentarily put aside, the image of love's food is extended to the beloved woman. The hunter himself feasts richly on consolation (152); sometimes hope offers food (244). He begs the lady to allow him to be nourished by her, spiritually: "I know I am quite unworthy of your worth. So let me feed on that alone; toward you I am undesirous of unlawful desire" (177). And, in a similar vein, he utters: "If you don't wish to show favor, may you nourish my heart with a greeting!" (479). But when *heart* breaks from its leash and is wounded by the stag and by Minne's anchor, the lover suffers and is heard to groan: "I said, 'if I make a profit from *this* bargain, and feed for long on this food, I may well consume my youth here without joy and solace!' " (124).

But these diverse banquets of the mind serve merely to replace the hunt's true object—the quarry. The Minne hunter willingly acknowledges genuine pangs of hunger for the game he pursues. He longs for food like a hawk, or even a raven that circles the place where quarry is being prepared and thrown to the hounds: "For the food of your bounty I cry like a hungry, preying hawk" (175). "Natural desire, like the raven, hovered over the hounds. He, too, wanted to have his share if it could be captured" (529).

Yet the prospect of a feast of love which the quarry offers does stir uneasiness within the Minne hunter. He confesses, at the poem's turning point, that he is eager to devour the quarry— unroasted—but for the pain it would cause (350). Distaste and anger inform his account of how large hounds surreptitiously slay and consume quarry in hidden places (163), how poachers feed their dogs on wounded game (547), how a "bad" hunter urges him to hunt with *ende*, a hound he says has fed quite often "on the hide" (*auf der hiute*, 415). The unprincipled hunter, by alluding explicitly to the custom of arranging the hounds' dainties on the flayed hide of the stag (OF *cuire* < *curée*, quarry), succeeds in making visually grisly the metaphorical comparison between sexual consummation and the hounds' feasting. In the Minne hunter's view, all such gluttonous feeding depends upon "murder" (419, 163, 355). There are even those rakes who would steal each others' "food." In a passage on *geselleschaft*, friendship, Hadamar conjoins three metaphors to deplore the greed of the uncomradely: the game of chance, the love of sweets, and an empty bag, a reference to the hunter who ends up without a portion.

> Whoever would, in all games of chance, pick up [winnings] without laying down [stakes], play tricks, have stolen tidbits without observing temperance; whoever wants to snatch sweets in an arrogant, uncomradely way—is it his comrade's fault if at the end his bag becomes empty? [399]

The game metaphor indicates those lovers who play to win, hoping to risk nothing; by means of the *genäsche-naschen* images, the poet expresses his dismay at those amorous gourmands who dishonorably steal their friends' girls; and finally the empty bag betokens the portionlessness of any Minne hunter who would engage in such dishonorable tricks. False lovers are eventually losers.

Finally, the image of *spîse* recurs in a culinary metaphor (509), in which the lover imagines himself and his lady engaged in cooking a repast. What he would boil (*versieden*), she would roast (*brâten*), she who is given to lordly procrastination!

Hadamar is the only poet of the love chase to develop the notion of the Quarry of love so specifically and so extensively. But love's food and love's kitchen, as conceits, are well known among medieval writers. There is a brief, ecstatic, reference in *Wigalois* to the food of the beloved's favor—*"dîner minne spîse"*— which fills the lover with a sense of being in Paradise.[69] In clear contrast to such an attitude, however, Hadamar wishes to amplify the image of *spîse* as quarry to evoke the sense of the lover's deep

[69] *Wigalois, der Ritter mit dem Rade* [ca. 1210], von Wirnt von Gravenberc, ed. J. M. N. Kapteyn (Bonn, 1926), 409, lines 9654–60.

ambivalence, rather than joy, gratitude, or humor. His suppliant and dependent position places him in an infantile relation to the powerful lady who feeds him on goodness and hope alone. But he suffers guilt and terror over his wish to be fed more substantially, and to feed his hounds, lest he may hurt or maim the stag, the beloved woman. The choice of the hunt metaphor produces and confirms these anxieties: quarry is eaten. His sustenance, as he eventually confesses, must come from a tame *wilt* that nourished him in secret (490). Perhaps this detail actualizes the maternal relationship of deer to man, whereas the stag—"mother of tender spirit" (*zarten mûtes mûter*, 138) can be expected only to give spiritual food. Otherwise it must yield up its life.

Leckerîe: The Wiles of the Beloved

As a complement to his feasting and culinary images, Hadamar has developed a system of imagery associated with heat and thirst. The source of the heat may be Minne, felt by the man who engages in this kind of hunting: "On the gridiron of hot love a man must begin and end the chase, where it [the stag] is locked within a pure heart." It is, moreover, the beloved who radiates that killing heat which only she can assuage: "Pure, clear, bright, translucent, you can wither my heart. But also your solace bedews it" (176). As love's physician, too, the lady is a source both of cooling dew—her loving glance—and warmth for the chilled invalid, with her lips (473).

In connection with the love chase, it is the Minne hunter and his hounds who feel the heat. *Heart*'s burning is compared to that of earth baked and cracked (additional strophe 605). The hunter wishes he might enlist *Amor*'s help, along with *faithfulness*, the hound's, to drive the stag to such a run that it would feel a kindred heat (151). Then there might be hope for the hunter, for presumably the stag's heat would draw it to the water where both stag and hunter might be refreshed. The old *weideman* makes such an observation: "You hunt in a Minne-hot sun; you'll broil in it unless the stag cools you in joy's brook" (191).

The beloved's refreshment becomes expressed as *kiss*, a hound that is "like a hot iron plunged hissing in a cold stream" (356). We may recall the well-irrigated terrain of Andreas' afterlife of fulfilled lovers. Hadamar's allusions to heat and thirst contribute to the sense of adventure associated with the brook of *leckerîe*. With this feature of the *Jagd*, Hadamar refers to the stream of water usually sought by the stag when extremely harried. Hadamar devotes the better part of twenty strophes (427-447), with some interpolated general comment, to *leckerîe*, a stream to which a stag would entice an entire hunting party and threaten the very lives of the pursuers. Stejskal defined *leckerîe* in this instance as "Schelmerei"—playfully dishonest behaviour—and E. E. Hese notes that both Wolfram and Albrecht employed *leckerîe* in the sense of immoral or lascivious conduct.[70] Dalby's *Lexicon* entry for this word, containing examples only from Hadamar, suggests that earlier scholars have missed the poet's intention which was probably "soiling," from *lecken*, to moisten. Thus *leckerîe* must mean the splashing of the stag. While the cynegetic definition is certainly plausible, it becomes clear from Hadamar's strophes on *leckerîe* that in his characteristic punning

[70] Hese, *Die Jagd Hadamars*, 83, citing *Willehalm*, 193. 25 and *Der Jüngere Titurel*, 229, 250, 439.

Old Low Franconian *likkon*, "lecken," to lick, passed into Latin in the forms *lecacitas, lecator, leccaria* (F. Blatt, *Novum Glossarium Mediae Latinitatis* ab anno DCCC usque ad annum MCC). The earliest occurrence of *lecator* in medieval Latin is in the work of the eleventh century satirist Sextus Amarcius, *Sermones* (ed. Karl Manitius, *MGH*, Weimar, 1969), III 933, IV 409, according to the research of Professor B. Bischoff, who kindly permitted me to refer to his paper, "Living with the Satirists," delivered April 11, 1969 at the King's College, Cambridge, Conference on "Classical Influences, A.D. 500–1500." J. F. Niermeyer (Lexicon Minus Mediae Latinitatis), makes the following distinctions among its various forms: *lecacitas:* gluttony, impudence; *leccaria:* dissipation; *lecator:* gourmand, drunkard, lecher, also wheedler; *leccatria:* gluttony. Tobler (*Altfranzösisches Wörterbuch*) gives the following meanings under *"lecherie":* daintiness, fastidiousness, "lickerishness"; a dainty dish; lasciviousness, debauchery; jesting, deceit, false pretences. The MHG *lëckerîe*, which must have passed back into German from OF, is defined in Lexer (*Mittelhochdeutsches Handwörterbuch*) as lasciviousness; rascality; gourmandise; buffoonerie; toadying.

fashion he has incorporated the moral meaning as well. Once a
hunting party is brought plunging into the water, men and
hounds are, as in the *Jagd*, in mortal peril.

The reader is first informed of *leckerîe* when the hound *luck*
(*gelücke*) is brought forth (11): he must be managed with care,
we are told, lest he lead the hunter straight to the perilous brook.
A fuller account comes much later in the poem. The Minne
hunter has turned away from that reprehensible rival who feeds
his dogs on wounded quarry, only to discover that the pursued
quarry has unscrupulous ways of its own. A few paraphrased strophes from the *leckerîe* passage will convey Hadamar's meaning:

> Game that is started in *schalkeswald* will fly swiftly to the water,
> no matter who is pursuing. *Leckerîe* has a great many rivulets;
> whoever wants to drive the game from there, must indeed know
> [true] companionship. [428]

> Many a hunter gets his saddle soaked thinking to follow the trail
> through the water. There his heart becomes submerged in an-
> guished weeping so that he curses his lot. Many a man who has
> hunted with *faithfulness*, and then lost the stag in *leckerîe*, laments
> that he was ever born. [429]

> Anyone who would abide in that water only a little while—how
> many a lord's hounds he would see there beside him in the brook!
> *Leckerîe* has become well known to the quarry from many a wood,
> and that gives me and many unfortunates cause for anguish. [435]

> Running in full cry upon the trail, *perseverance* must make fresh
> discoveries there: in the mocking waves, the hound glides out of
> sight so that he might be blinded. I don't think any one of the
> three—old *perseverance*, the whelps, *desire* and *endurance*—can
> escape *leckerîe*'s swift current by swimming. [437]

Although in an actual chase the stag sought water to save its
life, this event in the *Jagd* becomes the stag's practice of care-
lessly tormenting its pursuers. The awful attractions of *leckerîe*,
its false offer of refreshment after the heat of the chase, its
damage to hounds and hunters, the guile of the stag that plays
there at no risk to itself (except for the few that aren't quite

skillful enough), the importance of luck—all these reveal Hadamar's intention: that *leckerîe* is a woman's frivolous, teasing promise of favors. *Leckerîe* is a flirtation in which she can for the most part easily "float" while her earnest wooer flounders and "sinks." This realization brings the fervent outburst from the Minne hunter:

> I wish with all my heart that the eyes of good women could see, without distress, the secret of [mens'] hearts in all their love-longing, and would fully recognize their intentions. Then the good would be shown to the good and the impure would be avoided. [441]

Why must the cruel, provocative rusing of the stag, romping in *leckerîe* for its own amusement, be engaged in at the expense of the most faithful and loving of pursuers? *Leckerîe* is in a sense the final affront. The Minne hunter has been determined in abiding by his pure vows—to hunt without hopes of capture—only to be rewarded by the prospect of the stag's teasing him in this brook. The association of water with such unhappiness is prepared for in the poem. Both before and after the episode of *leckerîe* Hadamar uses the imagery of deep or flooding water to express uncertainty and despair. The old *weideman* exclaims: "My memories enable me to sink my fluttering heart in lamentation's pool" (229). The lover himself dramatizes the rapid play of his emotion with images of water:

> Ah, how I dam up the flood of my sorrow, whenever I, in my thoughts, conjoin my love and me with true constancy. [503]

> But then the dam of all my joys becomes turbulently flooded, and the tide of cares swirls my joy away. [504]

> Amid sighs my heart mounts again in my breast, but unhappily it cannot long stay afloat, it sinks down again, freighted with cares. [533]

In addition to this imagery of unquiet water, the occasional allusion to unwholesome drink—the drunken glee of the murderer of game (547), the terrible quaffing of the hanging man

(366)—lends support to the sense of perilous refreshment which the brook of *leckerîe* develops most fully.

In an actual pursuit the soiling of the stag indicated its weariness, hence its readiness to be taken; so the whole troop's plunge into the stream marked a penultimate stage of the chase. The crossing of the water, though dangerous on occasion, held out the likelihood of the hunter's triumph on the farther shore. In the *Jagd*, *leckerîe* is perceived when the poem is two-thirds over. This is the water that would appear to separate the longing hunter, coursing through a wilderness in which hunger and thirst have been his principal share, from the other bank upon which, according to usual expectations, he might soon become "one" with the stag. The anticipated winning of the quarry has found expression throughout the *Jagd* in terms of gaining nourishment and refreshment, assuming a self-yielding and benign woman. The Minne hunter's descent into the water, and his emergence with all his hounds, would betoken his passage to a new condition of fulfilled love. His conquest of the food-giving stag, his union with the beloved, would constitute his restoration to the state of bliss of a child who is fed.

Leckerîe's waters divide the Minne hunter's state of want from one of anticipated fulfillment. In addition, *leckerîe* appears to be itself a life-giving well. The beloved has been identified as the source of *fiuchte*, moisture, that slakes love's thirst, just as she has meant the lover's nourishment, both material and spiritual. The plunge into *leckerîe* might be expected to culminate the *fiuchte* imagery, since, as the old *weideman* informed the hunter, he is doomed to broil unless the stag should cool him in joy's brook (191). His immersion in *leckerîe* would form an intenser parallel to an earlier erotic image, the plunging of a glowing iron into a cool stream to effect the hissing of a kiss (356). If the hunter can cross the refreshing stream with the stag, he may hope to be nourished on the far side by its *spîse*. Given the actualities of the chase—the conclusion of which is heralded by soiling, and given the emotional landscape of the *Jagd*, we might expect an ultimate union (like that envisioned by an ecstatic

Mechthild) between hunter and quarry on a distant shore, a union to which the very entering of the water is a promise.

This never takes place in the *Jagd*. The gushing forth of *leckerîe* is a lying tale. The significant experience that pervades the *Jagd* is the continuing denial of sexual love. A most important aspect of the poet's account of *leckerîe* is that he does not take his Minne hunter into the water as he has conducted him all along the *vart* in *schalkeswald*. What he gives us instead is the hero's grieved and cynical musing by the side of the water: "je meurs de soif auprès de la fontaine." On *leckerîe*'s verge, the Minne hunter engages in reflections upon what happens to those who do follow the stag into the water. Every stag in *schalkeswald* knows how to run there quickly and easily and will entice its pursuer to the stream. In the view of the Minne hunter, immersion in those waters brings about not fulfillment of the chase, but despair and dissolution: a hunter loudly laments, his saddle is soaked, his dogs may drown or be blinded in the waves. Above all he acknowledges the stag's betrayal: instead of looking toward a "new life," rebirth to the embraces of a nourishing beloved, the unfortunate weeps that ever he was born. In the world of the *Jagd*, where the expectations of normal love (and normal hunting) are subverted, the woman is a perfidious destroyer, deriving sustenance from the element that sinks her wooer, just as the stag may float in *leckerîe* while the hounds battle the current and go under. Reflecting thus, the Minne hunter does not in fact enter *leckerîe*; for him the distant shore will never come into view. Instead, the poet edges away from this metaphor and substitutes a new one, *triege*, the hound *deceit*. Now it is *deceit* that nuzzles the hunter, misleads him into new regions of despair, and *leckerîe* is left forever.

In contrast to the deceptive waters of *leckerîe* is the tangle of *schalkeswald*, a forbidding, masculine world in which rivals are brutal and successful, and where would-be friendly counsellors do not encourage the consummation of the love chase. The *forstmeister*'s business is to protect game from rude and hungry hounds; he looks askance at "easy prey." The most spiritual of the counsellors, the *weideman*, urges the hero to give up the love hunt altogether, to follow the track of God. Through this wood whose terrain is fatiguing and whose inhabitants are, at the worst menacingly efficient and at best out of tune with the Minne hunter's desires, there runs the path. Seemingly it leads to whatever may be good in *schalkeswald*—joy's brook, or the stag that provides food. However, both objects are demonstrated to be impossible: to taste the food he craves makes the hunter a murderer; to enter the water confirms to him the ruinous perfidy of the beloved quarry.

In fact, the path leads nowhere. The *vart* comes finally to suggest the journey's futility. Remaining upon this track is the hunter's sole destiny. It is a course upon which he must forever engage in two opposing labors that re-enact the dialectic of Minne. These labors annihilate each other: one is the onward drive toward a hopeless vision; the other is the imposing of restraint with the leash that threatens to destroy life and manhood. The Minne hunter's purposeless coursing, alternately driving and withdrawing, finds a parallel in the single striking gesture of the stag that recurs most constantly, the *widerganc* and the *widerlouf*, its perpetual tracing and retracing of its footsteps. As stag and hunter run back and forth in an endless courtship, the whole journey comes to dramatize the denial of sexual love in a collection of remarkably apt and timeless images. Hadamar has contrived to divert the pattern of the chase from its normal end of fulfillment, and symbolically, of initiation, and to force from it an expression of forbearance. The journey is all the more arduous since the conventional contraries relating to love, which in Minnesang reside in the mind, have here been writ large into a narrative as act, and located in time on a path of lasting pain.

Epilogue: After Hadamar

Germany

The grand scale of the *Jagd*, and the complex effects, both verbal and psychological, that Hadamar achieved, mark the high point of the allegorical love chase. While love poets everywhere continued to exploit hunting conventions and figures, their attempts were more modest than Hadamar's and generally less original. Those writing in German or Dutch appear to owe their inspiration directly or indirectly to him, tending as they do to isolate some feature of the *Jagd* to develop in briefer compass, though occasionally with touches of individuality. Their work can be grouped under three heads: the lyric, the didactic and the altercative. Poems of the first type include those in which the narrator voices joy, hope, or despair about his amatory hunting, reflecting thus the large segments of the *Jagd* given to such emotional utterances. In the didactic group, discourse or instruction displaces much of the hunting action, or all of it. Guides appear, frequently allegorical huntresses such as Minne or one of her accompanying virtues, to give counsel, either of a general amatory nature or in hunting practice, notably in the use of the allegorical hounds. Here the rôles of the several counsellors from the *Jagd* tend to be expanded so as to form the main business of the poem. Works in the third category, the altercative, dwell upon the typically Hadamaresque strife among rivals: two hunters employ different methods, one with "good" hounds, the other with "bad" ones, and these compete with varying success.

Lyric poems

Three representative lyrics may be mentioned here, each of them distinct in tone: the tender *Daz gejaid* of Peter Suchenwirt (d. 1395), Hugo von Montfort's (d. 1423) exuberant *liet*, and the wry, anonymous *"Ich bin eyn bracke vp rechter vart."* Peter Suchenwirt's lyric[1] falls into four parts, each unified by an idea or a set of related images. The narrator labors in a chase with *love* (*lieb*), his hound that can run over stone and timber, while *trôst*, his huntsman—the lover's hope of consolation—races far ahead with his *hertze* tightly leashed (8-24). The poet shifts to a conceit of the storms that watchers cause, storms that bedim his mistress's eyes and his own, and that interfere with hunting:

> Two storms bring me heavy sorrow: when I am eager for hunting, bad weather comes unhappily to me and ruins the gold of high spirits. One storm is *tattle* (*meld*) that makes my strong joy falter; the other is *spy* (*merk*) from which I endure much sorrow. It brings fog and rain and ruins many of my hours. I call therefore to my hound, *"love, love,* leave off your hunting until fine weather comes to us. *Tattle* and *spy* are storms to blind shining eyes that ought to see with fourfold glancing . . . ." [25-42]

He returns to the chase; the hunter listens anxiously to the shouts of others who pursue the small elusive deer flying through the thickets. He plods on himself in hopes that Lady Joyful (*vraw selde*) may appear to free him of sorrow (43-55). At the last he begins to despond; yet he ends on a new note—if only the deer would grow tame for him! (66). Here is a possibility that changes the aim of the hunt with its usual predicament of a guilty hunter that "murders" game; it offers instead a wish for reciprocal love between the man and a gently acquiescent creature.[2]

---

[1] "Ich hör die weisen sprechen," 66 lines, ed. Felix Bobertag, *Deutsche National-Literatur* 10, *Erzählende Dichtungen des späteren Mittelalters* (Berlin and Stuttgart, n.d.), 162–64.

[2] The tamed deer motif recurs in Spenser's "Lyke as a huntsman":

> There she beholding me with mylder looks
> Sought not to fly, but fearlesse still did bide:
> Till I in hand her yet halfe trembling tooke,

Hugo's *liet*,[3] full of animation, celebrates the healthy joys of the *Minne jäger* without any of the familiar regrets or laments. Its three 10-line strophes are linked by the refrain: "Loosen the leash, let [the hounds] run on; I am eager for the chase. In this will I persevere: May it succeed for us!" The hunter gives a confident account of his sport: his methods are noble, he courses with horse and hounds (*ich jag gar fürstlich über land*, ii, 7). He engages in no trapping by night, no stalking. He offers advice, however, to the uncaptured deer to be wary of game preserves where other men may set their nets for lecherous purposes, tying them to hedges and rough thorns and hoping to ensnare quarry that hasn't its wits about it. His own hounds in the *"überlant" jagd* are, first, his desire (*will*), bliss (*wunn*), and fidelity (*trüwe*). To one of these he addresses the exhortation to "watch the path" (*"gsell, huet der vert"*, 3. 7)—an echo of Albrecht and Hadamar. The deer is young and inexperienced at rusing in a side leap; in fact, it knows nothing of the chase as yet (*umb jagen ist im och nit kunt*, 3. 9). He ends the verse by saying he will nevertheless uncouple his hound *perseverance* (*harre*). Hugo's song reflects the *persona* of the self-absorbed lover, sounding, however, a note of sanguine optimism quite unheard in earlier hunt allegories.

The lugubrious and weary laments of the older poets, on the other hand, come in for a share of satirical treatment in the fourteenth century-*Brackenjagd*[4] if we accept the judgment of

---

And with her owne goodwill hir fyrmely tyde.
Strange thing me seemd to see a beast so wyld,
So goodly wonne with her owne will beguyld.

And cf. the final couplet in Wyatt's "Whoso list to hunt," where the inscription on the hind's collar reads:

Noli me tangere for Caesar's I ame
And wylde for to hold: though I seme tame.

[3] "Es ist mir nu beschehen zwir," ed. Paul Runge, *Die Lieder des Hugo von Montfort mit den Melodien des Burk Mangolt* (Leipzig, 1906), 25; Hans Naumann and G. Weydt (eds.) *Herbst des Minnesang* (Berlin, 1936), 36–37.
[4] David Dalby, ed., "Two Middle Franconian Hunting Allegories," *Medieval German Studies Presented to Frederick Norman* (London, 1965), 259–61: "[I]ch bin eyn bracke vp rechter vart" (46 lines).

Dalby, the editor, that the role of the scenting hound here is a
phallic one, and that "the bawdy content is concealed skillfully
within the ambiguous framework of the poem . . . [which is]
intended as a parody of the many other hunting allegories of this
period." The brachet opens the poem, declaring that he has been
running up the right track. He addresses his plea for a reward to
a most glorious woman; instead of describing her as quarry, he
claims: "I never saw a lovelier person, since I pursued a footstep."
Alas, she is far ahead of him, farther than from here to Rome. He
begs her to wait—to a good hound the way will not seem too
great. Alternating hopeful cries with laments, the hound concludes his monologue with: "If only she would offer me a kiss
with her little red mouth, I would run to the death." At this point
the lady speaks to the huntsman, perhaps viewing this impetuous
hound with some alarm: "Master huntsman, leash up your
hound." In the dialogue that follows and ends the poem (33-46),
the lady protests, but the master praises his hound: no frost or
snow can stop him, nor any bridge; he can swim over any water.
The lady's last words seem to betoken encouragement: "I think
there will be no doubling ruse: let him run, perhaps honor will
come to him."

Altercative poems

The fourteenth-century *Jagd der Minne*[5] (478 ll.) and the
"Königsberger" Jagdallegorie (316 ll.)[6] center upon the disagree-

[5] J. M. C. Lassberg, ed., *Lieder Saal, das ist: Sammelung altteutscher
Gedichte* (St. Gall, 1846), 209-307.

[6] Karl Stejskal (ed.), *Zeitschrift für deutsches Altertum*, 24 (1880), 254-
68; later edited again by Fritz Schultz, *Festschrift zum siebzigsten Geburtstage Oskar Schade* (Königsberg, 1896), 233-237.

We may also include under the altercative allegories of the love chase
the Dutch "Ene beschedene Jacht" of Jan Dillo (C. P. Serrure, ed.,
*Vaderlandsch Museum voor nederduitsche Letterkunde, Oudheid en
Geschiedenis*, [1858], 2:151-6): A noble lady invites the poet (*Ic*) to a
place "where we shall be well received"; it is a forest where they see a
glorious lady playing with her hounds. A company of men and women
are about to hunt at her direction. The hounds (allegorical) are named.
The poet's guide explains: the lady is called Justice (*Gherechticheit*).
The hounds find a hart and bring it *te bile*. A hunter with six hounds

ment between hunting methods upon the preserve of love: a
"good" hunter endures misadventures as he finds himself
threatened, interrupted, or supplanted by a rival whose hounds
represent dishonorable qualities. The normal struggle of the
chase, that between hunter and quarry, becomes displaced to
the two hunting rivals. In the *Jagd der Minne* (*"Ich wolt jagen
durch frien mut"*), the hunter who tells his tale admits that he has
pressed after other *hinds* before he found the *deer* that was
runnable and sweet (*waidenlich und zart*, 46), one after his own
heart's delight. But his hopeful efforts with a pack of good
hounds—all of them to be found in Hadamar's *Jagd*—meet with
frustration as he runs into a *heck jäger* with his evil pack,[7] and
his net and snare (*netz und sail*, 145 and *passim*) with which he
sets traps across constructed hedges. The two dispute, the "hedge
hunter" taunting the narrator for his lack of wits and his child-
ishness in being willing to chase "über lant" (157 and *passim*)
without winning anything. The narrator attempts to shame and
berate his rival. They part, but the competitor's hounds mingle
with the good hunter's, confusing him by their barking, and
enraging him. He is chagrined to observe that the unscrupulous
rival shouts to his hounds and uses his horn in ways that are
maisterlich and *waidenlich* (311, 312). Yet he returns bad manners
with good, remaining courteously silent (hating himself for it),

---

renews (and disturbs) the chase. Justice follows with her pack, and
laments that the hunter—Injustice (*Onrecht*)—has interfered. The six
hounds of *Onrecht* are named: *Scone-Groete* (fair-greeting) is the *leithont*,
then come *Wankelmoet, Loesheit, Loghenaere, Runen,* and *Scalc* (vacilla-
tion, looseness, liar, secret murmuring, and rogue). The poem ends
with an injunction to virtuous men and women to hunt with Lady
Justice.

I am indebted to Peter Dronke for this account, as well as for the
references to the Dutch poems in n. 10 below.

[7] The good hounds are: *wil, lieb, trost, har, stät, trü, trur, zwifel, müge,
fröd, mase.*

On the other hand, the *heck jäger* ("I have more hounds than you,"
line 151) gives chase with *unverswigen* (his lead hound), *valsch, drieg,
unstätt, trüwe, losz, wanckel, nid, kall, rüg, schand,* and *schalck; rum*
joins the pursuit later.

while the formidable rival hunts noisily on his course. The deer is brought to bay (399), but as the *heck jäger* and his hounds close in with a big net,[8] the deer leaps high and escapes. This turn causes the interloper to roar and beat himself while the narrator laughs. Encouraged, he will press on with his good hounds, not knowing whether he will ever win a portion.

In the Königsberger hunt allegory (*Haet ich ze jagende sinne guot*"), a "bad" hunter, full of regret now, actually tells his own story: how with false hounds he quelled a hind that had been already hunted by an unsuccessful "good" predecessor. How had he come to such a pass? First, as an observer of a virtuous hunter's failure: that man now lay on the ground weeping and lamenting sorely having given futile chase for ten years with *trost, triuwe, stête, harre*. Hiding in a hedge, the narrator over-hears *ein wîser man* giving advice to the earnest and portionless hunter urging him to hunt instead with *zwîfel, wenk*, and *falsch*. When the wretched Minne hunter rejects this expedient—threatening to run after his counsellor and pluck out his hair—the eavesdropper decides to try his own luck. He finds the false dogs readily enough, and allows them to strike the same hind. "I took the deer in a net; my portion fell to me easily without any trickery. Yet it was painful to me, the unseemly thing that happened there." At once he catches sight of Minne and her company riding by. The hind takes alarm. The "bad" hunter

---

[8] The *heck jäger's* hunting style and his sinister glee are meant to evoke the ways of the devil, who sought to ensnare his victims with net, noose and trap. A lost soul in *Der jüngste Tag* cries, "der tüfel hat mich geseilt," as Adam too had lamented, "Belgibuz tient jà la corde pour moy fort lier et estraindre" (cited in F. Mone, *Schauspiele des Mittelalters* [Karlsruhe, 1846], 1:296, 268–69). In a poem called *Des Teufels Netz* a dialogue occurs between a hermit and the devil, who has a following of seven knights, *hoffart, neid, hass, frass, zorn, unkeuschheit*, and *mord*. The hermit asks the devil where his knights are so that he can avoid their nets and snares:

Das ich mich kunn warnen
von iren striken und garnen. [K. A. Barack, ed., *Bibliothek des literarischen Vereins in Stuttgart*, Vol. 70 (Tübingen, 1863)].

now complains to Minne, recapitulating the story with words of sympathy for the luckless man who had hunted before him. Minne and her son agree with this judgment that man is to be pitied; but Minne's son expresses his further view that the hind, not the false hunter, is blameworthy. She should be driven down and both her eyes put out, presumably for her "blindness" to her pursuer's merits. The rest of the poem is taken up with pious thoughts, expressed with homely force. If only such counsels had never been given! As for those who do give them and corrupt the innocent, let the devil carry them off on a spear, far away from earthly folk: "Since this charlatanry is come indeed into the world, make a tent for it, Lucifer, I pray, as it is appropriate, and strew it within with straw and dung, and tell your mother that she should give them fisticuffs for fodder!" The poem has a tri-partite structure: the "good" hunter's lament over not winning; the chase; the "bad" hunter's lament that he *did* win.

Didactic poems

Advice or discourse concerning the love chase receive primary attention in *Die Jägerin*, a fragment of 87 lines,[9] and the fifteenth-century *Die verfolgte Hindin*.[10] In the first work, the poet is not

[9] "Wil gy weten wo myr ghescach" (15th century), D. Dalby, ed., "Two Middle Franconian Hunting Allegories," 255–259.

[10] Adelbert von Keller, ed., "Die verfolgte Hindin," *Fastnachtspiele aus dem fünfzehnten Jahrhundert*, Bibliothek des literarischen Vereins in Stuttgart, Vol. 30, Pt. 3, (Stuttgart, 1853), 1392–1399.

In a similar tradition of didactic allegory are the Dutch poems, "Her Erentrijc, die haet geleden" (110 lines) and "Dit is van der hinde" (344 lines), both in *Die Haager Liederhandschrift, Faksimile des Originals mit Einleitung und Transkription*, ed. G. F. Kossmann (Haag, 1940), 32–33, 104–107. In the first work, Lord Erentrijc rides to a field, and meets a hunter. His hounds are *wille, moet, geer, denke, troest, heerde*, and *rast* (will, courage, desire, thought, comfort, obedience and repose). *Erentrijc* has two companions, Lords *Blijscap* (joy), and *Goetcompaen* (good companion). They see a knight and a lovely lady beneath a tree, each with a leadhound in hand. These two are perfectly equipped for the chase: her hound was called *trouwe*, his *stede*. The hunter uses these, and the lords talk of matters of love, hunting, and chivalry.

Dit is van der hinde shows the poet entering an enchanting wood where he finds a beautiful lady beneath a tree. He greets her, and they

himself a hunter but an observer and pupil. Riding forth into the wood he hears the sweet yelping of hounds, and encounters there *vrouwe stede* with her pack. In response to his questions she explains that she is pursuing *daz wilt*, whom she declines, however, to name precisely.[11] She then tells of her five pairs of hounds and their functions: *leyfft* and *lust* (love and delight), *troest* and *waen* (consolation, confidence), *tzwiuel* and *hoffen* (doubt and hope), *herden* and *helffen* (persevere and help), and *heelen* and *hoden* (concealment and watch, i.e., "huëten"). The last part of the poem exhorts to virtuous behavior anyone who would hunt such quarry, and urges the avoidance of "evil-willed hounds" (*vnwillegen hunden*) that go into deep mountains and thick hedges.

The various kinds of wisdom received by a hopeless hunter in *Die verfolgte Hindin* (lines unnumbered) tend to urge him *away* from the chase of his beloved deer. There is a wistful quality about the poem, unique too in its winter landscape and its delicate praise of a girl-like hind (ignoring now or perhaps forgetting the disparagement of hinds in the earlier German allegories). The poem opens:

---

talk of love. She urges him to hunt and shows him the right path. On this he finds a hind of the greatest beauty, tries to approach it, fails, and returns to the lady for advice. She suggests he take a pack of allegorical hounds. He pledges himself to *arbeyt*, she advises him how to use the hounds, and to hunt modestly (*Nu jach als een besceyden man!*). He asks, What is your name? And how shall I distinguish between the various hounds? She answers: the forest belongs to my lady, Venus, the park is called *Venus-velt*; I am *Minne*, her daughter. The hind must be hunted first by *coenraet* (bold counsel) and *hoefschermont* (fair speech), or else she flees to *schemelhorst* (the copse of shyness?). She tells the functions of the other hounds and concludes: see that you hunt rightfully, so that the hind is preserved—if she met with misfortune, you would be to blame.

See above, n. 6.

11   Sin name iss l m r,
        Ich enkaen dirss nyt ghesagen mer. [65–66]

Dalby, p. 258, proposes "l'ameir" for the cipher, echoing Gottfried's three-fold pun in Tristan, 11986 ff.

The wood has lost its leaves
and robbed are we
of small woodbirds singing;
one sees no more little blooms
springing upon the heath.
The little deer must seek and find
their grazing places with great effort.
It is the cold snow's doing
that troubles the ease of many hearts.

Riding out into the wood, the narrator is struck by a *mynniglich* hind whom he describes like a lady, with her bright clear eyes, her soft throat, firm breast shaped for delight, her slender and elegant legs, her *two* slim and arched feet, and finally the noble crown upon her head. If only he had a garden in which to keep her! But the would-be Minne hunter feels himself inept in the use of hunter's jargon, he has set no nets in hedges, he has no hounds, and when he falls from his horse, he is as heartsick as a broken-necked man and his laments increase.

His advisers are of two sorts: the allegorical ladies who appear to him, and later a wise old man. Without ado, *fraw stette* tells him to be steadfast in the love of God, never departing from this if he would grow old happily and be prepared for the day of Judgment. *Trew* advises fidelity, though not specifying to whom, in order to ward off sorrow and heal pain. *Ere* urges him to hold his dearest love in honor: in this he shall find peace. The old man's advice centers upon hunting first, though not of the hind. He suggests that the unsuccessful hunter take up hawk and hound in an effort to forget the hind that has caused him such pain. But as the hunter finds himself unable to follow these counsels, he consults the old man a second time. Now, says his adviser, he ought to have a painter do the hind's portrait. Sleeping and waking through the night, the lover reflects upon this. In the morning he rises, rides out upon the hunting track, still thoughtful. There at last he espies the deer on the heath. As he gazes he receives her lovely impression pressed (*gedruckt*) upon his heart—a figure reminiscent of Hadamar's *insigel*, the sealed footprint within the lover's heart. The concluding allusion to a "portrait" echoes the description of the girl-hind early in the poem.

Do the wintry landscape, the wish for a garden, the hunter's sense of ineptitude and lack of gear, together with the directives of the allegorical ladies—to think on God, last things, a happy old age, to keep his love in honor—suggest an elderly lover repining for a young girl?[12] Before actually going in pursuit of her, he had uttered the wish for a garden in which to keep her, while at the poem's close he prays that "Maria heavenly queen" may watch over her heart's desire and keep her from all sorrow. The hunter's sense of tender protectiveness toward the dainty girl-hind contrasts utterly with Hadamar's poem, where the hunter sighs and weeps for a strong, elusive stag.

France

La Chasse of Octovien de Saint-Gelais

The actual hunt of Octovien's poem, printed in 1509 by Antoine Vérard,[13] is preceded by an elaborate prologue in

[12] The dainty quality of the deer and the landscape, residing in such diminutives as *füsslein, beimlein, tierlein, plümlein, kleinen waltfogelin*, share in the convention, found notably in the lyric, of the miniature. (Cf. André Moret, *Les débuts du lyrisme en Allemagne* [Lille, 1951], 258).

[13] Bound together as a single volume, entitled *La Chasse et Le Depart d'Amours*, this incunable (Bibliothèque Nationale, Vélins 583) is in fact a collection of separate poetic pieces. One of these is *La Chasse* (folios Di r⁰–Li r⁰), a self-contained work whose hunt is not alluded to in *Le Depart d'Amours*, following immediately afterward. Six courtly political and moral pieces on the troubles of France, not taken into account by the book's title, precede *La Chasse*. The works contained are, in this order: *Plaings de la France*; *Complainte d'Arras*; *Plaintes de Justice et de la Paix*; *Hymne à la Paix*; *Le livre des vices et vertues* (a treatise of advice to princes); *Le debat du Seigneur de Court et du Seigneur des Champs*; *La Chasse*; a collection of rondeaux, ballades, and triolets which form the conclusion of *La Chasse*; and *Le Depart d'Amours*. This last work is a separate allegory; its principal villains are *Oblivion, Absence, Aage, Manage, Prison, Religion* and *Maladie*, none of whom have the final force of *Mort* in causing the departure of Love.

There has been a controversy over the authorship of the book or

the aureate diction of the late Middle Ages. The poem opens:

> Au temps de ver qu'est saison taciturne
> Doulce et paisible: gracieuse nocturne
> Que les estoilles cleres ne sont point cabres
> Phébus luysant / Aurora et Saturne
> Et que d'yver / froidure diuturne
> Au paravant / a enseiché les arbres
> Lonc admortis / semblant plus froictz que marbres
> Enveloppez un peu de seicheresse
> Sans liqueur estre pour tout vray seicher est ce.
>
> [D i rº]

of parts of it. The title page attributes the whole book to two men:

> La Chasse et le depart damours
>
> faiet et Compose par reverend pere en
> dieu messire Octovien de /
> sainct gelaiz evesque dangoulesme et par
> noble homme blaise da /
> vriol bachelier en chascun droit demourant
> a Thoulouze. /
>
> Cum preuilegio

Exactly in what relation Octovien de Saint-Gelais and Blaise d'Auriol stood to one another and to the pieces in the book, is the subject of the dispute. L'Abbé H.-J. Molinier (*Essai Biographique et littéraire sur Octovien de Saint-Gelays, Évêque d'Angoulême* [Paris, 1910], p. 194) demonstrated that a great number of the lyrics were taken from Charles d'Orléans: he suggests that Blaise d'Auriol, publishing the work seven years after Octovien's death, added the plagiaries. A. Piaget had expressed the view that Octovien actually wrote the *Chasse* and plagiarized passages from Charles throughout the poem as well as in the lyrics ("Une Édition Gothique de Charles d'Orléans," *Romania*, 21 [1892]: 581–596; and see Piaget's note appended to Emil Picot's article, "Une Supercherie d'Antoine Vérard," *Romania* 22 [1893]: 254–260). It was the opinion of Henry Guy that the whole book, including *La Chasse*, was a confection got together by Blaise d'Auriol and Antoine Vérard, head of the well-known printing house from which the book was first issued, and that it was falsely attributed to Octovien (*Histoire de la poésie française du XVI siècle*, Vol. 1: *L'École des Rhétoriquers* [Paris, 1910], p. 155 ff. and see Picot, Ibid., pp. 244 ff.).

In addition to Vélins 583, there are three other copies of the Vérard edition known to be extant (see John McFarlane, *Antoine Vérard* [London Bibliographical Society, 1900]). These are British Museum C. 34 M. 16; Chantilly 1739; and Fairfax Murray 493. After the first folio edition of

Phoebus in his brilliance forces the burgeoning of all Nature: liquors, honeys, balms and waxes are followed by butterflies, flies, larks, nightingales, violets, roses, princes, dukes, emperors, popes, and burghers, who swarm out of the earth as it were, in response to that beneficent heat. The author—*l'Acteur*—then explains how he, hard and dry as a nut, and saddened by winter, contains within himself the germ of an idea. As he walks in a pleasant orchard his winter-roughened spirit responds like the rest of the earth to the sun's virtue, which causes the germ to blossom finally into a great tree of erudition.

A *cerf amoureux* is being held prisoner in the sombre *Forest de Gracieulx Désir*. The chase in Octovien's poem takes the form, therefore, of a rescue. In the forest there are two forces, the one composed of *Amours*, the Queen of Love and her followers, holding court at the *Chasteau de Plaisance*, the other of her churlish enemies lurking in the *Buisson de Tristesse*. It is *Dangier* and his consorts who have stolen the *cerf amoureux* around whose neck the Queen's heart is suspended. The Queen laments.

Meanwhile a Perfect Lover (*L'Amant Parfait*) sits sighing in the little orchard, with three close companions, *Cueur Liberal*, *Ardant Desir*, and *Bon Confort*. Metaphors of the chase begin to occur: The Lover feels enmeshed in love's nets and fillets (*rethz et las*, E iv r⁰); *Cueur Liberal* urges him to remain unswervingly true to the Lady who has his heart tightly leashed without deceiving her (*qui vostre cueur | fermement tient en lesse sans la ruser*, E v r⁰).

Antoine Vérard, other houses reprinted the book in cheaper quarto editions. Of these the Bibliothèque Nationale possesses four, none of which bears a date. Three of these (Rés. Ye. 297, 298, 299) were printed in Paris for Philippe le Noir as *Sensuyt la Chasse et le départ damours.* . . . An allied house, that of Veuve Jehan Treperel and Jehan Jehannot, then acquired the le Noir plates to produce a blurred further edition, represented by the Bibliothèque Nationale copy, Rés. Ye. 300. Of these later editions, there is also a le Noir copy at Versailles, and a Treperel-Jehannot copy in the Fairfax Murray Collection. This last is said to have been printed in 1520 (see H. W. Davies, *Catalogue of a Collection of Early French Books in the Library of C. Fairfax Murray*, Vol. 2 [London: By the author, 1910]).

Received at the Court, the lover reveals his clumsiness and must be tutored by various gracious courtiers before he can be of use to the Queen. Then, from a second group—*Bonne Foy, Loyaulté, Déduyt Joyeulx*, and the hunter *Espoir de Parvenir*—the lover receives advice about hunting. Three hounds are brought forth. The first is the greyhound, *Légier Couraige*. He is "Bel / noble et gentil de corsaige. . . . Prompt / actif et trèsdilligent" (H i v°). *Légier Couraige* is light, runs well to the sound of a horn, and can force a beast out of the brush. But the hunter gives a word of warning about *légierté*. The lover should keep this quality in control, and beware of frivolous dancing, running, sallying and singing.

The limer *Soing* comes forth. *Soing* is a large hound that will keep the quarry in a corner, preventing its escape (H i iv°). *Soing* is said, moreover to be effective in guarding Love against presumptuous people who would steal her noble Heart. (Where was *Soing* earlier?) Finally, there is *Travail*, a gruff running hound, which would tirelessly bite the quarry, give it no rest, and drive it to the death. (H i iv°)

The "hunt" is in fact to be a contest between those forces that restrain and inhibit the "heart," fastened here to the collar of the stag of love, and those which encourage it to love's fulfillment. The hunt's object will be to dislodge the captive stag from the *Buisson de Tristesse*, and entice it to run straight along the *Chemin d'Esperance* into the net which *Amours*, the Queen, holds taut with the aid of *Beaulté* and *Plaisant Regard*. The powers inimical to love, that is, *Faulx Semblant, Faulx Rapport, Craintise, Trop Envyeux, Ennuy* and *Dangier*, are guarding the Bush. The lover with the three hounds, together with *Hardyesse, Jeunesse* and *Deduyt Joyeulx*, cluster upon one side of the *Chemin d'Esperance*: on the other side are gathered *Bonne Foy, Loyaulté, Bel Acueil* and the Queen's son *Cupido*. The hunter *Espoir de Parvenir* runs from one group of hunting courtiers to the other, giving directions, and ordering all to await the signal of his horn. When he spies the stag he cries *"Harau: hau / harau je le voy"* and urges the entire company on down the *Chemin d'Esperance*

The god of love, the queen of love, the perfect lover, and others of the court hold three hounds as they leave the Château de Plaisance and set out for the Forest de Gracieulx Desir to hunt the Stag of Love, visible in the thicket. Miniature in Octovien de Saint-Gelais, *La Chasse et le depart d'amours*, sixteenth-century incunable, Vélins 583, folio H 4 v°. Bibliothèque Nationale, Département de la Réserve.

with cries of *"Avant, Messieurs | avant | après | le cerf sans aultre demourance"* (K v r⁰) and *"Courons fort"* (K v v⁰). All rush forward toward the Bush, dislodge the stag, and drive it down the *Chemin d'Esperance* into the spread net. Despite the hounds' alleged ability to bite and harry the game the stag is not to be harmed; captured, it is to be safely, happily enclosed in the green fields beside the Queen's palace. The heart retrieved from the neck of the *cerf amoureux*, the Queen gives it ceremonially to the *Amant Parfait* who gives her his in return. He then exchanges

Espoir de Parvenir, as hunter, sounds the horn, preparing to follow the three hounds into the Buysson de Tristesse, where the Stag of Love is hidden. Miniature in Octovien de Saint-Gelais, *La Chasse et le depart d'amours*, sixteenth-century incunable, Vélins 583, folio K 4 v⁰. Bibliothèque Nationale, Département de la Réserve.

the heart of *Amours* with his lady in return for hers. Further adventures follow (N ii r⁰–N v v⁰), no longer relevant to the hunt; Lover and Lady must continue to war against the irate *Dangier* and his cohorts. Defeated at the last the villains subside, and the Lover and his company return to the *Vergier d'Amours*, where he regales them with the *ballades* and *rondeaux* that conclude the poem.

England and France: Song, Sonnet, and Metaphor

By the sixteenth century, the amatory chase found its principal expression in short lyrics, songs, and sonnets. Four English songs are printed in *Anglia:* the first two, attributed to William Cornysh, the King's Chapel Master, are "Blowe thy horne hunter" and "Sore this dere stryken ys"; the others are "I have been a foster long and many a day" and "I am a joly foster."[14] One of the Cornysh songs goes:

> [B]low thy horne hunter
> cū blow thy horne one hye
> In yonder wode there lyeth A doo
> In fayth she woll not dye
> cū blow thy horne hunter
> cū blow thy horne hunter

Wyatt's "They flee from me" and "Whoso list to hunt," together with Spenser's "Lyke as a huntsman," contain the motif of the love quarry that may grow tame for the desirous hunter. Sonnets of Drayton and Ronsard focus upon the plight of the man as the quarry of his desires. In "Amour 35" Drayton describes the lover's "hart" roused from its lair, his breast, allowing itself to be wounded by rays from his lady's "darting eyes." The sonnet's last four lines reveal the hart dying at his lady's feet:

> And looking on thee, falls upon the ground,
> Smyling, as though he gloried in his death.

[14] Ewald Flügel (ed.), "Liedersammlungen des XVI jahrhunderts, besonders aus der zeit Heinrichs VIII," *Anglia* 12 (1889): 238–9, 244, 245.

Wallowing in his blood, some lyfe yet laft,
His stone-cold lips doth kisse the blessed shaft.[15]

The French poet closes his sonnet, "Comme un chevreuil,"
with a similar comparison between the death of the roe, its side
bleeding, and the lover's own death wounds, caused by darts
shooting from Cassandra's eyes:

De rets ne d'arc sa liberté n'a crainte
Sinon alors que sa vie est attainte
D'un trait meurtrier empourpré de son sang.
    Ainsi j'alloy sans espoir de dommage,
Le jour qu'un coup mille traits en mon flanc.[16]

And in Shakespeare's *Twelfth Night*, Orsino confesses his condition since first he beheld Olivia:

That instant was I turn'd into a hart
And my desires like fell and cruel hounds,
E'er since pursue me. [I.i. 21–23.]

D. C. Allen, in a richly documented essay on Andrew Marvell,
"The Nymph complaining for the Death of her Faun,"[17] has
surveyed the recurrences of the imagery of the love chase in
Renaissance poetry. It is a figure, by now, which can draw its life
from both the medieval tradition uninterrupted in its continuity,
and from the rediscovered ancient one.

In casting a retrospective look over the medieval chase, we
may make some distinctions among the poets of the chief ver-
naculars examined in this study. English authors, we observe,
tend to give a moral, religious, or didactic emphasis to the figure
of the chase, even where love enters the scheme of their literary
work. Nor does the love chase itself appear to be a favorite of
theirs. French and German poets reveal their preoccupation with

[15] "Ideas Mirror, Amours in Quatorzains" (London, 1594), in *The
Works of Michael Drayton*, ed. J. W. Hebel (Oxford, 1931), 1:116.
[16] Gustave Cohen, ed., *Ronsard, Œuvres Complètes* (Paris, 1950), 1. 26.
[17] Don Cameron Allen, *Image and Meaning: Metaphoric Traditions in
Renaissance Poetry* (Baltimore, 1959), pp. 93–114.

the chase as an amatory vehicle; yet, they differ markedly in their approaches and endings. In France, the stag is capturable; the capture is always identified in some fashion that varies from author to author with love's consummation. The German poets imitate French models in their own manner. The love chase in Germany, with certain exceptions, dramatizes yearning unfulfilled. The lover in Hadamar's *Jagd* may hunt forever, and Hadamar's imitators, by diverting the promised struggles of the chase to new objects, manage to express conflicts without resolution. Hugo's song, while it anticipates capture happily enough, nonetheless does not conclude with a capture. The Königsberger allegory consummates the love chase, yet so bitter is its savor that the poet asserts that it were far better had it not been so. Even *Tristan* ends its hunting with the elusive stag—happiness on the world's terms is quite unattainable for the lovers. Renunciation, strife, the spirit of contest characterize the amatory hunting of this literary culture. In medieval France, where western hunting was first codified, the anticipated anguish of the quarry was made, in the schooling of lovers, the prelude to love's joy and virtue.

Yet, do not all amatory poems founded upon the chase share an assumption? As "al shal passe that men prose or ryme," so too do the styles of their prosing and riming; this distinctively medieval figure, arising both from the books men read and emulated and from the life they saw, provides us with a means by which we may seek to comprehend the earthly love that concerned them. We have seen how the hunt could chart, with a sense of conflict, a hero's crucial moral, mental, or corporeal changes when he permitted himself to be drawn into its circle, or even should he be found palely loitering at its edge. When the chase is the love chase, it is love's harshness that emerges from the poet's choice of the figure—whatever else may be said about an ultimate hope of perfect joy. And this may be, after all, what mortal love, for a great number of medieval poets, was about.

Index

Actaeon, 53, 58, 60
Aelfric: *Colloquy*, 47; Life of St. Eustace, 59–66
Aeneid, 43, 46, 93–95, 95n.; medieval versions: *Énéas*, 152n.; Heinrich von Veldeke's *Eneit*, 128
Albrecht von Scharfenberg, 195, 200, 204, 213; *Titurel*, 167–168, 183–184
Andreas Capellanus: Art of Love, 99, 197 and 197n., 223
Arabic literature, hunt in, 26 and 26n., 94 and 94n., 154n.
Aucassin and Nicolete, 104–105

Bacchae, 52–53
Beowulf, 17–18
Berners, Juliana: *Book of St. Albans*, 26, 129
Bestiaries, 20, 41
Bible: Canticles, 46; Exodus, 148, 166; Jeremiah, 81; Mark, Matthew, 81; Psalm 41, 41; Psalm 78, 166; Psalm 105, 166
Boar, 18, 19 and 19n., 59, 75, 97, 99, 140, 176
Brackenjagd, Die, 231–232
Burkart von Hohenvels, 167–171, 172

Cerf amoreus, Li dis dou (The Stag of Love), 144–148, 149–153
Cerf blanc, Le dit du (The White Stag), 146–148, 161–165

Cervantes: hunting allusions in the work of, 49, 120
Charlemagne, 23 ff., 27; *Karolus Magnus et Leo Papa*, 18
Chaucer: "An ABC," 44–45; *Boece*, 47, 82n., 210; *Book of the Duchess*, 115–127; Friar's Tale, 81n.; *House of Fame*, 127; Melibee, 76; Parson's Tale, 45, 76; Second Nun's Tale, 76; *Troilus and Criseyde*, 60, 77, 90n., 99, 100, 121–122, 127, 159n.
Chrétien de Troyes, 144, 152n.; *Erec*, 77, 106, 108–115; *Yvain*, 77

Devil as hunter, 76, 80, 81, 148, 234n.; demons as hunters, 46

Eustace, St., 43, 59–66, 105

Falcons and other birds, 17, 99, 109, 112–114, 135–137, 170n., 176 and 176n., 189
Fishing, 81, 97, 99
Fox, 82–85, 169; *see also* Quarry

Gaston "Phoebus," Count of Foix: *Chasse*, 27, 78–79, 115n.
Gawain and the Green Knight, Sir, 71–88, 128
Gottfried von Strassburg, *see* Tristan
Grail quest, 19, 173–176

THE STAG OF LOVE

Designed by R. E. Rosenbaum.
Composed by St. Catherine Press, Ltd.
in 11 point monotype Imprint, 2 points leaded,
with display lines in monotype Centaur.
Printed offset by Vail-Ballou Press, Inc.
on Warren Olde Style India, 60 pound basis,
with the Cornell University Press watermark.
Bound by Vail-Ballou Press
in Columbia book cloth
and stamped in All Purpose foil.